E. S. Riley

Message of the Governor Maryland to the General Assembly

in Extra Session

E. S. Riley

Message of the Governor Maryland to the General Assembly
in Extra Session

ISBN/EAN: 9783337213381

Printed in Europe, USA, Canada, Australia, Japan

Cover: Foto ©Suzi / pixelio.de

More available books at **www.hansebooks.com**

[Document A.]

BY THE HOUSE OF DELEGATES,

APRIL 27, 1

Read and 5,000 copies ordered to be printed.

MESSAGE

OF THE

GOVERNOR OF MARYLAN

TO THE

GENERAL ASSEMBLY.

IN EXTRA SESSION, 1861.

FREDERICK:
E. S. RILEY, PRINTER
1861.

MESSAGE OF THE GOVERNOR

TO THE

Legislature of Maryland.

STATE OF MARYLAND, EXECUTIVE CHAMBER,
ANNAPOLIS, April 25th, 1861.

Gentlemen of the Senate and House of Delegates:

The extraordinay condition of affairs in Maryland has induced me to exercise the constitutional prerogative vested in the Governor to summon the Legislature in special session, in the hope that your wisdom may enable you to devise prompt and effective means to restore peace and safety to our State.

I shall detail briefly the startling events which have induced me to summon you together, and which have so suddenly placed us in the state of anarchy, confusion and danger from which I sincerely trust you may be able to extricate us.

Believing it to be the design of the Administration to pass over our soil troops for the defence of the City of Washington, and fearing that the passage of such troops would excite our people and provoke collision, I labored earnestly to induce the President to forego his purpose. I waited upon him in person and urged the importance of my request. I subsequently communicated with him and his cabinet by special despatches, entreating an abandonment of their designs. To all my requests I could get but the reply: "that Washington was threatened with attack—that the government had resolved to defend it—that there was no

other way of obtaining troops than by passing them over the
soil of Maryland—and that the military necessity of the
case rendered it impossible for the Government to abandon
its plans, much as it desired to avoid the dangers of collision.''
My correspondence with the authorities at Washington is
herewith submitted.

The consequences are known to you. On Friday last a
detachment of troops from Massachusetts reached Baltimore,
and was attacked by an irresponsible mob, and several persons on both sides were killed. The Mayor and Police
Board gave to the Massachusetts soldiers all the protection
they could afford ; acting with the utmost promptness and
bravery. But they were powerless to restrain the mob.

Being in Baltimore at the time, I co-operated with the
Mayor, to the fullest extent of my power, in his efforts.
The military of the city were ordered out to assist in the
preservation of the peace. The railroad companies were requested by the Mayor and myself to transport no more troops
to Baltimore city, and they promptly acceded to our request.

Hearing of the attack upon the soldiers, the War Department issued orders that no more troops should pass through
Baltimore City, provided they were allowed to pass outside
its limits. Subsequently, a detatchment of troops was
ascertained to be encamped at or near Cockeysville, in Baltimore County. On being informed of this the War Department ordered them back.

Before leaving Baltimore, Col. Huger, who was in command of the U. S. Arsenal at Pikesville, informed me that
he had resigned his commission. Being advised of the probability that the mob might attempt the destruction of this
property, and thereby complicate our difficulties with the
authorities at Washington, I ordered Col. Petherbridge to
proceed, with sufficient force, and occupy the premises in the
name of the United States Government ; of which proceeding I immediately notified the War Department.

On Sunday morning last, I discovered that a detachment
of troops, under command of Brig. Gen. B. F. Butler, had
reached Annapolis in a steamer, and had taken possession of
the practice ship Constitution, which, during that day, they
succeeded in getting outside the harbor of Annapolis, where
she now lies. After getting the ship off, the steamer laid
outside our harbor, and was soon joined by another steamer,
having on board the Seventh Regiment from New York City.

Brig. Gen. Butler addressed me, asking for permission to
land his forces. It will be seen, from the correspondence

herewith submitted, that I refused my consent. The Mayor of Annapolis also protested. But both steamers soon afterwards landed at the Naval Academy and put off the troops. Subsequently, other large bodies of troops reached here in transports and were landed. I was notified that the troops were to be marched to Washington. They desired to go without obstruction from our people ; but they had orders to go to Washington, and were determined to obey those orders. In furtherance of their designs, they took military possession of the Annapolis and Elk Ridge Railroad ; in regard to which act I forwarded to Brig. Gen. Butler the protest, and received the reply herewith submitted. On Wednesday morning the two detachments first landed took up the line of March for Washington. The people of Annapolis, though greatly exasperated, acting under counsel of the most prudent citizens, refrained from molesting or obstructing the passage of the troops through the city.

Seriously impressed with the condition of affairs, and anxious to avoid a repetition of events similar to those which had transpired in Baltimore, I deemed it my duty to make another appeal to the authorities at Washington. Accordingly, I sent a special messenger to Washington, with a despatch to the administration advising that no more troops be sent through Maryland ; that the troops at Annapolis be sent elsewhere ; and urging that a truce be offered with a view of a peaceful settlement of existing difficulties by mediation. I suggested that Lord Lyons, the British Minister, be requested to act as mediator between the contending parties. The result of the mission will be seen from the correspondence herewith submitted.

These events have satisfied me that the War Department has concluded to make Annapolis the point for landing troops, and has resolved to open and maintain communication between this place and Washington.

In the brief time allowed, it is impossible for me to go more into detail. The documents accompanying this message place before you all the information possessed by me. I shall promptly communicate such other information as may reach me.

Notwithstanding the fact that our most learned and intelligent citizens admit the right of the Government to transport its troops across our soil, it is evident that a portion of the people of Maryland are opposed to the exercise of the right. I have done all in my power to protect the citizens of Maryland and to preserve peace within our borders.

Lawless occurrences will be repeated, I fear, unless prompt action be taken by you.

It is my duty to advise you of my own convictions of the proper course to be pursued by Maryland in the emergency which is upon us. It is of no consequence now to discuss the causes which have induced our troubles. Let us look to our distressing present, and to our portentous future. The fate of Maryland, and perhaps of her sister Border Slave States, will undoubtedly be seriously affected by the action of your Honorable Body. Therefore should every good citizen bend all his energies to the task before us ; and therefore should the animosities and bickerings of the past be forgotten, and all strike hands in the holy cause of restoring peace to our beloved State and to our common country. I honestly and most earnestly entertain the conviction that the only safety of Maryland lies in preserving a neutral position between our brethren of the North and of the South. We have violated no rights of either section. We have been loyal to the Union. The unhappy contest between the two sections has not been fomented or encouraged by us, although we have suffered from it in the past. The impending war has not come by any act or any wish of ours. We have done all we could to avert it. We have hoped that Maryland, and the other Border Slave States, by their conservative position and love for the Union, might have acted as mediators between the extremes of both sections, and thus have prevented the terrible evils of a prolonged civil war. Entertaining these views, I cannot counsel Maryland to take sides against the General Government, until it shall commit outrages upon us which would justify us in resisting its authority. As a consequence, I can give no other counsel than that we shall array ourselves for Union and Peace, and thus preserve our soil from being polluted with the blood of brethren. Thus, if war must be between the North and the South, we may force the contending parties to transfer the field of battle from our soil, so that our lives and property may be secure. It seems to me that, independently of all other considerations, our geographical position forces us to this, unless we are willing to see our State the theatre of a long and bloody civil war, and the consequent utter destruction of every material interest of our people, to say nothing of the blood of brave men and innocent women and children which will cry out from our soil for vengeance upon us if we fail to do all that in us lies to avert the impending calamity.

The course I suggest has all the while been the sole groundwork of my policy. But for the excitement prevailing among our people during the past few days, I believe the object I have kept steadily in view during my administration would have been consummated. If it has failed, I have the full consciousness that, throughout the whole of my harassing and painful incumbency of the Gubernatorial Chair, I have labored honestly and faithfully for the peace, the safety, and the interests of Maryland, and of our common country. This consciousness has fully sustained me in all my troubles, and has enabled me to endure patiently all the cruel, unmerited, and heartless attacks that have been made upon my integrity.

I have also comfort in the conviction that my policy has been sustained by a large majority of the people, and nothing that has transpired since the recent lamentable occurrences within our State has shaken that conviction. A momentary frantic excitement took the place of reason and good judgment, and men for the time threw aside all prudent thoughts of the future in the burning desire to avenge what they considered wrongs.

I submit my suggestions to your wisdom; and I appeal to you not only as devoted citizens of Maryland, but as husbands and fathers, to allow that prudence and christianlike temper, so honorable to all men, to guide your counsels; and I implore you not to be swayed by the passions which seem to be so fully aroused in our midst, to do what the generations to come after us shall ever deplore.

In conclusion, gentlemen, I ask your indulgence if I have omitted to present to you any other matter of interest in connection with the important subject which you are summoned to consider. The short time I have had in which to prepare this communication, and the turmoil and excitement around me may have caused omissions; if so, they will be promptly supplied when indicated by you.

THOMAS H. HICKS.

CORRESPONDENCE WITH THE AUTHORITIES AT WASHINGTON.

WAR DEPARTMENT, }
April 17th, 1861. }

HIS EXCELLENCY,

THOS. H. HICKS,

Governor of Maryland.

DEAR SIR:—

The President has referred to me your letter of this day, and, in reply, I have the honor to say that the troops to be raised in Maryland will be needed for the defense of this Capital, and of the public property in that State and neighborhood. There is no intention of removing them beyond those points.

Very respectfully,

SIMON CAMERON,

Secretary of War.

BALTIMORE, April 17th, 1861.

To the President of the United States:

SIR:—

From the conversation I had yesterday, in Washington, with the Secretary of War, and with Lieutenant-General Scott, I understood that the four regiments of militia to be called for from Maryland were to be posted and retained within the limits of this State, for the defense of the United States Government, the maintenance of the Federal authority, and the protection of the Federal Capital. I also understood it was the intention of the United States Government not to require their services outside of Maryland, except in defense of the District of Columbia.

Will you do me the favor to state, in reply, whether I am right in this understanding, so that, in responding to the lawful demands of the United States Government, I may be able to give effective and reliable aid for the support and defense of this Union.

I have the honor to be your obedient servant,

THOS. H. HICKS,

Governor of Maryland.

WAR DEPARTMENT, }
WASHINGTON, April 17th, 1861. }

To His Excellency,

THOS. H. HICKS,

Governor of Maryland.

SIR:—

The President has referred to me your communication of this date, in relation to our conversation of the previous day, and I have the honor to say, in reply, that your statement of it is correct.

The troops called for from Maryland are destined for the protection of the Federal Capital and the public property of the United States within the limits of the State of Maryland; and it is not intended to remove them beyond those limits except for the defense of this District.

I have the honor to be yours, &c.,

SIMON CAMERON,

Secretary of War.

WAR DEPARTMENT, }
WASHINGTON, April 18th, 1861. }

To His Excellency,

THOS. H. HICKS,

Governor of Maryland.

SIR:—

The President is informed that threats are made, and measures taken, by unlawful combinations of misguided citizens of Maryland, to prevent by force the transit of United States troops, across Maryland, on their way pursuant to orders, for the defênce of this capital. The information is from such sources and in such shapes, that the President thinks it his duty to make it known to you, so that all loyal and patriotic citizens of your State, may be warned in time, and that you may be prepared to take immediate and effective measures against it. ◦

Such an attempt could have only the most deplorable consequences; and it would be as agreeable to the President, as it would be to yourself that it should be prevented, or overcome by the loyal authorities and citizens of Maryland, rather than averted by any other means.

I am very respectfully, yours, &c.

SIMON CAMERON,
Secretary of War.

——

STATE OF MARYLAND,

Executive Chamber, ⎫
Annapolis, April 20th, 1861. ⎬

HON. S. CAMERON,

Sir :—

Since I saw you in Washington last, I have been in Baltimore City, laboring in conjunction with the Mayor of that city to preserve peace and order, but I regret to say with little success. Up to yesterday there appeared promise, but the outbreak came, the turbulent passions of the riotous element prevailed, fear for safety became reality, what they had endeavored to conceal, but what was known to us, was no longer concealed but made manifest; the rebellious element had the control of things. We were arranging and organizing forces to protect the city and preserve order, but want of organization, of arms, prevented success. They had arms, they had the principal part of the organized military forces with them, and for us to have made the effort, under the circumstances, would have had the effect to aid the disorderly element. They took possession of the Armories, have the arms and ammunition, and I therefore think it prudent to decline, (for the present,) responding affirmatively to the requisition made by President Lincoln, for four regiments of infantry.

With great respect I am your obedient servant,

THOS. H. HICKS.

FREDERICK CITY, MD., April 20th, 1861.

HIS EXCELLENCY,

THOS. H. HICKS,

Governor of the State of Maryland,

Annapolis, Md.

SIR:—

In obedience to Special Orders, No. 106, Adjutant General's Office, Washington, D. C. of April 15th, 1861, (detailing me to muster into the service of the United States, the troops of this State called out by the President's proclamation, of that date,) I have the honor to report to you my arrival at this place.

I would be pleased to receive from you, at your earliest convenience, any information and instructions you may have to communicate to me, in reference to this duty.

I am sir, very respectfully,

Your obedient servant,

R. MACFEELY,

1st. Lieut. 4th Infantry.

———

STATE OF MARYLAND.

EXECUTIVE CHAMBER, }
ANNAPOLIS, April 23d, 1861. }

R. MACFEELY, Esq..

1st Lieut. 4th Infantry.

SIR:

Your letter of the 20th inst. was received this morning. I am directed by the Governor to inform you that no troops have been called out in Maryland, and that consequently your mission is at an end. And you will therefore report to the Secretary of War, who has been informed of the Governor's views in this matter.

Your obedient servant,

GEO. W. JEFFERSON,

Private Secretary.

ANNAPOLIS, April 20th, 1861.

To the Secretary of War:

I have understood that it is contemplated to send Northern Troops to garrison Fort Madison.

I would earnestly advise that none be sent.

Respectfully,

THOS. H. HICKS.

TELEGRAPHIC DISPATCH.

WASHINGTON, April 20th, 1861.

GOV. HICKS.

I desire to consult with you and the Mayor of Baltimore, relative to preserving the peace of Maryland. Please come immediately by special train, which you can take at Baltimore, or if necessary one can be sent from hence. Answer forthwith.

LINCOLN.

STATE OF MARYLAND.

EXECUTIVE CHAMBER, ⎫
ANNAPOLIS, April 22d, 1861. ⎬

To HIS EXCELLENCY,

A. LINCOLN,

President of the United States.

SIR:

I feel it my duty, most respectfully to advise you that no more troops be ordered or allowed to pass through Maryland, and that the troops now off Annapolis be sent elsewhere, and I most respectfully urge that a truce be offered by you, so that the effusion of blood may be prevented. I respectfully suggest, that Lord Lyons be requested to act as mediator between the contending parties of our country.

I have the honor to be, very respectfully,

Your obedient servant,

THOS. H. HICKS.

DEPARTMENT OF STATE,
April 22d, 1861.

HIS EXCELLENCY,

THOS. H. HICKS,
Governor of Maryland.

SIR :—

I have had the honor to receive your communication of this morning, in which you inform me that you have felt it to be your duty to advise the President of the United States to order elsewhere the troops then off Annapolis, and also that no more may be sent through Maryland, and that you have further suggested that Lord Lyons be requested to act as mediator between the contending parties in our country, to prevent the effusion of blood.

The President directs me to acknowledge the receipt of that communication, and to assure you that he has weighed the counsels which it contains with the respect which he habitually cherishes for the Chief Magistrates of the several States, and especially for yourself. He regrets, as deeply as any magistrate or citizen of the country can, that demonstrations against the safety of the United States, with very extensive preparations for the effusion of blood, have made it his duty to call out the force to which you allude. The force now sought to be brought through Maryland is intended for nothing but the defense of this Capital. The President has necessarily confided the choice of the national highway, which that force shall take in coming to this city, to the Lieutenant-General commanding the army of the United States, who, like his only predecessor, is not less distinguished for his humanity than for his loyalty, patriotism, and distinguished public service.

The President instructs me to add, that the national highway thus selected by the Lieutenant-General has been chosen by him upon consultation with prominent magistrates and citizens of Maryland as the one which, while a route is absolutely necessary, is farthest removed from the populous cities of the State, and with the expectation that it would therefore be the least objectionable one.

· The President cannot but remember that there has been a time in the history of our country, when a General of the American Union, with forces designed for the defense of its Capital, was not unwelcome anywhere in the State of Maryland, and certainly not at Annapolis, then, as now, the Capital of that patriotic State, and then also one of the Capitals of the Union.

If eighty years could have obliterated all the other noble sentiments of that age in Maryland, the President would be hopeful nevertheless that there is one that would forever remain there and everywhere. That sentiment is, that no domestic contention whatever, that may arise among the parties of this Republic ought, in any case, to be referred to any foreign arbitrament, least of all to the arbitrament of an European monarchy.

I have the honor to be,

With distinguished consideration,

Your Excellency's most obedient servant,

WILLIAM H. SEWARD.

CORRESPONDENCE WITH THE MAYOR OF BAL-
TIMORE.

[*Telegram from Mayor Brown.*]

BALTIMORE, April 20, 1861.

To Governor Hicks:

Letter from President and Gen. Scott. No troops to pass through Baltimore, if, as a military force, they can march around. I will answer that every effort will be made to prevent parties leaving the city to molest them; but cannot guarantee against acts of individuals not organized. Do you approve? GEO. WM. BROWN.

16

[Telegram in Reply.]

ANNAPOLIS, April 20, 1861.

To the Mayor of Baltimore:

Your dispatch received. I hoped they would send no more troops through Maryland; but, as we have no right to demand this, I am glad no more are to be sent through Baltimore. I know you will do all in your power to preserve the peace.

TH. H. HICKS.

[Telegram to the Mayor of Baltimore.]

ANNAPOLIS, April 20, 1861.

I have received the following dispatch:

"I desire to consult with you and the Mayor of Baltimore relative to preserving the peace of Maryland. Please come immediately by special train, which you can take at Baltimore, or, if necessary, one can be sent from here. LINCOLN."

Have you received a similar dispatch? If so, do you intend going, and at what hour? My going depends upon you. Answer at once. TH. H. HICKS.

[Telegram in reply, without signature.]

To the Governor of Maryland:

The Mayor is in Washington. We have no knowledge of any such movement.

[*Telegram to Mayor Brown.*]

ANNAPOLIS, April 21, 1861.

To the Mayor of Baltimore:

It is rumored here that men have been sent for from Baltimore to come here to prevent the landing of troops. Do not let them come. The troops will not land here.

TH. H. HICKS.

CORRESPONDENCE WITH BR. GEN. B. F. BUTLER.

STATE OF MARYLAND, }
Executive Chamber, Annapolis, April 20, 1861. }

To the Commander of the Volunteer Troops on Board the Steamer:

SIR:—I would most earnestly advise that you do not land your men at Annapolis. The excitement here is very great, and I think that you should take your men elsewhere. I have telegraphed to the Secretary of War, advising against your landing your men here.

Very respectfully,

Your obedient Servant,

TH. H. HICKS,
Governor of Maryland.

SEAL OF THE STATE OF }
MASSACHUSETTS. }

OFF ANNAPOLIS, April 22d, 1861.

His Excellency Thos. H. Hicks, Governor of Maryland:

In reply to the communication from you on the 21st, I had the honor to inform you of the necessities of my command, which drew me into the harbor of Annapolis. My circumstances have not changed. To that communication I have received no reply. I cannot return, if I desire so to do, without being furnished with some necessary supplies, for all which the money will be paid. I desire of your Excellency an immediate reply, whether I have the permission of the State authorities of Maryland to land the men under my command, and of passing quickly through the State, on my way to Washington, respecting private property, and paying for what I receive, and outraging the rights of none—a duty which I am bound to do in obedience to the requisitions of the President of the United States?

I have received some copies of an informal correspondence between the Mayor of Baltimore and the President of the Baltimore and Ohio Railroad, and a copy of a note from your Excellency, enclosing the same to Capt. Blake, Commandant of the Naval School. These purport to show that instructions have been issued by the War Department as to the disposition of the United States militia, differing from what I had supposed to be my duty. If these instructions have been in fact issued, it would give me great pleasure to obey them.— Have I your Excellency's permission, in consideration of these exigencies of the case, to land my men—to supply their wants, and to relieve them from the extreme and unhealthy confinement of a transport vessel not fitted to receive them? To convince your Excellency of the good faith towards the authorities of the State of Maryland, with which I am acting, and I am armed only against the disturbers of her peace and of the United States, I enclose a copy of an order issued to my command before I had the honor of receiving the copy of your communication through Capt. Blake. I trust your Excellency will appreciate the necessities of my position, and give me an immediate reply, which I await with anxiety.

I would do myself the honor to have a personal interview with your Excellency, if you so desire. I beg leave to call your Excellency's attention to what I hope I may be pardoned for deeming an ill-advised designation of the men under my command. *They are not Northern troops—they are a part of the whole militia of the United States, obeying the call of the President.*

I have the honor of being your Excellency's obedient servant.

BENJ. F. BUTLER,
Brig. General in the Militia of the United States.

P. S.—It occurs to me that our landing on the grounds at
the Naval Academy would be entirely proper, and in accordance with your Excellency's wishes.   B. F. B.

SEAL OF THE STATE OF }
MASSACHUSETTS.   }

Special Brigade, Order No. 37.

HEADQUARTERS SECOND DIVISION MASS. VOL. MILITIA, }
On board steamer Maryland, off Annapolis, April 22d, 1861. }

Col. Munroe is charged with the execution of the following order:
At five o'clock A. M. the troops will be paraded by company and be
drilled in the manual of arms. Especially in loading at will, firing
by file, and in the use of the bayonet, and these specialties will be observed in all subsequent drills in the manual. Such drill to continue
until 7 o'clock, when all the arms will be stacked upon the upper
deck—great care being taken to instruct the men as to the mode of
stacking their arms, so that a firm stack, not easily overturned, shall
be made. Being obliged to drill at times with the weapons loaded,
great damage may be done by the overturning of the stack and the
discharge of the piece. This is important. Indeed, an accident has
already occurred in the regiment from this cause, and although slight
in its consequence, yet it warns us to increased diligence in this regard. The purpose which could only be hinted at in the orders of
yesterday has been accomplished. The frigate Constitution has lain
for a long time at this port substantially at the mercy of the armed
mob, which sometimes paralyzes the otherwise loyal State of Maryland. Deeds of daring, successful contests and glorious victories had
rendered "Old Ironsides" so conspicuous in the naval history of the
country, that she was fitly chosen as the school ship in which to train
the future officers of the navy to like heroic acts.

It was given to Massachusetts and Essex county first to man her;
it was reserved for Massachusetts to have the honor to retain her for
the service of the Union and the laws.

This is a sufficient triumph of right, and a sufficient triumph for us.
By this the blood of our friends shed by the Baltimore mob is in so
far avenged. The Eighth Regiment may hereafter cheer lustily on all
proper occasions, but never without orders. The old Constitution, by

their efforts, aided untiringly by the United States officers having her in charge, is now safely "possessed, occupied and enjoyed" by the government of the United States, and is safe from all her foes.

We have been joined by the Seventh Regiment of New York, and together we propose peaceably, quickly and civilly, unless opposed by some mob, or other disorderly persons, to march to Washington, in obedience to the requisition of the President of the United States. If opposed we shall march steadily forward.

My next order I hardly know how to express. I cannot assume that any of the citizen soldiery of Massachusetts or New York could, under any circumstances whatever, commit any outrages upon private property in a loyal and friendly State. But fearing that some improper person may have by stealth introduced himself among us, I deem it proper to state, that any unauthorized interference with private property will be most signally punished, and full reparation therefore made to the injured party, to the full extent of my power and ability. In so doing I but carry out the orders of the War Department. I should have so done without those orders.

Col. Munroe will cause these orders to be read at the head of each company before we march.

Col. Leffert's command not having been originally included in this order, he will be furnished with a copy for his instruction.

By order of

B. F. BUTLER,
Brig. General.

{ Signed. }

WILLIAM H. CLEMENS,
Brig. Major.

STATE OF MARYLAND,
Executive Chamber, Annapolis, April 22, 1861.

To Brig. Gen. B. F. Butler:

Sir—I am in receipt of your two communications of this date, informing me of your intention to land the men under your command at Annapolis, for the purpose of marching thence to the city of Washington. I content myself with protesting against this movement, which, in view of the excited condition of the people of this State, I cannot but consider an unwise step on the part of the Government. But I most earnestly urge upon you that there shall be no halt made by the troops in this city.

Very respectfully,

Your obedient servant,

TH. H. HICKS.

STATE OF MARYLAND, }
Executive Chamber, Annapolis, April 23, 1861. }

To Brig. Gen. B. F. Butler:

Sir: Having. in pursuance of the powers vested in me by the Constitution of Maryland, summoned the Legislature of the State to assemble on Friday, the 26th instant; and Annapolis being the place in which, according to law, it must assemble; and having been credibly informed that you have taken military possession of the Annapolis and Elk Ridge Railroad, I deem it my duty to protest against this step; because, without at present assigning any other reason, I am informed that such occupancy of said road will prevent the members of the Legi-lature from reaching this city.

Very respectfully, yours,

THOS. H. HICKS.

SEAL OF THE STATE OF }
MASSACHUSETTS. }

HEADQUARTERS THIRD BRIGADE, }
UNITED STATES MILITIA, }
Annapolis, Md, April 23, 1861. }

To His Excellency Thos. H. Hicks,

Governor of Maryland.

You are credibly informed that I have taken possession of the Annapolis and Elkridge Railroad. It might have escaped your notice, but at the official meeting between your Excellency and the Mayor of Annapolis, and the authorities of the government and myself, it was expressly stated as the reason why I should not land, that my troops could not pass the railroad, because the company had taken up the rails, and they were private property. It is difficult to see how it could be, that if my troops could not pass over the railroad one way, the members of the Legislature could pass the other way. I have taken possession for the purpose of preventing the carrying out of the threats of the mob, as officially represented to me by the Master of Transportation of this city, "that if my troops passed over the railroad, the railroad should be destroyed."

If the government of the State had taken possession of the railroad in any emergency, I should have long waited before I entered upon it. But, as I had the honor to inform your Excellency in regard to insurrection against the laws of Maryland, I am here armed to maintain those laws, if your Excellency desires, and the peace of the United States, against all disorderly persons whatever. I am endeavoring to save and not to destroy; to obtain means of transportation, so I can vacate the capital prior to the sitting of the Legislature, and not be under the painful necessity of occupying your beautiful city while the Legislature is in session.

I have the honor to be

Your Excellency's obedient servant,

Br. Gen. B. F. Butler.

HEADQUARTERS THIRD BRIGADE, }
MASS. VOL. MILITIA, }
Annapolis, Md., April 23, 1861. }

To His Excellency Thos. H. Hicks,

Governor of the State of Maryland:

I did myself the honor, in my communication of yesterday, wherein I asked permission to land the portion of the militia of the United States under my command, to state that they were armed only against the disturbers of the peace of the State of Maryland and of the United States.

I have understood within the last hour that some apprehensions were entertained of an insurrection of the negro population of this neighborhood. I am anxious to convince all classes of persons that the forces under my command are not here in any way to interfere with or countenance any interference with the laws of the State. I am, therefore, ready to co-operate with your Excellency in suppressing most promptly and effectively any insurrection against the laws of Maryland.

I beg, therefore, that you announce publicly that any portion of the forces under my command is at your Excellency's disposal, to act immediately for the preservation and quietness of the peace of this community.

And I have the honor to be,

Your Excellency's obedient servant,

B. F. BUTLER,

General of Third Brigade.

·

·

STATE OF MARYLAND,
Executive Chamber, Annapolis, April 23, 1861.

To Brig. Gen. B. F. Butler:

Sir—I have the honor to acknowledge the receipt of your letter of this morning, tendering the force under your command to aid in suppressing a rumored insurrection of the slaves in this county.

I thank you most sincerely for the tender of your men; but I had, before the receipt of your letter, directed the Sheriff of the County to act in the matter; and am confident that the citizens of the county are fully able to suppress any insurrection of our slave population.

I have the honor to be,

Your obedient servant,

TH. H. HICKS.

COPY OF DISPATCHES FROM BRIG. GEN. BUTLER TO GOVERNOR CURTIN.

To His Excellency Andrew Curtin, Commander in Chief of the Forces of Pennsylvania:

Sir: Should this dispatch be forwarded to you, countersigned by His Excellency Thomas H. Hicks, Governor of Maryland, you will please to understand that the insurgents have surrendered Pikeville Arsenal, and that it, therefore, will not be necessary to advance your troops, as you were yesterday requested by me.

B. F. BUTLER,

Brigadier General.

Annapolis, April 24, 1861.

State of Maryland, }

Executive Chamber, Annapolis April 24th, 1861 }

To Brig. Gen. B. F. Butler:

Sir—A dispatch signed by you, addressed to Gov. A. Curtin, has been received by me, with a verbal request that I countersign it, and have it forwarded to its address.

In reference to the Arsenal at Pikeville, I have no official information. I do not know who is now in possession of it. I am cut off from all communication with other parts of the State; and have no means to forward your dispatch, if I were willing to countersign it.

I am compelled, therefore, to decline to accede to your request.

Very respectfully,

Your obedient servant,

TH. H. HICKS.

BY THE HOUSE OF DELEGATES.

April 27, 1861.

Read and ordered to be printed.

CORRESPONDENCE

BETWEEN THE

GOVERNOR OF MARYLAND

AND THE

SHERIFF OF FREDERICK COUNTY.

EXECUTIVE CHAMBER,

Frederick City, April 27, 1861.

Gentlemen of the House of Delegates:

1 herewith transmit to your honorable body a copy of a correspondence between this department and the Sheriff of Frederick county.

The subject matter thereof being an incident of the peculiar condition of affairs which you are assembled to consider. I respectfully submit it for your action.

THOMAS H. HICKS.

CORRESPONDENCE.

STATE OF MARYLAND,

EXECUTIVE CHAMBER,

Frederick City, April 26, 1861.

To the Sheriff of Frederick county:

Sir: I have information to the effect that the Virginia troops, now stationed at or near Harper's Ferry, have seized upon and appropriated to their use some property belonging to a citizen of Maryland, said property being at the time of seizure within the limits of Maryland. I am also informed that you have official cognizance of the matter. Will you do me the favor to furnish me, in writing, with such information as you possess in reference to said seizure?

Very respectfully, your obedient servant,

THOMAS H. HICKS.

SHERIFF'S OFFICE,

Frederick City, April 27, 1861.

To His Excellency, the Governor of Maryland:

Sir: In reply to your inquiry of the the 26th inst., I herewith give you a copy of the dispatch received by me, dated Point of Rocks, April 24th, 1861:

To the Sheriff of Frederick county:

My boat, loaded with grain, bound from Berlin to Georgetown is detained at this point by order of officers in command at Harper's Ferry. I demand your protection, and will

hold the State of Maryland responsible for said detention and
for all damages done said cargo. Answer.

C. F. WENNER.

POINT OF ROCKS, April 25, 1861.

To the Sheriff of Frederick county,

And the State or Prosecuting Attorney :

I command you to protect my property that is now being
loaded in the cars to go to Harper's Ferry against my wishes
or instructions, and I fall on my State for protection and
damages. I demand your presence at this point. I will
have my rights. The State is bound to give it to me.

Your's, in haste,

C. F. WENNER.

There is about two hundred Virginia troops here—every
thing under their control. Since they have taken my boat,
it is truly warlike here, with clashing of swords. They will
have discharged by noon—feeding the troops with the oats.
They are all troops here.

C. F. WENNER.

Mr. Wenner also called at my office in this city, on the
25th inst., and stated the same as above detailed; and also
stated that he gave some resistance, until the officers ordered
the soldiers to fire after a minute's notice; and that they refused to give him one of his mules to go home with; and
while loading the grain on the cars, he insisted on the grain
being weighed by the Agent of the Baltimore and Ohio Railroad Company, that he might seek redress, which was denied him by the officer, who stated that he might go to Harper's Ferry to see it weighed. He also states they took from
him grain to feed near one hundred horses without weighing
or measuring; and the bridge was then ready for destruction,
having about six cords of wood and other combustible materials thereto attached, to burn and blow it up.

The above is all the information that has come to my
knowledge respecting the matter.

Respectfully submitted,

MICHAEL H. HALLER.

BY THE HOUSE OF DELEGATES.

April 30, 1861.

Read and ordered to be printed.

COPY

OF

PROPOSED AMENDMENT

TO THE

CONSTITUTION OF THE UNITED STATES.

STATE OF MARYLAND,

Frederick City, April 30, 1861.

Gentlemen of the House of Delegates:

I herewith transmit to your honorable body a copy of the proposed amendment to the Constitution of the United States, which was adopted, as a joint resolution, by Congress, and approved by the President; and which is authenticated under the Seal of the Department of State at Washington.

. THOS. H. HICKS.

COPY OF PROPOSED AMENDMENT

TO THE

CONSTITUTION OF THE UNITED STATES.

To his Excellency,
The Governor of the State of Maryland,
Annapolis:

WASHINGTON, March 16, 1861.

SIR :—I transmit an authenticated copy of a joint resolution to amend the Constitution of the United States, adopted by Congress, and approved on the 2nd of March, 1861, by James Buchanan, President.

I have the honor to be,

Your Excellency's ob't servant,

ABRAHAM LINCOLN.

By the President.

WILLIAM H. SEWARD, Secretary of State.

UNITED STATES OF AMERICA,

DEPARTMENT OF STATE.

To all whom these presents shall come, Greeting:

I certify that the paper hereunto annexed, has been compared with the original roll, and is a true copy of the "Joint Resolution to amend the Constitution of the United States;" approved March 2, 1861.

In testimony whereof, I, William H. Seward, Secretary of State of the United States, have hereunto subscribed my name and caused the seal of the Department of State to be affixed.

L. S.

Done at the city of Washington, this 13th day of March, A. D. 1861, and of the Independence of the United States of America the 85th.

WILLIAM H. SEWARD.

JOINT RESOLUTION.

Thirty Sixth Congress of the United States, at the second Session, begun and held at the city of Washington in the District of Columbia, on Monday, the third day of December, one thousand eight hundred and sixty.

JOINT RESOLUTION TO AMEND THE CONSTITUTION OF THE UNITED STATES.

Resolved, By the Senate and House of Representatives of the United States, of America in Congress assembled, that the following article be proposed to the Legislatures of the several States as an amendment to the Constitution of the United States, which, when ratified by three-fourths of said Legislatures, shall be valid, to all intents and purposes, as part of the said Constitution, viz :

ARTICLE XIII.

No amendment shall be made to the Constitution which will authorize or give to Congress the power to abolish or interfere, within any State, with the domestic institutions thereof, including that of persons held to labor or service by the laws of said State.

WILLIAM PENNINGTON,

Speaker of the House of Representatives.

JOHN C. BRECKINRIDGE,

Vice President of the United States, and

President of the Senate.

Approved March 2, 1861.

JAMES BUCHANAN.

[Document D.]

BY THE HOUSE OF DELEGATES,
MAY 4, 1861.
Read and 3,000 copies ordered to be printed.

REPORT

OF THE

BOARD OF POLICE

OF THE

CITY OF BALTIMORE.

IN EXTRA SESSION, 1861.

FREDERICK:
E. S. RILEY, PRINTER.
1861.

REPORT.

To the Honorable
THE GENERAL ASSEMBLY
OF MARYLAND :

The Board of Police of the City of Baltimore, created and
appointed by your Honorable Body by the provisions of the
4th Article of the Code of Public Local Laws, sections 806,
&c., deem it their duty respectfully to report,

That the said Board was duly organized, and entered upon
the discharge of their duties. For full information respecting all their proceedings to the 1st of January, 1861, they
respectfully ask leave to submit to your Honorable Body, as
a part of this report, the accompanying copy of a report,
made by the Board, in pursuance of the 821st section of the
Article of the Code above mentioned, to the Mayor and City
Council in January last. It should have been stated in said
last mentioned report, that the Board had likewise performed
the duties imposed upon them in reference to elections by
sections 199, &c., of the same article of the Code. The
City had been divided into election precincts, Judges and
Clerks of Election appointed, and all the duties of the Board
with regard to holding elections had been performed. An
election was held in the City on the 10th day of October,
1860, for a Mayor and for members of both branches of the
City Council of Baltimore, and another was held on the 6th
day of November following, for electors of President and
Vice President of the United States. The Board have great
satisfaction in stating, that on both those days the utmost
quiet and good order were preserved throughout the City,

that none of the polls were in any manner obstructed, and
that not a single complaint was either then, or has subsequently, been made, that any person desiring to vote was,
at either election, impeded or hindered in presenting himself
before the judges and voting with perfect freedom for whomsoever he thought proper, if the judges found him to be a
legal voter.

The Board continued from the date of their above report
to exercise their regular functions until Friday the 19th
April. On that day a large detachment of, it is understood
about 1800 men of the Massachusetts and Pennsylvania
Militia arrived in the forenoon in the City, via the Philadelphia, Wilmington and Baltimore Railroad. No member of
the Board of Police had any information that these troops
were expected on that day, until from half an hour to one
hour of the time at which they were to arrive. The Marshal of Police was immediately notified, and called out at
once a large portion of his force to preserve order during
their transit through the City. When they arrived, there
were manifestations of a disposition to interfere with their
passage, and after some had been transported by cars
through the streets to the Washington Depot, obstructions
were placed on the track in the City, which stopped the
progress of the remainder, these alighted, to march to the
Depot, and to prevent any diffiulty the Mayor placed himself at their head, and they thus proceeded on their route.
Missiles were notwithstanding thrown at the troops, and
some of them were injured, their assailants were fired upon,
and in some instances, with fatal effect. An intense and
irrepressible feeling appeared to be at once aroused, and
repeated conflicts between parties of citizens and the Massachusetts troops took place, several being killed on both sides.
The Marshal who had been on active duty at the Camden
Street Depot, and did not know that these troops were on
their route or expected, hearing of this, hastened to meet
them with a force of the Police, and under their escort they
reached the Washington Depot, and after some delay, the

train finally started for Washington ; attempts were made to hinder it, by placing obstructions on the track of the Rail Road, but by the interference of the police these were soon removed.

The City authorities were meanwhile informed that there had been another arrival of military, who were then at the Philadelphia Depot. The Marshal of Police hastened to that point, and as it was impossible for them at that time to be taken through the streets, without a general and bloody conflict, he protected them with a party of his Police, until they were sent back by the Rail Road Company in the cars to Havre de Grace. During the afternoon and night a large number of stragglers from some of the above datachments of troops sought the aid and protection of the Police ; they were safely cared for at the several station-houses, and were sent off in security, by the earliest opportunity to Havre de Grace or Philadelphia in the cars.

The same night the Board had a meeting, when the opinion was unanimously expressed, that it was utterly impossible from the state of the public mind, that any more forces from other States, could by any probability, then pass through the City to Washington, without a fierce and bloody conflict at every step of their progress, and that whatever might be the result, great loss of life, and imminent danger to the safety of the City, would necessarily ensue. The Board were equally unanimous in their judgment that as good citizens, it was their duty to the City, and to the State of Maryland, to adopt any measures whatsoever, that might be necessary at such a juncture, to prevent the immediate arrival in the City of further bodies of troops, from the Eastern or Northern States, though the object of the latter might be solely to pass through the City. It was suggested that the most feasible, if not the most practicable mode, of thus stopping for a time, the approach of such troops, would be to obstruct the Philadelphia, Wilmington and Baltimore and the Northern Central Rail Roads, by disabling some of the bridges on both roads. His Honor the

Mayor stated to the Board, that his Excellency the Governor, with whom he had a few minutes before been in consultation in the presence of several citizens concurred in these views, they were likewise those of the Board, and instructions were given for carrying them into effect. This was accordingly done. The injury thus done on the Rail Roads amounted to but a few thousand dollars on each ; subsequently as has been stated, further and greater damage was done to other structures on the Roads by parties in the country or others, but this was without the sanction or authority of the Board, and they have no accurate information on the subject. The absolute necessity of the measures thus determined upon by the Governor, Mayor and Police Board, is fully illustrated by the fact, that early on Sunday morning, reliable information reached the City, of the presence of a large body of Pennsylvania troops amounting to about twenty-four hundred men, had reached Ashland near Cockeysville, by the way of the Northern Central Rail Road, and were stopped in their progress towards Baltimore, by the partial destruction of the Ashland Bridge. Every intelligent citizen at all acquainted with the state of feeling then existing, must be satisfied, that if these troops had attempted to march through the City, an immense loss of life would have ensued, in the conflict which would necessarily have taken place. The bitter feelings already engendered, would have been intensely increased by such a conflict; all attempts at conciliation would have been vain, and terrible destruction would have been the consequence, if as is certain, other bodies of troops had insisted upon forcing their way through the City.

The tone of the whole of the Northern press, and of the mass of the population, was violent in the extreme. Incursions upon our City were daily threatened, not only by troops in the service of the Federal Government, but by the vilest and most reckless desperadoes, acting independently, and, as they threatened, in despite of the Government, backed by well known influential citizens, and sworn to the commission of all kinds of excesses. In short every possible effort was made to alarm this community. In this condition of things, the Board felt it to be their solemn duty to continue the organization which had already been commenced, for the purpose of assuring the people of Baltimore that no effort would be spared to protect all within its borders to the full extent of their ability. All the means employed were devoted to this end, and with no view of producing a collision with the General Government, which the Board were particularly anxious to avoid, and an arrangement was happily effected by the Mayor with the General Government that no troops should be passed through the City. As an evidence of the determination of the Board to prevent such collision, a sufficient guard was sent in the neighborhood of Fort McHenry several nights, to arrest all parties who might be engaged in a threatened attack upon it, and a steam-tug was employed, properly manned, to prevent any hostile demonstration upon the receiving-ship Alleghany, lying at anchor in the harbor, of all which the United States officers in command were duly notified.

Property of various descriptions, belonging to the Government and individuals, was taken possession of by the Police force, with a view to its security. The best care has been taken of it. Every effort has been made to discover the rightful owners, and a portion of it has already been forwarded to order; arrangements have been made with the Government agents satisfactory to them, for the portion belonging to it, and the balance is held subject to the order of its owners.

Amidst all the excitement and confusion which have since prevailed, the Board take great pleasure in stating that the good order and peace of the City have been preserved to an extraordinary degree. Indeed, to judge from the accounts given by the press of other cities, of what has been the state of things in their own communities, Baltimore, during the whole of the past week, and up to this date, will compare favorably, as to the protection which persons and property have enjoyed, with any other large City in the United States.

All which is respectfully submitted.

By order of the Board,

CHARLES HOWARD,

President.

Office Board of Police,
Baltimore, May 3d, 1861.

REPORT

OF THE

BOARD OF POLICE.

To the Honorable, the Mayor

           and City Council:

The Board of Police of the city of Baltimore have the honor, in obedience to the provisions of Sec. 821 of the 4th Article of the Code of Public Local Laws, to report:

That the Commissioners, named in Section 807 of said article, met on the 6th day of February last, and organized the Board of Police by taking and subscribing the several oaths prescribed by law. His Honor, the Mayor of the city, had been invited to attend the meeting, but he declined to do so, or to recognize the Board as clothed with any lawful authority; as he was advised by counsel, that the act creating the Board was unconstitutional, and therefore void. The Marshal and Deputy Marshal of the City Police, in like manner, refused to attend upon or pay obedience to the orders of the Board, alleging that they considered themselves as acting under the authority of the Mayor and City Council. Under these circumstances, the Board, whilst taking measures to procure, with as little delay as practicable, a decision by the proper judicial tribunals of the important questions at issue, deemed it their duty to forbear any other attempt, to exercise in the meanwhile the high power vested in them. Proceedings were accordingly instituted, in the mode designated by the law; and the counsel for the city having expressed their desire to have a final decision upon them obtained as soon as possible; all the points raised in the case were fully and elaborately argued in the Superior Court of Baltimore city. On the 13th of March that court pronounced its opinion, entirely sustaining the constitutionality and validity of the law, and rendered judgment accordingly. An appeal having been taken, the judgment of the Supreme Court was, on the 17th of April, unanimously affirmed by the Court of Appeals.

On the rendition of this judgment the Mayor of the city promptly surrendered to the Board the station houses, arms, equipments, &c., provided for the use of the Police force previously established by the city, and on the 21st of April the said force passed under the sole and exclusive management of the Board of Police. On the 7th of May the Board revoked all the commissions previously given by the city authorities, and gave new appointments to the officers and men whom they had selected, and they continued to exercise their authority over the force according to law, making such changes in the composition of the same by removals and new appointments as they deemed advisable, until the 3d day of October, when they publicly declared by advertisement in the newspapers, that the organization of the Police force, created by the authority of the State, was complete.

The Board take pleasure in stating that the introduction of the new system, which it was made their duty to inaugurate, was followed by a marked improvement in the general good order of the city, and a cessation of those scenes of riotous and lawless violence which were before of such constant occurrence in the streets and public places of the city, as well as on private premises. The efficiency of the present Police system for the preservation of order, has been, since its establishment, well tested. The visits of strangers of high public positions, under circumstances which attracted large crowds to the city. The holding of several political conventions of delegates from every part of the country, in whose proceedings the most intense interest was felt, and the occurrence of two important elections, have all taken place without any serious disturbance or breach of the peace. In this respect the most sanguine hopes of those who anticipated such results from the organization of a Police force, entirely disconnected with, and independent of the influence of any political party, have been fully realized.

Crimes of other descriptions, the Board regret to say, continue to be far too prevalent in the city. Burglars and thieves pursue their avocations, and in many instances have as yet escaped detection. The Board have given much attention to this subject, and have adopted such measures as seem to them best calculated to arrest the evil. Diligent observation is kept by the police upon those in the community who are known to lead dissolute and profligate lives, without having or being able to show any visible means of support; and in all such cases the provisions of the Vagrant Act will continue to be rigidly enforced. Other steps have also been taken, which the Board trust will have the effect of detecting and bringing to justice the perpetrators of such crimes.

The experience of the Board has already satisfied them that improvements may be made in the present Police system, which would much increase its efficiency. Some of these would require, before they could be adopted, alteration in the Law of the State under which the force is organized. Of such the Board do not propose now to speak, preferring to wait until time shall more fully test the correctness of their views. There are others of an important character, which the Board have had under consideration, and which they have already sufficient authority to make; but they have refrained from doing so as yet on account of the additional expense in which they would involve the city. The chief of these would be to increase the number, and improve the condition of the station houses, none of which are suitable for the purposes for which they are designed. They neither afford sufficient accommodation for the number of men now employed on the force, nor for the detention, in a proper manner, of persons taken to them, charged with various offences, of very different grades. The drunkard, in a disgusting state of intoxication; the common loafer, whether white or colored; the suspected murderer, or other felon; the respectable and orderly citizen, who may, in a moment of excitement, have committed an offence against the laws, have all to be treated alike, and detained in the same description of cells, and those by no means of a suitable description. There surely ought to be provision made which would allow of some classification being made of parties detained in custody at the station houses. The Board are also satisfied that the number of the station houses should be at least doubled. The extent of the city is now so great that many portions of it are far removed from any of the station houses; and, when an officer makes an arrest, much time is necessarily lost whilst he is taking his prisoner to one of the stations and returning to his proper post. The Board deem it highly important that, whenever the financial condition of the city may justify such a measure, an entire change should be made in the present division of the same into police districts, and new and additional station houses should be provided.

Many complaints have been made to the Board of the inconveniences to which citizens are subjected by the strict enforcement of various city ordinances, when there is, in particular instances, no apparent necessity for requiring them to be literally observed, and where individuals are subjected to serious interruption and embarrassments in their business by being required rigidly to conform to them. It cannot be denied that cases have been presented in which the violation of an ordinance would seem not in any manner to affect either the public or any individual injuriously. For instance, whilst the ordinances respecting obstructions in streets are necessarily general in their provisions, there are some portions of streets, near ship-yards, and on the outskirts of the City, which are scarcely ever used except by the owners of property fronting upon them, who have long been in the habit of making use of such streets, in a manner prohibited by the ordinances, but without complaint being made from any quarter. In such cases, it has for many years past been the practice of successive Mayors of the City, to give directions to the Police not to enforce the ordinances, and sometimes to give permit to parties who applied for the privilege of acting contrary to their letter. If, at the instance of individuals, proceedings were instituted against such person to recover the penalties incurred, which it is believed has seldom or ever happened, the city's portion of the fine imposed would of course be remitted. Numerous applications have been made to the Board to give, in like manner, instructions to the police to refrain from enforcing the ordinances in special cases. But, whatever grounds there might have been for a Mayor of the city, as being a part of the Legislature, as well as the chief executive authority of the Corporation, assuming to exercise such powers, it seems very clear that the Board of Police can with no propriety undertake to do the same. It is made expressly their duty by the law creating the Board to "enforce all the ordinances of the city, which may be properly enforceable by a police force," and this they must do in all cases alike.

In the account of the disbursements of the Board, which accompanies this report, will be found a charge for "pay and expenses of detectives," whilst on the roll of the force no names appear of persons employed in that capacity. The Board have made no permanent appointments of detectives, but have, from time to time, temporarily engaged suitable persons to act as such. They respectfully submit that they deem it important for the detection and prevention of crime, that they should, as occasion may require, engage the services of confidential agents; but that the efficiency and usefulness of the latter would often be impaired, if not destroyed, if their names and the nature of their employment were made public. The Board have therefore thought it proper, not to place upon the regular rolls of the force, any of the persons whom they have thus employed.

In the communication addressed to the Honorable the Mayor and City Council, on the 18th of April last, it was stated that the estimates then presented by the Board, for the ensuing twelve months, did not include the cost of such arms as would be required for the police force, it being presumed that those which had been provided by the city for the police organized under its authority, and which were by law to be delivered over to the Board of Police, were of a kind and description, and were in such proper order and condition as would be required by the Board; and it was anticipated that, should such prove not to be the case, the Board would be compelled to make a further and special requisition for the funds needed to procure a further supply. The Board have found it necessary to purchase an additional quantity of arms, and among the expenses incurred under the head of "Arms and Equipments for the Police Force," is included the amount of $2,418 paid for new arms. These have, however, been paid for out of the monies already received from the city, without its having as yet been necessary to make any further requisition to defray their cost.

The following statements are herewith respectfully submitted, viz :

That marked A being an account of the receipts and disbursements of the Board, for the organization and maintenance of the police force.

Statement B, of the amounts credited and charged to the special fund, directed to be established by section 814 of article 4 of the Code.

C, a list of all the officers and men of the permanent police force on the 31st December, 1860, with a statement of the number of resignations and dismissals from the 7th of May, 1860.

D, the number of arrests made, and for what offences, during each month of the past year. Those for the first four months are taken from the books of the late Marshal, Mr. Benjamin F. Herring, and the remainder from the reports made to the present Marshal, Col. Kane.

E, a printed copy of the general rules and regulations which were adopted for the government of the police. Other general orders and regulations have been from time to time issued, but none of them are deemed of sufficient interest or importance to make it necessary to furnish copies herewith.

Respectfully submitted by order of the Board.

CHARLES HOWARD.

7

A.

RECEIPTS AND DISBURSEMENTS OF THE BOARD OF POLICE *on account of the Organization and Maintenance of the Permanent Police Force.*

RECEIPTS.		
From the Mayor and City Council pursuant to requisitions of the Board made every two weeks, from May 5th to December 27th, 1860, inclusive...........................		$167,049 80
From proceeds of sale of two horses...	$273 40	
Less charge for livery..................	19 00	
		254 40
		$167,304 20
DISBURSEMENTS.		
For salaries of Commissioners and Treasurer of Board of Police, from February 6th to November 5th, 1860.....................................	$6,250 00	
For salary of Clerk, from February 9th to December 31st, 1860.......	712 28	
For office expenses, (repairs, fuel, furniture, &c.).......................	520 16	
For office expenses, (printing stationary, advertising, &c.)..........	259 10	
For expenses in Superior Court and Court of Appeals, and counsel fees in Mandamus case vs. Mayor and City Council...........................	3,944 50	
For counsel fees and legal expenses in other cases.........................	315 72	
Amount receipts carried forward,		$167,304 20

Amount receipts brought forward,	$167,304 20

DISBURSEMENTS CONTINUED.

For arms and equipments, (revolvers, belts, clubs, shields, &c.)...	$3,779	29
For B. W. Herring, for salaries of Marshal, Deputy and Clerks, from May 1st to May 7th, 1860..........	144	02
For pay rolls of Police force under B. W. Herring, Marshal, from April 22d to May 7th, 1860—fifteen days.,.............................	8,519	97
For George. P. Kane, salaries of Marshal, Deputy and Secretary, from May 7th to December 31st, 1860.....................................	1,969	91
For Captains of Districts, for pay rolls of officers and regular Policemen, from May 7th to December 31st, 1860..............................	132,486	79
For pay of persons employed from time to time as Detectives..........	1,577	27
For pay of special Policemen for October and November elections.....	1,492	00
For pay of four "Justices" at station houses—eight months..............	266	67
For expenses of Marshal's office, from May 7th to December 31st, 1860, (for repairs, fuel, stationary, cost of telegrams, &c.)..............	1,441	62
For expense of Eastern District, from May 7th to December 31st, 186), (repairs of watch boxes and station house, fuel, furniture, bedding, &c,).............................	707	59
Amount receipts carried forward,	$167,304	20

NOTE.—From the foregoing amount of $132,486 79, paid to Captains for pay rolls of officers and men of the regular Police force, there has been returned by them to the Board, in instalments, the aggregate amount of $13,047 81, to pay for their uniforms. Of this the Board have paid to the various parties furnishing uniforms $12,578 57, and have in hand a balance of $469 24—said balance being applicable to the liquidation of some accounts not yet settled.

Amount receipts brought forward,		$167,304 20
DISBURSEMENTS CONTINUED,		
For expenses of Middle District, from May 7th to December, 31st, 1860, on same account...............	1,194 48	
For expenses of Southern District, from May 7th to December 31st, 1860, on same account...............	728 89	
For expenses of Western District, from May 7th to December 31, 1860, on same account...............	650 25	
Balance...................................	343 69	
		$167,304 20

B.

SPECIAL FUND.

RECEIPTS.

Received from Japanese Embassy, per A. Belmont, Esq., N. Y.	$300	00
Received from Policemen, rewards paid them for arresting deserters, runaway negroes, &c.	52	11
Received from proceeds of sale of unclaimed old iron,	1	65
Received from Policemen, amount paid them for serving warrants, &c.	17	30
Received from Policemen of Eastern District for fines imposed by the Board for violations of the Rules of the department.	52	00
Received from Policemen of Middle District, for fines imposed by the Board for violations of the Rules of the Department.	87	71
Received from Policemen of Southern District, for fines imposed by the Board for violations of the Rules of the Department.	70	00
Received from Policemen of Western District, for fines imposed by the Board for violations of the Rules of the Department.	135	00
	$715	77

DISBURSEMENTS.

Amounts paid to members of the Force for injuries received in person and property, as follow :—				
To Eastern District	$11	42		
To Middle District	200	36		
To Southern District	23	78		
To Western District	59	28		
	$294	84		
Balance	420	93		
			$715	77

C.

PERMANENT POLICE FORCE
OF THE CITY OF BALTIMORE.
December 31st, 1860.

BOARD OF POLICE.

President.
CHARLES HOWARD.

Treasurer.
WILLIAM H. GATCHELL.
CHARLES D. HINKS,   JOHN W. DAVIS.
(*Ex-Officio.*) HON. GEO. WM. BROWN, *Mayor of the City.*

Clerk to the Board.
WM. F. McKEWEN.

Marshal.
COL. GEORGE P. KANE.

Deputy Marshal.
THOMAS GIFFORD.

Clerk at Marshal's Office.
JNO. H. T. JOYNES.

EASTERN DISTRICT.

Captains.

Aaron W. Stockton...No. 1   Benjamin F. Kenny...No. 6

Lieutenants.

Geo. S. Spofford........No. 5   Silas E. Parsons........No. 6

Sergeants.

Robt. Hamill............No.	1	Francis W. Perry......No.	4
Wells R. Hall......... "	2	Edward Hutson......... "	5
Benjamin F. Auld.... "	3	Joseph H. Price........ "	6

Turnkeys.

David Nichol.   P. McLarney.

Police.

Aaron, Geo. W.........No.	2	Fuller, Joseph.........No	25
Barrenger, John L.... "	35	Galloway, Greenbury "	56
Birmingham, A........ "	33	Gardner, Isaac......... "	53
Baker, Henry........... "	8	Gough, W. R......... "	54
Brown, Thomas........ "	55	Glenn, Samuel........ "	65
Claridge, John H...... "	19	Glass, James A........ "	6
Cooper, Geo. W....... "	21	Hall, George........... "	39
Connelly, James....... "	32	Heurd, Wm............ "	13
Colfer, John J.......... "	20	Horseman, Wm. B.... "	40
Cox, Stephen G........ "	17	Horne, Samuel........ "	28
Diggs, Beverly......... "	1	House, Geo. W........ "	29
Dobson, Wm............ "	22	Horney, Thomas E... "	166
Dobson, Thomas H.... "	30	Hammond, John S.... "	9
Donohue, James........ "	23	Hanson, Thos. P...... "	36
Dove, M. E.............. "	11	Jay, Stephen P........ "	57
Downs, Harris.......... "	14	Johnson, Jackson L.. "	63
Francis, Robert........ "	37	Jones, Geo. W......... "	50
French, Robert......... "	72	Jordon, Robert........ "	59
Foreman, Jos. E...... "	73	Keer, John............. "	64
Lambdin, Thos......... "	68	Sahm, Geo. F......... "	73
Lambie, Wm. C....... "	45	Sapp, John F........... "	43
Lewellyn, James...... "	16	Shea, John............. "	60
Logan, Wm. C........ "	70	Sheldon, Alexander... "	31

MIDDLE DISTRICT.

Captains.

Samuel W. Bowen...No. 2   John T. Gray..........No. 7

Lieutenants.

Robert O. Elliott.....No. 1   One vacancy.

Sergeants.

Chas. McComas........No. 7	Chas. B. Aldrick.....No. 10
A. J. Maloney......... " 8	Geo. V. Metzel....... " 11
Samuel M. Linzey..... " 9	Benj. R. Norwood... " 12

Turnkeys.

John Bush.   Thomas Cafferty.

Policemen.

Baker, Henry.........No. 79	Coliins, James.........No.172
Baker, John T........ " 188	Cornelius, James S... " 189
Ball, John L.......... " 81	Cowman, Richard.... " 183
Barker, Wm.......... " 189	Clark, Jos. C.......... " 84
Bates, Charles W.... " 136	Clautice, Geo. T...... " 184
Biggs, Joseph........ " 77	Chuillou, Augustus.. " 127
Brown, John......... " 102	Darling, Jas. T....... " 185
Brown, James........ " 140	Darling, John........ " 85
Brandt, John L...... " 139	Drohan, David........ " 186
Bracken, James...... " 190	Davidson, S. G........ " 86
Bransby, John C.... " 137	Davidson, Wm........ " 109
Bouchett, Jos. A.... " 152	Degoy, John.......... " 149
Bradley, Alexander. " 141	Erdman, John......... " 126
Busick James H..... " 124	Eckert, Wm. W...... " 155
Burns, Henry......... " 88	Faucett, James H.... " 128
Canavan, James..... " 124	Foreman, Evan M... " 108
Carroll, Thos. B..... " 142	Foxcroft, Nicholas... " 173
Carlisle, Wm. H.... " 83	Freeman, Levin....... " 87
Campbell, Geo. L.. " 103	Fields, Thompson.... " 76
Garvey, James H.... " 175	Myers, Daniel........ " 135
Gaunt, John.......... " 131	McLaughlin, Jas..... " 80
Gibson Andrew...... " 176	Offut, J. F. C......... " 169
Gilmore, Robert..... " 129	O'Neil, Lewis......... " 113
Gorman, Wm. H.... " 119	Parker, Jas. A. S.... " 147

Gladson, Chas. A....No.110
Guy, Moses............ " 144
Harman, Littleton S " 120
Hamilton, Jos. E.... " 89
Hay, Robert W...... " 177
Hollins, John T...... " 90
Hyatt, Chas. C....... " 122
Hyms, Alex. H...... " 145
Hanson, Wash. R.... " 194
Harrison, Francis.... " 174
Hughes, James....... " 154
Jamison, James...... " 167
Johnson, Wm. R..... " 178
Jollie H. G............ " 146
Kees, Lawrence....... " 91
Killman, Thos. T.... " 125
Kelly, John........... " 94
Knox, Wm. F........ " 138
Linzey, John H...... " 104
Loftis, Thomas....... " 179
Lalor, Lawrence..... " 180
Lingenfelter, Jas. D " 193
Lowery, Alex. F.... " 200
McAdams, Jas........ " 168
McCann, Wm......... " 191
McCabe, Jas.......... " 161
Merryman, John.... " 112
Miskelly, Jas. F..... " 93
Moran, Charles...... " 109
Murphey, Daniel A. " 130
Murray, Andrew V.. " 156
Moran, Geo. E....... " 171
McIntire, Owen...... " 197
Phillips, Edwin...... " 95
Poole, Edwin R....... " 157
Peregoy, Wm. C..... " 192

Peirce, John J........No.115
Poston, John F....... " 101
Quinn, James......... " 158
Redgraves, Samuel... " 96
Robson, John......... " 116
Rutherford, Alex.... " 97
Robinson, Geo. W... " 98
Roberts, Wash...... " 106
Rogers, John .... " 170
Saunders, Geo. C.... " 162
Smith, Geo. T........ " 151
Seidenstricker, John " 159
Stewart, John M.... " 160
Stevenson, John...... " 117
Slater, Robert......... " 100
Staylor, Philip........ " 161
Shipley, Wm. C...... " 150
Sutherland, John.... " 195
Smith, Wm. M....... " 82
Sutton, Joseph J...... " 196
Schimp, Geo. W..... " 99
Shaw, Bernard....... " 111
Thomas, James....... " 118
Thompson, R. G...... " 163
Toner, John........... " 148
Treadway, Nicholas. " 164
Tindle, Robert W.... " 198
Williams, Wm. H.... " 165
White, Samuel J...... " 153
Weller, Geo. P........ " 78
Ware, Peter............ " 182
Wallis Wm T......... " 107
Weitzel, John......... " 132
Weitherstine, John. " 92
Waltgen, Henry..... " 199

SOUTHERN DISTRICT.

Captains.

Isaiah Gardner.........No. 3   Fred'k Boyd...........No. 4

Lieutenants.

James McMillan........No. 2   Wm. O. Wright......No. 4

Sergeants.

James E. Crangle.....No. 13   Thomas Mortimer.....No. 16
George Short........... " 14   Frederick Nagle....... " 17
Henry Creighton...... " 15   Jonathan Parsons.... " 18

Turnkeys.

David Simmont.   Jacob Ledley

Policeman.

Abell, Ignatius......No. 216   Cordery, James C....No. 239
Adams, Benj. F..... " 231   Clemmance, Jno...... " 241
Bateman, Samuel... " 215   Clipper, Wm.......... " 206
Brannan, Chas. S... " 204   Davis, Wm. J......... " 244
Brown, Samuel...... " 225   Davis, Wm. B........ " 209
Bowers, Martin H... " 236   Dancker, David...... " 243
Butler, Wm. T...... " 218   Dewalt, Wm. H...... " 229
Brooks, Peter B..... " 214   Doll, George.......... " 219
Chisholm, Henry.... " 201   Fairbanks, Wm. J... " 269
Collins, W. H....... " 262   Floyd, Wm. T....... " 205
Crawford, R. J...... " 263   Garderer, Wm........ " 212
Creamer, Anthony... " 264   Garton, Wm. C...... " 271
Cross, Wm. H......... " 224   Graham, James....... " 227
Griffith, Barzillai..... " 272   Norfolk, John W.... " 259
Groves, George........ " 207   Newell, Peter......... " 265
Hawkins, Geo. W.... " 217   Parks, John A........ " 256
Hamilton, Maxwell... " 249   Phelps, Richard...... " 255
Hammett, Jos. A..... " 121   Pennington, A. N... " 257
Hays, David........... " 208   Pumphrey, Geo. S... " 211
Harris, Wm. T........ " 270   Pumphrey, Ebenezer " 258
Hennick, John C...... " 230   Rae, Robert.......... " 220
Hause, John........... " 228   Rhodes, John F...... " 203
Hussell, Geo. W...... " 242   Sanders, Geo. P...... " 266

WESTERN DISTRICT.

Captains.
Wm. H. Brown......No. 5 Geo. H. Zimmerman.No. 8

Lieutenants.
John T. Lawson......No. 3 Theodore Essender...No. 7

Sergeants.
Wm. Stanfield	No. 19	Wm. T. Pittenger	No. 22
Wm. J. Jamison	" 20	James J. Chalmers	" 23
Geo. W. Kries	" 21	Wm. B. Meredith	" 24

Turnkeys.
Geo. Kielholtz. Wm. B. Abell.

Policeman.
Allen, John	No. 307	Hitchcock, Alex	No.341
Akers, Charles	" 301	Handy, Edward H.	" 339
Byrne, Thomas F.	" 304	Hughes, Charles E.	" 316
Brown, Benj. J	" 245	Herring, Wm. T.	" 347
Biddison, Zachariah	" 303	Hosfrous, Lewis	" 287
Carns, Wm.	" 305	Jones, Francis W.	" 340
Chandley, Jno. H.	" 327	Johnson, James M.	" 332
Cook, John	" 306	Keefer, John	" 311
Clinton, Henry D.	" 312	Kielholtz, Jacob	" 317
Collier, Richard J.	" 313	Knott, Corelius L.	" 331
Conrad, John F.	" 350	Lare, Edward	" 298
Cox, Wm. A	" 187	Larracy, Matthew G	" 395
Conway, Wm.	" 336	Lambright, Philip.	" 330
Councell, J. F.	" 284	Long, John T.	" 329
Carter, Wm. H.	" 348	Logue, Peter	" 288
Dennis, Wm. H.	" 338	Lineweaver, Geo. W	" 279
Delanty, Wm.	" 308	Lucas, Edward C.	" 297
Eney, Oliver N	" 309	McCain, John W.	" 289
Fitzgerald, Thomas	" 310	McCurley, Felix	" 344
Ford, Gustavus	" 349	McGee, James W.	" 290
Gettier, Cornelius E	" 285	Melville, Samuel J.	" 326
Gillaspy, Robt.	" 286	Morrow, William.	" 318
Hardy, James C.	" 342	Moorhead, David.	" 280
Harner, Fred'k	" 281	Marriott, Elijah J.	" 333

Neidhammer, Wm..	No.	319	Smith, Samuel A...	No.	276
Null, David..........	"	302	Thomas, Alexander	"	282
Patrick,Samuel......	"	283	Thornton, Thomas.	"	229
Perry, James C......	"	343	Throught, John T..	"	334
Russell, Wm. H....	"	322	Timmons, Geo.......	"	314
Sands, John H......	"	293	Vansant, W. H......	"	324
Steel, Benj. F.......	"	294	Wagner, Geo. L....	"	300
Stipes, Richard W..	"	346	Walters, Robert B..	"	323
Story, John W......	"	292	Wright, Thomas...	"	321
Switzer, Lewis.......	"	296	Wysham, Joseph...	"	337
Shipley, Samuel A.	"	276	Wilkinson, Wm. F.	"	320
Summers, Wm......	"	335	Walters, Wm. C....	"	114
Shipley, Andrew...	"	295	Young, John R......	"	291
Spindler, Peter A...	"	277	Zellers, George......	"	278

RECAPITULATION

Of Officers and Number of Policemen in service Dec. 31st, 1860.

OFFICERS.

Marshal........................ 1	Deputy Marshal.............1
Captains.......................8	Lieutenants(one vacancy,) 7
Sergeants.....................24	Turnkeys......................8

Total number of Officers, 49.

POLICEMEN.

Eastern District............77	Middle District............119
Southern " 77	Western " (one vacancy)76

Total number of Policemen, 349.

Number of Resignations and Dismissals of Officers and Policemen from May 7th to December 31, 1860.

	Resigned.	*Dismissed.*	*Total.*
Captains................................	3	0	3
Lieutenants............................	2	0	2
Sergeants.............................	3	2	5
Turnkeys..............................	0	0	0
Policeman.............................39		28	67
Total........................47		30	77

29

D.

Showing the number of Arrests made by the Police Department, and how disposed of, during the year, 1860.

MONTHS.	Assault and Battery.	Assault with Intent to Kill.	Assault with Intent to Commit Rape.	Assault with Intent to Rob.	Assault on Officers.	Assaulting and Stabbing.	Assaulting Wives.	Arson.	Abusing.
January.........	71	11	......	......	6	......	9	2	6
February........	70	6	......	......	4	1	7	5	23
March...........	68	10	......	5	4	4	5	3	25
April...........	40	6	......	....	9	4	14	......	26
Total 4 Months.	249	33	......	5	23	9	35	10	80
May......	145	11	......	1	......	3	17	2	54
June..............	114	10	......	......	......	4	8	1	52
July	134	11	......	......	9	2	23	......	62
August	131	5	......	......	......	2	17	......	110
September........	78	9	......	2	6	1	21	1	109
October	66	6	......	......	2	3	18	......	62
November........	95	3	......	......	9	......	16	1	74
December........	79	2	......	......	2	1	24	......	60
Total 8 Months.	842	57	......	8	28	16	144	5	583
Total 4 Months.	249	33	......	5	23	9	35	10	80
" 8 "	842	57	......	3	28	16	144	5	583
Total year 1860.	1091	90	......	8	51	25	179	15	663

TABLE D.—*Continued.*

Months.	Abusing Parents.	Abusing Families.	Abusing Horses.	Abduction.	Breach of Ordinances.	Breach of the Peace.	Burglary.	Bigamy.	Committed to House of Refuge.
January..........	2	4	1	......	50	128	......	......	......
February........	3	......	......	......	59	12?	......	......	......
March.............	......	2	......	......	66	188	......	......	......
April.............	3	4	......	......	64	132	......	......	......
Total 4 Months.	8	10	1	......	239	571	......	......	......
May...............	7	3	......	3	180	159	1	......	1
June..............	1	2	......	......	141	170	......	......	......
July	2	8	......	1	134	182	1	......	......
August...........	4	3	......	6	121	252	1	......	......
September.......	......	8	......	......	122	217	......	1	......
October	3	4	......	1	71	119	......	......	......
November........	......	5	2	......	90	165	......	......	......
December........	......	1	......	......	116	186	......	......	......
Total 8 Months.	17	34	2	11	975	1450	3	1	1
Total 4 Months.	8	10	1	......	239	571	......	......	......
" 8 "	17	34	2	11	975	1450	3	1	1
Total Year 1860.	25	44	3	11	1214	2021	3	1	1

Table D.—*Continued.*

Months.	Committed for Safe Keeping.	Desecration of the Sabbath.	Disturbing Public Worship.	Fast Driving.	Fraud.	Forgery.	False Pretences.	False Imprisonment.	Fornication.
January			2	4			2		
February						1	3		
March				6			1		
April			5	7					
Total 4 Months.			7	17		1	6		
May	4					1	1		
June		1		4			1		
July			3	11			2		
August				16			1		
September		1		15		2	6		
October		1		6	1		1		1
November				9			2		
December				10					1
Total 8 Months.	4	3	3	71	1	3	14		2
Total 4 Months.			7	17		1	6		
" 8 "	4	3	3	71	1	3	14		2
Total Year 1860.	4	3	10	88	1	4	20		2

TABLE D.—*Continued.*

Months.	Fighting in the Street.	Fugitive from Justice.	Gambling.	Gambling on the Sabbath.	Horse Stealing.	House Breaking.	Inciting to Riot.	Interfering with Officers.	Insulting Ladies on the Street.
January	14	......	......	5	......	......	......	3	1
February	16							2	......
March	15	1	......	......	......	......	......	16	......
April	8	......	......	4	......	......	......	16	......
Total 4 Months..	53	1	......	9	......	......	......	37	1
May................	26	......	8	11	......			15	1
June	19	1	......		......	7	......	14	2
July	38	......	......	2	......	4	......	13	2
August...........	46	1	......		......	2	......	14	1
September	24	......	......		......	1	......	15	1
October	38	1	......	5	......	2	1	6	2
November	19	4	......	9	......	......	3	3	4
December.........	13	......	......	2	......	4	......	3	1
Total 8 Months.	223	7	8	29	......	20	4	83	14
Total 8 Months.	53	1	......	9	......	......	......	37	1
" 4 "	223	7	8	29	......	20	4	83	14
Total Year 1860.	276	8	8	38	......	20	4	120	15

TABLE D—*Continued.*

Months.	Intoxication.	Indecent Exposure.	Keeping Disorderly Houses.	Larceny.	Illegal Voting.	Mania-a-potu.	Murder.	Murder, suspicion of.	Suspicious Characters.
January	211	......	......	30	......	......	1	......	......
February	290	......	......	20	......	......	1	......	......
March.............	297	5	......	30	......	......	......	......	......
April	189	4	......	25	......	......	......	......	......
Total 4 Months.	987	9	......	105	......	......	2	......	......
May................	245	1	......	25	......	......	......	......	......
June................	172	1	......	30	......	......	......	......	......
July	259	3	......	33	......	......	......	......	......
August............	357	6	......	45	......	......	1	7	......
September........	386	......	......	39	......	......	1	1	......
October	468	......	3	45	2	......	5	1	4
November	445	......	......	46	......	......	......	......	......
December.........	526	......	......	43	......	......	1	......	......
Total 8 Months.	2858	11	3	306	2	......	8	9	4
Total 4 Months.	987	9	......	105	......	......	2	......	......
" 8 "	2858	11	3	306	2	......	8	9	4
Total Year 1860	3845	20	3	411	2	......	10	9	4

Table D—*Continued.*

Months.	Peddling without License	Pick-Pockets.	Passing Counterfeit Money.	Rioting.	Rioting at alarms of fire.	Rape.	Receiving Stolen Goods.	Robbery.	Selling Liquor on Sunday
January		2		1			1	2	
February		1	1				4	9	2
March			1			1	2	5	
April	1	1					1	1	
Total 4 Months.	1	4	2	1		1	8	17	2
May				8	1		2	5	2
June	1	5		8		1	1	2	
July	1			11	1	2		4	1
August	2	1	2	5		1		3	1
September				4				2	1
October		5		11				7	2
November			3			1	3	3	
December	1		1	2			7	6	5
Total 8 Months.	5	11	6	49	2	5	13	32	12
Total 4 Months.	1	4	2	1		1	8	17	2
" 8 "	5	11	6	49	2	5	13	32	12
Total Year 1860	6	15	8	50	2	6	21	49	14

4

Table D.—*Continued.*

Months.	Shooting at Persons.	Selling Liquor without License.	Shooting with Intent to Kill.	Swindling.	Threatning to Kill.	Threatening to Assault.	Threatening Arson.	Vending Lottery Policies.	Vagrants.
January			1				3		
February			2		1				
March	4				1				1
April	1	1					2		
Total 4 Months.	5	1	3		2	5			1
May	4	2	1	1	3				21
June		1			3				47
July					1			28	39
August					1				36
September					2				23
October						1			20
November					1				20
December		1	1					4	36
Total 8 Months.	4	4	2	1	11	1		32	242
Total 4 Months.	5	1	3		2	5			1
" 8 "	4	4	2	1	11	1		32	242
Total Year 1860	9	5	5	1	13	6		32	243

TABLE D—*Continued.*

MONTHS.	Perjury.	Destroying Property,	Harboring Colored Persons.	Dealing with Minors.	Absconding.	Bastardy.	AGGREGATE.	Committed for Trial.
January	1	2					576	62
February	1	3					657	60
March.............		2	1				770	80
April.............		3					571	62
Total 4 Months.	2	10	1				2574	264
May...............							974	122
June..............					2		827	86
July					3		1030	77
August............					2	6	1209	105
September........					2	3	1102	88
October		8			3		1007	69
November	1						1036	67
December........				1			1140	55
Total 8 Months.	1	8		1	12	9	8325	669
Total 4 Months.	2	10	1				2574	264
" 8 "	1	8		1	12	9	8325	669
Total Year 1860	3	18	1	1	12	9	10899	933

TABLE D.—*Continued.*

MONTHS.	Committed for Examination.	Bailed for Trial.	Bailed to keep the Peace.	Committed in Default of Bail.	Fined.
January	14	57	92	282	69
February	27	54	69	351	96
March	15	58	121	407	89
April	11	35	84	312	67
Total 4 Months..........	67	204	366	1352	321
May..................	24	56	225	435	113
June.................	21	65	206	349	100
July	27	65	262	486	113
August...............	27	66	351	599	61
September............	30	47	304	573	60
October	23	37	259	549	70
November.............	26	40	223	605	75
December.............	23	55	266	653	88
Total 8 Months..........	201	431	2096	4248	680
Total 4 Months..........	67	204	366	1352	321
" 8 "	201	431	2096	4248	680
Total Year 1860..........	268	635	2462	6600	1001

RULES AND REGULATIONS

FOR THE GOVERNMENT OF THE

PERMANENT POLICE FORCE

OF THE CITY OF BALTIMORE.

The "Board of Police of the City of Baltimore" are charged, among other high and responsible duties, with those of preserving the public peace, preventing crime, and arresting offenders, and protecting the rights of persons and property, at all times of the day and night, within the boundaries of the city of Baltimore, as well on water as on land. To enable them to discharge their duties, they have been entrusted with all powers which, in the judgment of the Legislature, were deemed necessary or proper.

The Board are authorized and required to appoint, enroll, and employ a permanent police force, which they shall equip and arm, as they shall judge necessary, and to make all such rules and regulations, not inconsistant with the law creating the Board as they may judge necessary for the appointment, employment, uniforming, discipline, trial and government of the police. In discharging this duty, it has been the desire of the Board to call into the public service a body of men, whose individual character and habits of life will afford a guarantee for the faithful discharge of their respective duties, and for their cheerful and cordial co-operation with the Board in executing, according to its spirit as well as letter, the provisions of the law, under which they are alike appointed.

In preparing the following rules and regulations, which are hereby prescribed for the discipline and government of the police force, the Board of Police have had in view the single object of raising to the highest standard the efficiency and respectability of the entire force, and are satisfied that a strict and rigid observance of them by every member of the police will materially tend to this result. Such alterations and modifications of them as experience may demonstrate to the Board to be advisable, will from time to time be made. But until so altered, a literal and punctilious adherence to them will be positively required; and it will be expected that every member of the force will give his willing and zealous aid in carrying out the views of the Board and the provisions of the law.

GENERAL REGULATIONS.

1. The marshal, deputy marshal, captains, lieutenants, sergeants and turnkeys, first appointed, will hold their offices until the 10th day of March, 1861, and until they be re-appointed, or their successors shall have duly qualified. They are hereafter to be appointed for one year from and after the 10th day of March next ensuing the date of appointment. They shall at any time be removable by the Board for cause.

2. The policemen shall be employed, as the law prescribes for five years on the permanent police, and any such policeman whose term of service shall expire, and who, during his appointment, shall have faithfully performed his duty, shall be preferred by the Board in making their new appointments. Policemen shall be subject to removal only for cause, after hearing by the Board.

3. All the officers and men of the police force shall devote their entire time to their duties as such, and are prohibited from engaging in any other business. Though they will be divided into sections, and assigned in rotation for active service, they are to be considered as always on duty, and liable to be called on at any moment. They are therefore required invariably to wear their uniform dress when they appear in public, unless they are under suspension, or have the written authority of the Board of Police for a definite period of time to appear in plain dress, during which time they will be relieved from duty, unless specially called on by an officer of higher grade to execute the laws or preserve the peace.

4. No member of the police force will be allowed to wear any insignia of office, or embellishment of any part of the uniform, other than such as the regulations of the Board may prescribe.

5. Captains, lieutenants, sergeants and policemen, whenever on an actual tour of service, shall wear the shield or badge, on the outside of the outermost garment, over the left breast, so that the entire surface of the shield shall always be distinctly visable. At all other times they will carry it with them, and if called on to do active duty they shall immediately place it over the breast as above.

6. All arms, equipments, insignia of office, books of regulations, and other property of every description of the city of Baltimore or of the Board of Police, which have been furnished to any member of the police force, and which are not required to be paid for by him, must immediately upon his ceasing to be a member of it, be returned in good order, ordinary wear and tear excepted, to a captain of the district to which such member may have been attached.

7. Every member of the force must appear at all times neat and cleanly in his person in all respects, with his uniform and equipments in perfect order. His hair and beard must be kept neatly cut and trimmed, and proper regard paid to the bathing of the person. All inspections at the station-houses or elsewhere, will embrace all the above particulars.

8. Whilst firm in the discharge of their duties, the officers and men of the police force must at all times be civil and orderly, must maintain command of temper, observe decorum and exercise patience under personal provocation; the use by them of harsh, profane or insulting language on any occasion is possitively prohibited.

9. Whilst all members of the force are cautioned against allowing themselves to be readily provoked by uncivil or rude language, yet if the offence be of an aggravated character, or anything like an assault be made or attempted on their persons, they are authorised to arrest the offender, and take him to the station-house on a charge of a breach of the peace, or assault, as the circumstances may warrant. If such arrest be not made at the time, or if on any occasion a member of the force desires to take out a warrant for any offence against his person or property, the written consent of a captain of the district must first be obtained, and no complaint made by a member of the force of such offences shall be withdrawn without the written consent of the Board of Police.

10. Police officers and men are strictly fobidden to enter any public bar-room, or drinking room, except in the discharge of their duty; nor can they be allowed to smoke on the public streets. A charge of being at any time intoxicated will be a sufficient ground for the suspension, and, if proved, for the dismissal of any member of the police force.

11. Courtesy of demeanor among all the members of the

police foree, as well as respect to officers, is indispensable to discipline. Respect to superiors in rank will not be confined o obedience when on active duty ; but will be manifested on tall occasions. Every officer and policeman will, therefore, be expected, on meeting or approahing one of higher rank than himself, promptly to offer the customary salute, which must, in all cases, be immediately and respectfully returned.

12. The law positively prohibits every officer of police and policeman from receiving any money or gratuity or extra compensation for any services they may render, without the consent of the Board of Police ; and it provides, that all such moneys, as any of them may be so permitted to receive, shall be paid over to the Board, in aid of a fund for the relief of policemen injured in the discharge of their duties, and of their families, and for extra pay for gallantry and good conduct on extraordinary occasions. Members of the force will also not be allowed, in that character, to receive any complimentary gift or subscription, whether tendered by members of the police force or by other citizens.

13. The entire police force of the city constitutes one body, and any of its officers and men may be at any time placed on day or night duty, temporarily or permanently, anywhere within the jurisdiction of the Board of Police, without regard to the district to which they may have been before attached, or to the duty previously assigned them. And in making promotions, the Board will look to the whole force of the next grade in rank, without reference specially to the district in which a vacancy may have occurred, or to the numbers by which members of the same grade may be distinguished from each other.

14. No officer or policeman will be allowed to leave the city, or absent himself from duty, without the written consent of the Board of Police. If there be no opportunity for making application to the Board, such consent may be given by the Marshal, or Deputy Marshal, or in cases of extreme and pressing urgency, by a Captain. Officers granting such leave will report the reasons for the same to the Marshal.— Absence from duty without such permission will subject the party to being reported, and tried for neglect of duty.

15. It shall be the duty of every member of the force, whenever he may be called on by an officer of the same district of higher permanent rank or by the Marshal ,or Deputy Marshal to give all information in his possession touching any violation of the rules and regulations of the Board by any other member of the police force.

16. All bodies of policemen proceeding under charge of an officer to perform any service shall be marched in military order and preserve silence.

17. No officer or policemen shall communicate, except as directed by his superior in office, any information respecting his instructions, or give to any person any intimation or information which might enable any party to escape from arrest or punishment or facilitate the disposing or secreting of property stolen or embezzled.

18. All property found in the streets or elsewhere by, or which may otherwise come into the possession of a member of the police force, must be safely delivered to the captain at the station-house of the district, with a special report in relation to the same.

19. Members of the police force must not serve any process in civil cases, or render assistance or interfere in any such cases except to prevent an immediate breach of the peace or to quell a disturbance. If a warrant for the arrest of a party on a criminal charge be placed in the hands of a sergeant or policeman by any other authority than by an officer of police of higher rank, he will deliver the same to the officer in command at the station-house, who will designate by whom it shall be executed. But if the sergeant or policeman when such warrant is placed in his hands have an immediate opportunity of making the arrest, or, if it be necessary without delay to arrest the party charged, to prevent his escape from the city, he will at once execute the warrant.

20. No member of the police force shall on any occasion maltreat a prisoner or other person, by using unnecessary violence towards them.

21. Every member of the police force shall be protected in his right to entertain his own political opinions. But they are all required to refrain from attending any primary or other political meeting for the purpose of making nominations or promoting the election of any public officers, or of electing delegates to any political convention; neither can they be permitted to be delegates to any such convention, or members of, or connected with any club or other association, whose objects or other purposes may have reference to the nomination or election of any candidate for office. And it is particularly enjoined upon them carefully to avoid, at all times and in all places, entering into any political discussion of a character which may lead to recrimination and the use of harsh and intemperate language. On the days of any elections held under the ordinances of the city, or the laws of the State, or of the United States, it shall be the duty of every officer of police and policeman, whether specially assigned to attend at the polls or not, to preserve the peace, and repress disorder, and by all lawful means in his power to protect the integrity of the ballot-box, enforce the rights of legal voters, and prevent illegal voting. Every officer and man in command of parties of the police on such days, will give to each separate

5

member of the same, in turn, an opportunity during the day to vote at his proper election precinct, whenever, in the judgment of such person in command, this can be done without jeopardizing the public peace, or of affording an opportunity for creating disorder, or for a violation of law by such temporary diminution of his command.

22. No member of the police force will be allowed to make or to solicit from others, contributions for political purposes.

23. Every member of the force shall at all times carry with him a memorandum book, on which he shall enter, as soon as practicable after the occurrence, the names of all persons taken into custody by him, and the nature of the charges preferred against them, with such particulars as will be important at the trial of the case, especially noting the names of the witnesses present when the alleged offence was committed. Their books will be furnished by the Board, and must always be open to the inspection of any officer of higher rank, and returned as other public property when the party quits the service, or at any time when demanded by the Marshal, Deputy Marshal or a Captain of Police.

24. Every member of the police force will be required to pay prompt obedience to every order that may be given to him in the name of the Board of Police, by the President or President *pro tem.* of the Board.

25. Any officer may, if he deem the occasion to require it, suspend any subordinate in rank to himself for disobedience of orders, or gross neglect or violation of the rules and regulations; such suspension shall as soon as practicable be reported, if made by the Marshal or Deputy, directly by the Marshal to the Board, and if made by any other officer, to the Captain on duty at the station house of the district to which the party suspended was attached, together with the reasons for such suspension. Such report will, without delay, be transmitted to the Marshal, and by him to the Board.— An officer or policeman whilst under suspension must not wear his uniform. Any officer or policeman specially detailed to command a party may, for like causes, suspend any one of the same, or of a subordinate grade, who is under his orders, and shall make in the same manner a report of his proceedings.

26. Each officer and policeman will have assigned to him a separate number, to be worn at all times on the cap when in uniform; such number indicate no permanent superiority of rank, and they may at any time be changed, as the Board may direct. But as it is desirable that, at all times, when two or more are acting together, some one of them shall, in order to prevent confusion, be responsible for their action, and should consequently have for the time being the right to give all necessary directions to the others, the following rules are prescribed, viz., Every officer and policeman will at all time

obey an order given him by an officer of higher rank than himself. Should such order interfere with one previously given by any other officer, the party receiving it will respectfully state that fact, but if the last order be then repeated he will obey it. But if an officer thus countermands or interferes with the execution of a previous order, given by another officer of equal or superior rank to himself, he will be responsible for so doing, and will be required to show to the satisfaction of the Marshal that his action was justified and required by the urgency of exising circumstances.

a. Within the limits of the district to which he is attached, every officer and policeman will be temporarily superior to and will have the right to give directions to, all other members of the force from other districts who may be present, if they be of the same or of a lower permanent rank than himself, and such directions must be observed and obeyed.

b. When officers and policeman of the same district are acting together within its limits, the one wearing the lowest number will be temporarily superior to all others of higher numbers, excepting, however, that an officer or policeman who is at the time on his regular, active tour of duty, shall, without regard to number, take the direction of all other of the same rank temporarily required to assist him, and a policeman on duty within his own beat shall, in like manner, have the direction of all other policeman who may be required to assist him, though belonging to the same district.

c. When two officers of equal rank are present where any duty is to be performed, and neither of them belongs to the district in which their action is required, the officer of the lowest number will take the direction of all others of the same or of lower rank.

d. The last two above rules shall not apply to any case in which the Marshal or Deputy Marshal, or (in the absence of instructions from them) the Captain on duty within his district, shall assign to any particular officer or policeman the command of any part of the force ordered on any special service. In such cases the officer or policeman will have the command of all others of the same permanent rank with himself, who may be required to assist him, and an officer of higher rank, unless on active duty at the same place, shall not interfere with an officer, so detailed to command, unless it appear to him that the state of things is such that he ought to take the command, of which he shall make a full report.

The captains, lieutenants and sergeants are required to see that the above rules as to temporary rank are distinctly explained to, and understood by, every member of the police force in their respective districts.

27. Every officer and policeman commanding a reserve

force, which may on any special occasion have been ordered on active duty, shall immediately on the return of such party to the station-house call the roll, note absentees, if any, and report the same, together with anything material that may have occurred to the Captain of the station-house, unless he shall have been ordered to report directly to the Marshal or Deputy Marshal.

28. The officers and men of the police force will, in all things, co-operate with and aid the corporate authorities in the discharge of their duties, and pay prompt and respectful attention to all suggestions or requests made by the Mayor of the city or the heads of the several departments. They are not, however, in order to comply with any such suggestion or request, to neglect any duty or leave the post to which their previous orders or the rules and regulations may have assigned them, but will, in such case, report as soon as practicable to their immediate commanding officer for instructions.

29. It shall be the duty of the police at times of fire to place ropes, if any be at hand, or to establish guards across all streets, lanes and alleys on which there shall be any building situated, on fire, and at such other points as they may deem expedient and necessary; and they shall prevent any and all persons, except owners and employees of buildings endangered by the existing fire, and firemen, who shall be known by the badge of the fire Department or Company to which they may belong, from entering within the lines designated by guards or ropes.

30. The ordinary duties of Captains and of those under their command respectively are to be performed within the several districts to which they are attached, But it is the duty of every officer and member of the Police Force, whenever there is a call for their services, to detail a sufficient party, or if it seem necessary, to repair in person to any other part of the city where their action or assistance is actually required. In such cases, the officers and policeman of the district in which the force is called on to act, will temporarily take rank of, and have the right to command all others of the same or lower permanent grade, as provided by Sec. 26, sub. sec. a, of these Rules.

31. The law provides for the enforcement by the police of the laws of the State and the ordinances of the city, so far as the same may properly be enforced by a police force; special instructions as to the discharge of these duties will from time to time be issued.

32. Every officer and policeman will be held responsible for the proper discharge of the duties assigned him; and it will not be received as an excuse or justification for anything that he may do, or omit to do, that he followed the advice or suggestion of any other person, whether connected with the

police force or not, except when an officer of higher rank, who has the right so to do, may take upon himself the responsibility of giving to him direct and positive orders for his conduct.

33. Each member of the police force will be furnished with, and must keep in his possession a copy of these rules and regulations, with which he must make himself familiar, in order that his duties may be fully understood. If he cease to be a member of the force, such copy will be returned to the Board, or to an officer of police, as other public property.

Every police officer and policeman is also required to make himself well acquainted with the details of every order issued for his government, that may at any time be posted in the station-house of the district to which he may be attached.

34. The penalty for a wilful violation of any of the rules and regulations prescribed by the Board, or habitual inattention to them, will in all cases upon conviction, after a hearing by the Board of the party charged with "disobedience of orders," "violation of the rules and regulations," or "neglect of duty," be liable to dismissal from the service.

The Board may, if they think fit, in view of the peculiar circumstances of any case, impose the lesser penalties of fine and suspension. But they will never consider any officer or policeman as proper to be retained in the service, if, from the evidence before them on his trial, they shall arrive at the conclusion that he is unable or unwilling to discharge his whole duty, in such manner as will be creditable to the service, and satisfactory to his superior officers and to the Board.

SPECIAL DUTIES

OF

OFFICERS AND POLICEMEN.

The foregoing general Rules and Regulations, and such others as may be hereafter prescribed by the Board, will be considered as binding on all members of the Police Force, in every case to which they apply. The following Rules have relation more particularly to the special duties assigned to them individually.

DUTIES OF THE MARSHAL.

1. The Marshal is the chief executive head and commander, under the Board of Police, of the entire Police Force; and all officers and members of the same must respect him and obey his orders accordingly. It shall be his duty, under the instructions of the Board, to see that the laws of the State and ordinances of the city are enforced, and that the rules and regulations prescribed by the Board are strictly observed.

He shall, from time to time, submit to the Board for their consideration all such general orders as he may deem it desirable to issue for the better government of the Police Force, and if approved by the Board shall see that the same are duly observed. In any sudden emergency, requiring immediate action, before the Board can be consulted, he shall issue such special orders as he may deem necessary to prevent the commission of crime, or to preserve the public peace, and shall as soon as practicable report to the Board all such orders, and his proceedings in reference to the same.

He shall have made out, and shall keep in his office, such copies or abstracts of all reports made to him by officers and members of the Police Force as he may deem necessary, and transmit the original reports to the Board every morning, by 11 o'clock, with such remarks and suggestions as he may think required. He shall from time to time report to the Board upon all matters which he may deem to require their attention, and make also such special reports as they may at any time call for.

2. It shall be his duty to repair in person to all extensive conflagrations, and to the scene of all serious riot or tumultuous assemblages, take command of the Police Force present, and protect property and enforce the la vs.

3. He shall have power to direct temporarily any or all of the Police Force to any place within the limits of the jurisdiction of the Board, where in his opinion their services may be required.

4. He shall report to the Board of Police, when brought to his knowledge, the presence of any contagious or infectious disease in the city, or the existence of any nuisance which may be detrimental to the public health.

5. The returns and reports of commanding officers of any special force detailed for service beyond the city limits, shall be made to the Marshal.

6. He shall from time to time, (not less frequently than once a month,) report to the Board upon the condition of the several station houses as to order and cleanliness ; and upon the manner in which the books are there kept.

7. When charges are filed in his office, or preferred by himself against any member of the police force, he shall immediately transmit the same, with the names of the party making the charge, and all the names of witnesses given him, to the Board of Police, for such action thereon as they may deem proper.

8. Whenever the Marshal shall detail officers or policeman on special duty, he shall notify in writing the Captains of the Districts to which they may at the time be attached.

DEPUTY MARSHAL.

1. Under the direction of the Marshal, the Deputy Marshal shall have supervision of the entire Police Force, and in case of the sickness or absence from the City of the Marshal, shall exercise full command over the Force. He will be respected and obeyed accordingly.

2. His duty shall be to see that the Orders and directions of the Board of Police and of the Marshal,•in relation to the dress, discipline, deportment and duties of Members of the Force are promptly obeyed, and the rules and regulations prescribed by them enforced throughout the City.

3. He shall attend at the Marshal's Office at such times, and shall assist the Marshal by attending to such parts of his duties as the latter may designate. He shall make to the Marshal such regular and special Reports as he may direct.

4. He shall, at least once in every twenty-four hours, visit each station-house, and observe its condition.

5. Upon the occurrence of any extensive conflagration or serious riot or tumultuous assemblage, he shall repair to the spot, and if the Marshal be not present, take charge of the Police Force, and act as the Marshal is required to do. When the Marshal is on the ground, the Deputy will remain and assist him, or repair to the Office or elsewhere as the Marshal may direct.

CAPTAINS.

1. The Captains of Police will be held strictly accountable for the preservation of the public peace in their several districts ; and to insure good order, they are invested with the power to post the men under their command in such parts of their respective districts, and assign to them such duties as they may deem expedient ; subject at all times, however, to the orders of the Marshal or Deputy Marshal. Captains will also be responsible for the condition of their several station houses.

2. They will exercise constant vigilance over all supicious houses and places in their respective districts, and command their Policemen to carefully note the residence, within their beats, and the conduct of all suspicious persons. The Captains will keep a record of the same. and report the result to the Marshal from time to time, as he may direct.

3. They shall report to the Marshal in writing all violations of the prescribed rules and regulations, by any of their command, that may come to their knowledge.

4. They shall on the first day of every month, (and at any other times when necessary,) make out, and return to the Marshal, requisitions for supplies of all such articles as the Board of Police may authorize to be furnished for the use of the station-houses, and shall at the same time report the quantities of each article remaining on hand of supplies previously furnished. They will on the 1st days of May, August, November, and February, in each year, and also whenever at other times specially called on, return to the Marshal an accurate inventory of all furniture and property in, and will state the condition of, their respective station-houses.

5. They will be held responsible for the cleanliness of their respective station-houses ; and will permit no persons to remain about them but members of the Police Force, or other parties who may have business requiring their presence there.

6. The Captain, or Officer at the time in command at each station-house, will keep a Policeman or Turnkey constantly stationed at the door, who shall refuse admittance to persons not connected with the Police Force, unless their visit is on

business relating to Police Matters. When, however, any
person arrested may be under examination, all persons whom
the Police Justice, the party who made the complaint, or the
accused, may desire to be examined as witnesses, shall be
called in; and the Captains will also admit such friends of
the accused, to a limited and not inconvenient or unreasonable extent, as the latter may desire to be present,

7. It shall be the especial duty of Captains, as of all other
Officers, to see that their subordinates adhere strictly to the
regulations respecting cleanliness and neatness of uniform
and of person, and to report in writing to the Marshal all
violations of the same.

8. The captains will cause the Men of their respective
commands to be divided into such number of Platoons and
Sections as the Marshal shall direct, and designate the proper
Officers to command the same; and see that such Officers
properly discharge their duties.

9. They shall see that all the members of their commands,
are thoroughly instructed in their duties, and are acquainted
with the nature and extent of the powers delegated to them
respectively.

10. The roll shall be called at the station-houses, at the
commencement and at the termination of each hour of active
duty; and the Captains will cause the Men, as their Names
are called for Patrol Duty, to arrange themselves in line, that
they may be inspected by the Sergeants.

11. The Captains shall divide their respective Districts,
with the sanction of the Marshal, into proper number of patrol beats, both for day and night, and designate the Men
for patrol duty therein and the Sergeants to command them.
The beats shall be numbered, and records of the same, and of
the names of the Sergeants and Men assigned to each, be
kept at the station-houses.

12. When any person is brought to a station-house charged
with any offence against the laws, the Captain on duty will
ascertain from the party making the charge, whether the
alleged act constitutes an offence for which a person may lawfully be detained, and whether there is reasonable ground for
supposing that it was committed by the party accused. If
satisfied on these points, he will cause the party to be detained in custody at the station-house, until the case be acted
on by the Police Magistrate. If the party has been arrested
under a regular warrant, he will in all cases be detained
until the case is thus acted on. All persons who may be legally remanded for a further hearing, or finally committed,
the Captain will cause to be safely escorted, and delivered,
with the proper order of commitment, to the custody of the
Warden of the City Jail.

6

13. Captains will keep an accurate record of all persons arrested and brought to their station-houses in custody, whether they be detained or not. On such record shall be entered the names of the persons arrested, those of the parties who made the charge, and the Officers who made the arrest; any special circumstances which may have attended the same; the nature of the alleged offence; the names of any persons given in as witnesses of the same, and the disposition made of the case, viz: whether the party was released, and by whom, or sent to jail.

If he be detained at the station-house when brought in, the witnesses present will be notified to attend at the next regular hour for the visit of the Police Justice, or at such other time, as he may require their attendance.

14. They shall enter upon a book kept for the purpose, a correct list of all property found, or suppossed to be stolen, or that for any other cause may be delivered into their possession, with the name of any supposed owner. Such property shall, within 24 hours, be safely delivered to the Marshal, or such person, in his office, as may be authorized by him to receive the same, unless the Magistrate require the property to remain for a longer time at the station-house, in which case it must be safely cared for by the Captains.

A receipt is to be given by the Captains of whomsoever the property is delivered to at the Marshall's office, to the party from whom it is received.

15. Every morning at 9 o'clock, the Captains will report to the Marshal in writing, a detailed account of the occurrences in their several districts during the preceding 24 hours, embracing the names of absentees from roll call, the names of Officers and Men on duty, all violations of orders or of standing regulations, the names of all parties arrested and brought to the station-houses in custody, with the offence charged, the Officers by whom the arrest was made, and the disposition made of each case; and any information they may have received of offences committed within their districts.

They shall also report to the Marshal as often, as circumstances may require, throughout the day, any occurrences of special interest in their respective districts.

16. On an alarm of Fire being given, it shall be the duty of the Captain on active duty in the district, or in an adjoining district, near to the station-house of which the Fire may occur, to repair to the Fire with such Force, as he may have at once at command, and be diligent in preserving order, protecting property, aiding firemen to discharge their duty, and in carrying out the general regulations prescribed for cases of Fire. When the Marshal or Deputy Marshal are on the

ground, the Captains will place themselves immediately under their orders.

17. In cases of riot or any sudden emergency requiring the services of the Police, the Captains on duty in the districts in or near to which the event occurs, will forthwith proceed to the place at which the Police are wanted, with such force as they can command, or with part thereof as they may find necessary, and be vigilant and prompt in the discharge of their duties.

18. The Captains will attend to having all notices sent to them from the Board of Police or the Marshal's Office, and subpœnas issued by the Police Magistrates, promptly served.

19. They shall keep at the station-houses, a book in which shall be entered all complaints of violations of City Ordinances, by whom the violation is alleged to have been committed, the names of the complainants and the residence of all the parties, and send a copy of such entries to the Marshal every morning at or before 9 o'clock; unless in their judgment the circumstances of the case are such as to render it proper immediately to make a special report of any case.

20. The Captains shall have entered on another Book to be kept at each station-house, the time that the Captains, Lieutenants, Sergeants and Turnkeys were on duty at the station-house, the particular hours during which any of them were engaged in visiting the beats of the Policemen, and those during which they were absent on any special duty ; and also the names of such of the reserved Police Force, as may have been detailed for any special duty, and the time they were absent on such service.

21. All the entries upon the Books and Records required to be kept at the station-houses, shall be made by the Lieutenants or Sergeants on duty at the time at the Stations. In their absence, the Captain may designate any other member of the Force to make such entries. But in all cases, they shall be made under the supervision of the Captain at the time in command, who shall be responsible for their correctness. All such Books and Records shall at all times be freely open to the inspection of the Marshal, Deputy Marshal, and of every member of the Board of Police.

22. The Captains will be vigilant in enforcing the laws against lotteries, gambling and selling liquor on the Sabbath. And whenever they shall have reason to believe that gambling is being carried on in any house in violation of the law, or that any Landlord of a Public House is in the habit of violating the Sunday liquor law, they shall despatch a Sergeant as often, as may be necessary to ascertain the facts. They may station a Policenan, in uniform, near the door of any such house, or in the vicinity, to observe who frequent the same, in order that the necessary information may be

communicated, when called for by the Grand Jury of the Baltimore City Court.

23. They will be particular in reporting to the Marshal, in order that he may promptly notify the proper city authorities, all violations of the rules prescribed for the Lighting, &c., of the City Lamps, or of any other general regulations of the heads of any of the Departments, which may be reported by Policemen or others.

24. On the death, resignation or discharge from the Police Force of any member thereof, other than the Marshal, Deputy Marshal, or a Detective, it shall be the duty of the Captain at the time on day duty, of the district to which such member was attached, to demand the surrender of the arms, equipments, insignia of office, books of regulations, and of all other public property belonging to the City or to the Board of Police, which may have been placed in the hands of such member; for all of which that may be delivered to him, the Captain will give a receipt, in which he shall state the order and condition in which he received the same.

If such demand be not promptly complied with, the Captain will so report to the Marshal, in order that the surety on the bond of the party may be notified of his liability.

25. In the absence of a Captain form a station-house, all his duties, as prescribed by the regulations at the time in force, will devolve upon the Lieutenant or Sergeant who may be in command there, and who will be required strictly to perform them.

No station-house must ever be left without the presence of a Captain or Lieutenant, or in cases of urgency, of a Sergeant.

LIEUTENANTS.

1. The Lieutenants will exercise all the powers and discharge the duties of Captain, in the event of the sickness or absence of the latter from their respective station-houses; and will see that all the prescribed rules and regulations are strictly conformed to.

2. It will be their duty to see that the Sergeants are at all times diligent in the performance of their duties. For this purpose they shall visit the different sections of their respective districts, in such order and at such times as may be prescribed by any general order, or as their Captains on active duty may direct; and shall notice the deportment of the members of the police force, and see that the regulations in regard to neatness and cleanliness of uniform and person are properly observed. They shall report in writing to the Captain every violation of the prescribed regulations.

3. The Lieutenants will at all times act as assistants to, and will obey the orders of the Captains of their respective districts.

SERGEANTS.

1. Sergeants will be held responsible for the omission of policemen to conform to the regulations requiring neatness of appearance, and proper condition of uniform and equipments, unless they promptly report such omissions to the Captains or Lieutenants of the district to which they are attached. They must also carefully notice and report any case of neglect of duty by the men of their respective sections.

2. When ordered to the command of policeman going to their beats, the Sergeants will march them to their respective beats in military order, habitually in single file, see them properly placed, and instruct them as to the extent of their beats.

The Sergeants on active duty shall patrol their allotted precincts, and see each man of their respective sections on duty within the same at least once in every two hours.

3. The Sergeants will inspect every man of their respective sections, as soon as they are formed in line, preparatory to marching on patrol or any other duty, and see that in every particular the regulations are complied with; then at the proper hour proceed with them and relieve in succession the men previously on their beats, beginning with those nearest the station-houses, and ending with the furthest.

The men thus relieved will remain on their beats, until the return of the Sergeant, meet him at such point as he may have designated, and successively fall in with the relieved section and be marched to the station-houses.

4. The Sergeants are strictly enjoined to require at all times proper obedience and respect from their subordinates; and on no occasion indulge in unofficerlike familiarity with them. The particular attention of the Sergeants is called to this regulation.

POLICEMEN.

1. Policemen must make themselves familiar with every part of their respective beats; and vigilantly scrutinize all suspicious persons they meet with, in order that crime may as far as possible be prevented, and when committed, that the offender may be discovered and arrested.

2. They must, to the extent of their ability, prevent assaults, breaches of the peace, and all crimes about to be committed. The frequent occurrence of disorders on any beat, without the prompt arrest of offenders, will afford grounds for attributing negligence to the Policeman on such beat, unless the Board of Police are satisfied that such a state of things has been owing to causes beyond the Policeman's control.

3. They will be expected to acquire such knowledge of the

inhabitants within their respective beats, as to be enabled at once to recognize them.

4. They must carefully examine every part of their respective beats, especially in the night time, and see that doors and windows are not left unsecured. Should a Policeman be stopped or delayed in his regular patrol by any special cause requiring him to remain at a particular place, he must satisfy his superior officers that there was cause for his so remaining.

5. They shall strictly watch the conduct of all suspicious persons, or those of known bad character who may live or be found in their several beats, and take notice of the time and the particular part of their beats where such persons may be seen, and of any attending circumstances worthy of notice. When any serious offence shall be discovered to have been committed, the Policemen shall state to their respective Captains what persons of such character they may have observed and at what places.

6. They shall observe all houses and places in which they may have reason to think that gambling is being carried on in violation of law, and report the result of their observations to their commanding officers.

7. All persons arrested must be forthwith taken to the station-house of the district to which the Policeman making the arrest is attached. Whenever any person charges another with the commission of a crime, and requires the party to be taken into custody, the Policeman called on to make the arrest shall require the accuser to accompany him as a witness, along with the accused to the station-house—or if the former be a known responsible person, the Policeman may be satisfied with his assurance that he will immediately repair to the station-house. The Policeman will return as soon as possible to his beat, and inspect the same, to see that no depredation has been committed in his absence.

8. No Policeman shall leave his beat until regularly relieved, except for the purpose of taking a party arrested to the station-house, of rendering assistance when summoned by a Policeman on a neighboring beat, or of interfering to prevent crime or arrest offenders in cases falling under his own observation, in the adjacent parts of neighboring beats. Special instructions will be given at the station-houses and through the Sergeants, as to the mode in which signals for assistance are to be made, and the circumstances under which they are to be given, and to be attended to,

9. Whenever a Policeman is called from his beat in the discharge of his duty, he will return to it without delay, as soon as his services elsewhere can be dispensed with. Whilst he is absent, all the Policemen on adjoining beats, who may be

aware of the fact, will, as far as possible, extend their watchfulness to his beat as well as to their own.

10. Policemen must always give their names or show their numbers to any person who may require them to do so.

11. They must only use their Batons or other weapons in cases of self-defence, or of forcible or violent resistance to them when in the discharge of their duty.

12. Policemen detailed for special duty, will each day make a report to the Captains of their respective districts, at such hours as the latter may designate.

13. It will be a neglect of duty for a Policeman carelessly to lose any part of his equipments, or insignia of office, his copy of rules, memorandum book, &c, ; or to omit to make an immediate report to his commanding officers of the loss of any such articles.

14. Policeman will carefully note and report all drinking houses that are kept open at unusually late hours, or at which they may have reason to suppose that the Sunday liquor law is violated ; and they shall also observe and report anything on the streets, or elsewhere within their beats likely to produce danger or public inconvenience ; or anything offensive or unpleasant to the residents within their respective beats.

In these, and all other cases where they may report any offences or nuisances, they will also report, if known, the names of one or more credible witnesses by whom they may have reason to suppose, evidence on the subject can be given.

15. They are strictly enjoined to remove all persons found begging in the streets, and at or about the entrances to Hotels and Public Buildings, or at Steamboat Landings and Railroad Depots, and to take them to the station-houses of their respective Districts, to be disposed of by the Officers there in command, as the law provides.

16. Policemen will be vigilant in performing the duties prescribed in section 29 of the "General Rules and Regulations" in cases of fire. They will observe the following directions as to giving alarms through the Fire Alarm Telegraph.

Whilst something must always be left to their own discretion as to the propriety of giving an alarm, they will in ordinary cases observe the following precautions :

a. If assured by a known and responsible person that it is proper to call out the Fire Department, a Policeman having a key to the Alarm Boxes, will give the alarm ; taking care to note the name and residence of his informant, which he shall give to any officer of the Fire Department who may ask it.

b. If a stranger, or one in whom a policeman may not have full confidence, requests an alarm to be given, the latter should first ascertain, by personal observation, that it is proper to do so. If, however, the alleged fire is not close at hand, and the informer is willing to remain with the policeman until the facts are ascertained, the latter will then be excused for giving the alarm, should it prove to be false ; but he will take care that such informer does not leave his side, until it shall be ascertained that his statement was correct ; and should he attempt to do so, the policeman will arrest him on charge of raising a false alarm, and will hand him over to the officers of the Fire Department on their arrival.

c. Unless a fire is distinctly visible from the box at which an alarm is given, the policeman will remain at the box until the arrival of the Fire Department, that he may direct the engines to the proper place.

d. Policeman will always be particularly on their guard to avoid being induced to give an alarm on account of a burning chimney, or the existence of any other fire, which there is good reason to believe may be extinguished by those who may be present, without the aid of the Fire Department. On the other hand, when the services of the latter are believed to be really required, no time should be lost in giving an alarm.

All policemen must make themselves well acquainted with the location of all alarm boxes on or near the confines of their respective beats. Those having keys will be particularly instructed by the Sergeants as to the mode of giving alarms ; and as to the duty of one of them attending at each box, every day at 12 o'clock, noon, precisely, to ascertain that the boxes and telegraph wires are in order.

All policemen on night duty, will be particularly careful to call up with the least possible delay all Members of the Fire Department residing on or immediately adjoining their several beats, who may have left their names and residences at the station-houses, with a request to be called when there is an alarm of fire. Policemen must make themselves familiar with the residences of all such persons. They will also on other occasions call persons attached to other city departments, who may in like manner have signified their wishes.

17. Notices will be placed in the station-houses of the hours at which the city lamps are required to be lighted and extinguished, and policemen will carefully note and report all violations of such rules, and all broken or defective lamps.

18. Policemen, when on a tour of service, must not, except when on duty together, walk or talk with each other, or with any other person whom they may meet on any part of their beats, unless it be to receive or communicate information appertaining to their duty or to answer civilly but briefly questions of strangers or citizens really requiring their assistance or direction. They must not under any circumstances, unless in the discharge of their duties, stop at the corners of the streets, or linger on their routes, or enter any house, but are expected constantly to patrol their beats.

BY THE HOUSE OF DELEGATES,

May 8, 1861.

Read and ordered to be printed.

REPORT

OF

THE ADJUTANT GENERAL

OF MARYLAND;

TO THE GENERAL ASSEMBLY;

SPECIAL SESSION, 1861.

STATE OF MARYLAND.

FREDERICK CITY, May 8, 1861.

Gentlemen of the House of Delegates:

In compliance with your order of April 29, I have directed the Adjutant General to furnish me with the information asked for in said order; and herewith transmit to your Honorable Body, the report and accompaning papers furnished me by him.

THO. H. HICKS.

WHITNEYVILLE, January 18, 1861.

To His Excellency, Gov. HICKS,

Annapolis, Md.

DEAR SIR:—I have received yours of the 16th inst., I am astonished at the contents.

All I have to say is, that I will receive back such as are worthless and make those that are perfectly serviceable at least as good as sample furnished you last summer. Will not your brother go to a place where there is any complaint collecting such arms as are not considered good serviceable— have the same carefully packed so that they can be transported without damage to me. Hence, giving me a prompt opportunity of making all right which I am sure you will be improved most fully. Let there be no unnecessary delay in this—I feel more about it than any one else can. I assure you if any unserviceable arms have gone to Maryland, it has been owing to the negligence and stupidity of my men and inspectors who has assured me when each lot of arms went from here that they were serviceable. I have discovered that some of the first arms I sent out have a breech pin a little too small, but there are not many I trust. You will oblige me by sending me at once a list of the defects. The guns that have left here for several months past I think are right, I have just discovered, too, that there may be some with the hammer a trifling too loose on the shank of the tumbler (this is wrong and as soon as discovered they should be laid aside for repair which can easily be done.) I am positive there is nothing in the guns but can be easily repaired and that in other respects the guns are good and serviceable.

Hoping that you will give this matter your most prompt attention and delegate your brother H. C. Hicks to go at once to every place where the arms are distributed and examine them—sending me those that are not every way right.

I want to know the faults and then I can correct the difficulties. Don't hesitate to assure parties that if their is any thing wrong about the guns they will be made right, I have 100 here now to substitute for any that prove defective.

Yours, very respectfully,

E. WHITNEY.

ADJUTANT GENERAL'S OFFICE.
Annapolis, May 3rd, 1861.

To His Excellency,

THOS. H. HICKS,

Governor of Maryland :

SIR :—

Your communication of the 30th enclosing an order adopted by the House of Delegates requiring us to report at an early day to the House in relation to the purchase of arms,

&c., did not reach me until late yesterday afternoon, and I hasten to furnish you with the information desired.

After the passage of the Act referred to, you and myself had a consultation and we determined to purchase the arms, &c., of the General Government, because we concluded by so doing we could obtain better arms and at more reasonable prices than if we should purchase of individuals or companies. Accordingly.I addressed a letter to Col. A. K. Craig of the Ordnance Department. He replied under date of April 14th, 1860, that he had no authority to sell arms; that a bill was then pending before Congress to give such authority, and that when the same should become a law he would afford us every facility. I herewith enclose you Col. Craig's letter marked H. C. K. The bill much to our regret did not pass and we were compelled to look elsewhere.

Accordingly we invited proposals for furnishing arms and accoutrements from the most prominent manufacturers in the United States. The proposals were received with samples of the articles to be furnished. Not trusting to our own knowledge we invited the assistance of Lieut. William T. Magruder a distinguished officer of the U. S. Army and other prominent and competent military men. The samples were opened in the Executive Department and fully and thoroughly examined. We thereupon awarded the contract for furnishing the muskets and revolvers to Eli Whitney of New Haven Connecticut and the sabres to Ames Manufacturing Company, Chicopee, Massachusetts.

There has been expended $64,415.05 of the appropriation, leaving in the State Treasury a balance of $5,584.85, and the proper vouchers for these expenditures are now on file in the Executive Chamber.

We had no agent for the purchase of arms—H. C. Hicks, Esq., was employed to procure samples &c., but the contracts were made by you and myself.

The Infantry arms purchased by us were two thousand Rifled Muskets of the Minnie patern, and one thousand Cavalry Sabres and Revolvers with the necessary accoutrements, &c.

After we had contracted for the purchase of the arms, &c., upon consultation, we concluded that it would be better and attended with less expense to the State to have them deposited in the city of Baltimore, and distributed from that place. We were led to this conclusion in the first place on account of the superior advantages and facilities afforded by steamboats and rail-roads for transporting them to their various places of destination, and thus with as little delay as possible granting the pressing demands of the Military companies for arms from the various counties in the State ; and in the second place from the consideration that the State armories were not in a fit condition for their reception, to say nothing of the delay and cost of unpacking and re-packing the same.

In furtherance of our object, we procured the services of H. C. Hicks, Esq., to act as Agent to inspect the arms and see that they conformed and were equal to the samples furnished and to forward them under orders received from the Adjutant General to the different Military companies throughout the State and to pay the cost of transportation. For these services he was to receive the sum of $500.

The warehouse of Woolford & Patterson had been selected as a proper depository for the arms. From this place I continued to distribute them by forwarding from time to time, orders on the agent in favor of the different Military companies throughout the State up to the 19th of April last, when during the excitement in Baltimore, I learn from the agent aforesaid, that the place of deposit was forcibly entered and the arms, &c., remaining undistributed taken violent possession of and borne off—there were at the time 370 Infantry arms and accoutrements and sixteen Cavalry arms and accoutrements. I have not as yet been able to ascertain in whose possession the arms, &c., are.

Enclosed I send you a statement of the arms, &c., distributed, with the names of the companies and counties—paper marked No. 1 contains an account of the Infantry arms and paper marked No. 2. of the Cavalry arms distributed.

In haste I remain, sir,

Very respectfully,

Your obedient servant,

N. BREWER, of Jno.,

Adj. Gen. of Md,

COLT'S PATENT, F. A. M. Co.,

Harford, Conn., 12th May, '60.

To HIS EXCELLENCY,

Governor HICKS,

Annapolis, Maryland.

SIR:—By request I sent to-day per Express, to your address a lot of sample arms and appendages, the prices of which are the same, as paid by the U. S. Government, viz :

One Revolving Holster Pistol Carbine................				30.50
"	"	Belt " "	....	26.00
"	"	Holster Pistol........................		22.50
"	" "	Belt Pistol............................		18.00
"	Single Barrel Minnie Rifle.......................			10.00

These Pistols and Pistol Carbines are of the same model and style of finish, as those now being furnished to the United States Government, for the use of the Army and Navy.

We could furnish immediately, say :—

1000 Revolving Belt Pistols, for Holster or Belt ;
200 Revolving Holster Pistols ;
75 " " " Carbines ;
350 Single Barrel Minnie Rifles.

We have such quantities of our various kinds of arms in progress of Manufacture, that we could furnish much larger quantities than the above, on very short notice.

We have also in store several hundred of our Revolving Breech Military Rifles, Artillery Carbines with Sabre Bayonets, Cavalry Carbines of different lengths and calibres, which we could furnish on the shortest notice, at the prices paid by the United States Government.

We have enclosed a few samples of our new and improved Combustible Envelope Cartridges packed in patent waterproof cases to wish to call your special attention. These cartidges are believed to be superior in many respects to any others ever yet manufactured either for military or sporting purposes.

I send herewith a list of the different sizes made with prices annexed.

I am sir, respectfully,

Your most ob't servant,

SAM'L COLT.

ORDNANCE OFFICE,

WASHINGTON, *April 14th*, 1860.

GEN. N. BREWER, of John,

    Adj't Gen'l of Maryland,

        Annapolis.

SIR :

I have to acknowledge the receipt of your letter of the 10th inst., and in answer to state, that the Rifle Musket and Long-range rifle, with sword bayonet, both of the cal. of 58 inch, are the latest models adopted for the U. S. troops ; the Rifle Muskets for foot troops, and the Rifle for the Regiment of Riflemen. They are considered so far as has been ascertained from experience, very efficient arms for military service.

The Rifle Muskets and Long-range rifles are manufactured at the National Armories ; but there is no authority for selling them. There is now a bill before Congress to authorize the sale to the States ; but it has not yet become a Law.

Our mounted Regiments are armed with Sabres, Revolver, pistols and Carbines. The pistols most in use were made by Mr. Samuel Colt, and are of two sizes, one for the belt, and a larger one for the holsters ; the price of the belt pistol is $18, and that of the holster pistol $22 50. A much cheaper and it is believed an equally good pistol, can be procured elsewhere.

The carbines are generally what are called breech-loaders. The most numerous in our service are of the "Sharps'" pattern ; which, on account of the greater simplicity of construction, are, I think, generally preferred. Amongst the others I would mention Burnsides, with a metallic cartridge ; Maynard's modification of Lafoucheux ; also with a metallic cartridge ; Merrill's (at Baltimore,) and Joselyn's. Burnside's received the award of a Board of officers appointed to examine and decide upon the merits of different arms of the kind.

The prices paid for these arms are as follows :

Sharp's Carbines manufactured by the Sharp's Arms
   manufacturing Company, Harford, Conn...................$30.
Burnsides Carbines, manufactured at Providence..........$30.
Merrill—at Baltimore......................................$35.
Joselyn's—Millbring Mass..................................$35.

Any assistance which this Department can furnish will be cheerfully rendered to the State authorities.

Respectfully your ob't serv't

H. D. CRAIG.

Col. of Ordnance.

AN ACCOUNT of the Infantry Arms distributed in different Counties in the State of Maryland, up to April 16th, 1861.

ALLEGANY COUNTY.

Cumberland Continentals	Capt. Horace Resley;	50

ANNE ARUNDEL COUNTY.

United Rifles,	Capt. Frank A. Bond,	36
Magothy Home Guard,	" W. F. Dunbar,	50

BALTIMORE COUNTY.

Towson Guards,	Capt. Chas. R. Chew,	60
Reisterstown Riflemen,	" R. I. Worthington,	40
Garrison Forest Rangers,	" W. E. Nichols,	48

CARROLL COUNTY.

Smallwood Infantry,	Capt. W. Scott Roberts,	50
Carroll Guards,	" Geo. E. Wampler,	45

CECIL COUNTY.

Union Rifles,	Capt. J. W. Taylor,	50
Cecil Guards,	" Jno. A. J. Cheswell,	50

CHARLES COUNTY.

Smallwood Riflemen,	Capt. E. Wells,	50

DORCHESTOR COUNTY.

Dorchester Guards,	Capt. Jas. Wallace,	50
Taylor Greys,	" Wm. W. Caton,	50

Carried over,

Brought Forward,

FREDERICK COUNTY.

Liberty Riflemen,	Capt. A. A. Sappington,	39
Maryland Defenders,	" Jas. Wood,	50

HARFORD COUNTY.

Harford Riflemen,	Capt. Herman Stump,	50
National Guards,	" Robert S. Rodgers,	50
Chesapeake Riflemen,	" J. T. Bradbury,	50

HOWARD COUNTY.

Border Guards,	Capt. E. A. Talbott,	50

KENT COUNTY.

Reed Rifles,	Capt. E. F. Perkins,	50
Chester Blues,	" W. W. Valk,	50

MONTGOMERY COUNTY.

Poolsville Guard,	Capt. Jno. T. Flelchall,	40
Rockville Riflemen,	" W. V. Bouic,	50

PRINCE GEORGES' COUNTY.

Piscataway Riflemen,	Capt. G. R. W. Marshall,	50

QUENN ANNES' COUNTY.

Scott Rifles,	Capt. R. Goldsborough,	50
Chesapeake Riflemen,	" R. W. Earickson,	50

ST. MARY'S COUNTY.

Riley Rifles,	Capt. J. T. M. Raley,	50

SOMERSET COUNTY.

Tyaskin Guards,	Capt. Jno. W. Moore,	50
Somerset Guards,	" J. W. Polk,	50

Carried over,

Brought Forward,

TALBOT COUNTY.

Home Guards,	Capt. Henry Strandberg,	50
Talbot Blues,	" Sam'l W. Waddawer,	40

WASHINGTON COUNTY.

Sharpsburg Riflemen,	Capt. R. E. Cook,	42
Boonsboro' Guards,	" Jno. E. Brining,	50

WORCESTOR COUNTY.

Worcestor Sentinels,	Capt. Jas. M. Moore.	40
		1630

N. BREWER, of Jno.,
Adjt. Genl.

AN ACCOUNT of Cavalry Arms distributed up to the 19th April, 1861.

ANNE ARUNDEL COUNTY.

Union Guards,	Capt. James A. Iglehart,	50
West River Guards,	" George B. Steuart,	50
Severn Guards,	" George D. Claytor,	40

BALTIMORE COUNTY.

Baltimore co. Horse Guards, Capt. Charles Ridgely,	50

CALVERT COUNTY.

Southern Guards,	Capt. Geo. Lyles,	40
Calvert Cadets,	" Basil D. Bond,	50

CHARLES COUNTY.

Charles County Mounted Volunteers, Samuel Cox,	60

FREDERICK COUNTY.

Manor Mounted Guard, Capt. Joseph N. Chiswell,	42
Liganore Mounted Guard, " Chas. A. Beavans,	40
General Edward Shriver,	10

HARFORD COUNTY.

Spesutie Rangers,	Capt. Robert H. Archer,	50
Harford Light Dragoons,	" Archer H. Jarrett,	40

HOWARD COUNTY.

Company B. Howard Dragoons, Cap. G. R. Gaither,	40

KENT COUNTY.

Columbian Hussars,	Capt. John T. Skirven,	40
Marion Blues,	" Richard C. Johnson,	40

Carried over.

MONTGOMERY COUNTY.

Montgomery Mounted Guards, Capt. Ed. W. Owen,		40
Poolesville Light Dragoons, " Benj. S. White,		40

PRINCE GEORGE'S COUNTY.

Vansville Rangers,	Capt. Nicholas Snowden,	40
Planter's Guards,	" John Contee,	50

QUEEN ANNE'S COUNTY.

First Troop Washington Blues, Capt. Solomon Betts	38
Col. Samuel T. Harrison,	4

ST. MARY'S COUNTY.

St. Mary's Dragoons,	Capt. Randolph Jones,	40

SOMERSET COUNTY.

Somerset Life Guard Dragoons, Andrew J. Crawford	50

TALBOT COUNTY.

Talbot Horse Guards,	Capt. M. T. Goldsborough,	40
		984

N. BREWER, of Jno.,
Adjutant General,

I hereby propose to furnish for the State of Maryland one thousand light cavalry sabres, of the last model issued by the U. S. Government, for seven dollars each. The blades of said sabres to be tested for strength in every respect, as for U. S. Government, and subject to the inspection of H. C. Hicks, Esq ; to be well packed in good strong cases and delivered at the port of Baltimore, at the expense of the Ames Manufacturing Co.

Four hundred of the above to be ready for delivery in thirty days from this date ; and two hundred at the expiration of each succeeding thirty days, or if preferred, will deliver three hundred in each thirty days after first delivery, provided we are notified at the time of first delivery that this will be required.

JAMES T. AMES,
Ag't Ames Manufacturing Co.

For Geo. Ames,
Chicopee, Mass., Aug. 23, 1860.

New Haven, May 23, 1860.

This may certify that Eli Whitney of New Haven, State of Connecticut, does hereby agree with N. Brewer, as Adjutant General, and Thomas H. Hicks, Governor of the State of Maryland, agents for said State for the purchase of Arms, to wit: as follows: to furnish said State of Maryland, two thousand Minnie long-range muskets, equal to the sample already furnished by said Whitney, and now at Annapolis, Md. The calibre of said Muskets being ⅝ of an inch in diameter, to be packed in cases and delivered in the city of Baltimore, Maryland. (Cost of cases and packing and cost of transportation to be paid by said Whitney) at his risk, subject to your order. The appendages to be as follows: 4 Minnie bullet moulds and 2 cone wrenches to every case of 20 Guns ; 1 screw driver and wiper to each gun. The price for the guns and appendages as above is ($15.00,) fifteen dollars per gun. These arms are to be delivered as follows: two hundred in 60 days, and the balance in lots of 300, to be manufactured and delivered without unnecessary delay. Said Whitney also agrees to furnish and deliver in Baltimore, Md., at his risk and expense, one thousand medium Army or Navy revolving pistols like and equal to the samples furnished by said Whitney and now at Annapolis, Md., at sixteen dollars and twenty cents each, appendages included; all packed and delivered in the city of Baltimore, subject to order.

The above arms are to be inspected at the factory by H. C. Hicks, and packed under his supervision. Four hundred of the above pistols to be delivered in thirty days, and the balance without unnecessary delay ; payments to be cash on delivery in Baltimore.

ELI WHITNEY.

BY THE HOUSE OF DELEGATES,

MAY 9TH, 1861.

Read and 10,000 copies ordered to be printed.

REPORT

OF THE

COMMITTEE ON FEDERAL RELATIONS

IN REGARD TO THE

CALLING OF A SOVEREIGN CONVENTION.

FREDERICK, MD.
E. S. RILEY, PRINTER,
1861.

REPORT

OF THE

Committee on Federal Relations.

To the Honorable,
  The Speaker of the House of Delegates:

The Committee on Federal Relations, to whom were re-ferred the Message and Correspondence of the Governor, the Bill calling a Sovereign Convention, &c., &c., ask leave respectfully to report, as follows:

The Message of his Excellency, the Governor, demands the consideration of the Legislature, from two points of view—first, in regard to the state of public affairs which it discloses, and secondly, as to the remedy which it suggests to the people of the State for the perilous contingencies which surround them.

So far as we can ascertain the views of the Governor, from the brief presentation of them, which the haste of our meeting had, as he states, permitted him to make, it appears that he regards the circumstances which have transpired since the attack upon the Massachusetts regiment in Baltimore, on the 19th of April, as constituting all the facts to which it is necessary your attention should be drawn. Your Committee, of course, recognize the propriety of avoiding at this moment all unnecessary recurrence to discussions which have already been far overstepped by the rapid progress of events; but they find it, at the same time, quite impossible to do justice to the questions before them, without a frank and explicit reference to at least a portion of the public events which had preceded and were so closely connected with the occurrence alluded to.

4

The President of the United States, by his Proclamation of the 15th of April, had called upon a portion of the States to place at his disposal a body of militia, to the number of seventy-five thousand men. The Proclamation was directed against the people of the newly-formed Southern Confederacy, and its purposes and policy were obvious, although its terms were technically shaped in conformity with the Act of Congress of 1795. It recited, with formal precision, in the language of the Act, "that the laws of the United States were opposed, and the execution thereof was obstructed," in the seven seceded States, "by combinations too powerful to be suppressed by the ordinary course of judicial proceedings, or by the powers vested in the Marshals," and it called forth the militia of the other States, in the further language of the statute, "to suppress such combinations, and to cause the laws to be duly executed." In pursuance of another section of the law, it then commanded "the insurgents to disperse and retire peaceably to their respective abodes" within twenty days. If there is any proposition clear beyond dispute, it must be, that if the occasion which authorizes the President to call out the militia, under the Act of 1795, existed at all, it was declared, by the explicit terms of the Proclamation, to exist only in the States of the Southern Confederacy, which were therein enumerated. It is equally indisputable, as matter of law, that the militia, if called out lawfully at all, were lawfully empowered to execute the laws and suppress unlawful combinations in the seven States named, and in none other. Such a conclusion of law is not only obvious and unavoidable, as matter of construction, but equally to be insisted upon as matter of principle and self-protection on the part of the people; for the exercise of the military power, in a free government, is never to be permitted, except within the limits and under the severest restrictions and checks of the law. If a President of the United States, under the fraudulent pretence of suppressing unlawful combinations in Louisiana and Florida, could be permitted to call out troops, to be used for any purpose in Maryland or Virginia, no soil of any State would be free from invasion, and no right of the citizen anywhere would be secure against overthrow.

It was not, however, because of any apprehension that the militia which were called out by the President would be used in other than the designated quarters, that the Proclamation created an intense and immediate excitement in the Southern and Border Slave States. On the contrary, it was the very purpose announced by Mr. Lincoln which kindled so intense a flame of resentment and resistance. His Proclamation was regarded as a declaration of war against the Southern Confederacy—as a deliberate summons to the people of the two sections, into which his party and its principles had so hopelessly divided the land, to shed each other's blood, in wantonness and hate. A scheme so full of wickedness—so utterly subversive of every principle upon which our government was founded, and so sure to involve the destruction of that government, let the fortune of war be what it might—could not but excite almost to frenzy every feeling of those who sympathized with the people against whom it was fulminated. Independently, too, of its wantonness and inhumanity, it was felt and known to be a gross violation of the Constitution, and without color of lawful authority. The people of the seceded States, whether constitutionally or unconstitutionally, had separated themselves from this government and established a federal government of their own, with all the forms of a constitution and all the substantial attributes of actual independence. Through their constituted authorities and in their collective capacity, as communities, they had withdrawn themselves from the Union —repudiated its laws and excluded its officers, of all sorts, from the exercise of all functions and jurisdiction. The United States Government no longer had among them either courts to issue, or marshals to execute process. They had substituted their own courts and their own processes, to which they yielded cheerful obedience. The authority of the Federal Government was in fact dead within their limits. They were in an attitude towards it, not only of independence, but of forcible resistance, for they had repelled the assertion of its authority over any portion of their soil, and had subdued, for their own protection, one of its fortifications within their borders. The Confederate Government and that of the United States were, in fine, belligerents, engaged in actual, though undeclared war, and with all the rights and responsibilities which it gives and entails. This last is none the less true, because of their being engaged in civil war, for that is like any other war, when waged among civilized people. Vattel defines the relations which exist in such cases in terms too clear to be misunderstood, and too well recognized to be disputed.

' "A civil war," he says, "breaks the bands of society and government, or at least suspends their force and effect. It produces in the nation two independent parties,

who consider each other as enemies, and acknowledge no
common judge. These two parties, therefore, must necessarily be considered as thenceforward constituting, at
least for a time, two separate bodies, two distinct societies. Though one of the parties may have been to blame
in breaking the unity of the State and resisting the lawful
authority, they are not the less divided in fact. Besides,
who shall judge them? Who shall pronounce on which
side the right or the wrong lies? On earth they have no
common superior. They stand, therefore, in precisely the
same predicament as two nations, who engage in a contest, and being unable to come to an agreement, have recourse to arms." (Vattel, Book 3, ch. 18, sec. 293.) To
attempt to apply, under such circumstances, to a belligerent people, an Act of Congress, which was meant as a
domestic remedy, in aid of civil process and to secure obedience to the laws under judicial proceeding—in States
still recognizing the authority of the Union and the jurisdiction of its tribunals—was to trifle with the understandings of educated men. To issue a proclamation to three
millions of free Americans, composing seven powerful
States, and asserting the sacred and indefeasible right of
self-government, with arms in their hands, and "command" them as "insurgents" to "retire peaceably to
their respective abodes," like a mob at a street corner,
was an absurdity too gross to be here respectfully discussed. No government would venture to palm such an
imposition upon a people, except in the well-assured confidence of absolute power. Nay, in the passionate excitement of the moment, the President forgot even the suggestions of politic decorum, and did not hesitate to transgress all possible constitutional limits, and confess a
purpose of animosity and revenge, by distinctly calling
on the people, whom he summoned to the field, "to redress wrongs already long enough endured." The Proclamation, therefore, meant war, and nothing but war. It
could signify nothing else, and to attempt to cloak its
meaning and purpose under the flimsy pretext of "executing the laws" and "suppressing unlawful combinations," was but to cover up a flagrant usurpation with
words.

Neither the Constitution nor the laws of the United States can be tortured into conferring the war-
making power upon the President in any contingency.
Where foreign nations are concerned, the plain language
of the fundamental law entrusts it to Congress only. As
against the States of the Union, the possibility of such a

thing is not even contemplated, much less provided for. Like parricide at Athens, it was held too heinous and impossible, to be named, even for the purpose of punishment. As early as the fifth day after the meeting of the Convention for the formation of the Federal Constitution, "the use of force against a State," by the rest of the Union, as contemplated in the plan of Mr. Randolph, was denounced by Mr. Madison, and on his motion the resolution providing for it was indefinitely postponed by unanimous assent. Mr. Madison announced it as his deliberate opinion that "a union of the States, containing such an ingredient, seemed to provide for its own destruction." From that day forward such an idea ceased to be a part of the theory of those by whom the Constitution was framed. When Gen. Hamilton was called to express his opinion upon it, he asked, "How can this force be exerted on the States collectively? It is impossible; it amounts to a war upon the parties. Foreign powers, also, will not be idle spectators. They will interpose; the confusion will increase and a dissolution of the Union will ensue." The reasoning was unanswerable, and the Constitution happily was not stained with the perilous folly, against which these two great statesmen so earnestly protested. There was not a discussion in the debates on the Federal Constitution, whether in the Convention which framed it or the State Conventions which adopted it, that does not confirm this view of its spirit and purpose. The essays of the Federalist are pregnant with demonstrations to the same effect, and there is no constitutional lawyer who does not know, that the whole theory of the Government is to act, through the courts, upon individuals, and not through the Army and Navy upon the States. The brave and wise men who framed and upheld it, would have died in the breach before they would have submitted themselves to it upon any other basis. It could never have been adopted, it would never have been ratified, upon any other understanding. The States would have endured anarchy, distracted counsels, and all the evils of the old Confederation, aggravated tenfold, before they would have surrendered themselves to any system in which the Federal Government, and least of all, the Federal Executive, was clothed with the constitutional power of coercing them by force of arms. They entered into a constitutional Union, depending for its permanence upon the good faith and good feeling of its members, and deriving its strength from their consent only. They did not abandon themselves to the bayonets of a military despotism enthroned upon popular majorities.

But, illegal and unconstitutional as was the war which the Proclamation summoned one section of the country to wage against the other, the causes and purposes of that war, made it chiefly obnoxious to the people of Maryland and of the Slave States of the Border. It was a war of propagandism and of sectional aggression and domination. It was a war of the North upon the South. It was a war in which the dominant section had seized upon the name and flag, and resources and powers, of the General Government, and was abusing them for its own ends, and for the permanent establishment of its dominion over the other section. It was a war, to the unholy purposes of which the sacred associations and memories of the Union were prostituted, and in which its honored name was taken in vain. It was a war waged against a people of our own name and blood; who sought peace and kindly relations with us, and who asked only to be let alone and to be permitted to govern themselves. It could bring no good, for it could end only in the defeat of the invaders or the subjugation of the invaded, and in either case the Union, which our fathers left to us, must be at an end. Subjugated provinces could not be sister States, and a Federal Government, professedly Republican, maintaining its authority by armies, could not be other than the worst and most unprincipled and uncontrollable of despotisms. The South had entrenched itself upon the principle of self-government. It had offered to negotiate, peaceably and honorably, upon all matters of common property and divided interest, claiming only that three millions of people had a right to throw off a Government, by which they no longer desired to be ruled, and to live under another Government of their own choosing. Unless the American Revolution was a crime, the declaration of American Independence a falsehood, and every patriot and hero of 1776 a traitor, the South was right and the North was wrong, upon that issue. The people of Maryland, therefore, could have but one choice in such a contest, and while as devoted to the Union and as loyal to the Constitution, as the people of any of the thirteen States, who had formed the one and pledged themselves to the other, they could not but throw the whole weight of their sympathies upon that side to which common interests and institutions inclined them, and with which they felt that the right and the truth were. Nor was it a matter of sympathy merely. The breach of the Constitution involved in the coercive policy of the Administration, was a breach of their rights, and not less than an unlawful aggression upon the rights of the Southern people. It was an overthrow of the principles of free government, and could end in nothing but an ignominious annihilation of the noble institutions of the Republic. The people of Maryland were summoned to take part, as soldiers, in the strife, and as citizens they were asked to contribute their means to its prosecution, and were to bear their share of its unconstitutional burdens; their stake in the struggle, therefore, was one of political and individual self-preservation. They were bound by every principle and pressed forward by every impulse of right and self-respect, to make every protest against the wrong to their brethren, and the oppression to themselves, which their situation and circumstances would permit. To the requisition upon them for troops, to take part upon the side of the Government in such a strife, their answer, if they could have given it with their own voice, would have been an instant and indignant refusal.

It is deeply to be regretted that the response of his Excellency, the Governor, should have fallen so far short, in this regard, of the manly and patriotic spirit with which the Governors of Virginia and North Carolina, Tennessee, Kentucky and Missouri, threw back the insulting proposition of the Administration. Indeed, the Committee are unable to determine, from the correspondence with which the Governor has furnished the Legislature, whether his Excellency does not still contemplate complying with the requisition as made. His letter of April 20th, to the Secretary of War, is the only one which gives a key to his intentions, and in that he merely announces that he thinks it " prudent to decline (for the present ")—not because of the illegality and wickedness of the demand, and the disgrace which the State would incur from acceding to it—but on account of the then alleged disorderly condition of the militia themselves. Your Committee are not prepared to admit the accuracy of the statement made by the Governor in the letter referred to, to the effect that " the principal part of the organized military forces " of Baltimore took part with the " disorderly element " in the affair of the 19th of April. On the contrary, they have every assurance and every reason to believe that the organized military of Baltimore, under the direction of the constituted authorities, and in implicit obedience to their orders, did all that could have been expected from brave men and good citizens to preserve the public tranquility. But whether the hasty statement of the Executive be well or ill-founded in that particular, the determination of the State of Maryland, upon the question of furnishing her quota of militia to make war upon the Southern States, ought not, in the opinion of your Committee, to rest a moment longer upon any such collateral and accidental issue. It becomes the self-respect of the State that she should speak out openly and decidedly upon the point, and the question should no. longer be left dependent upon what may be hereafter regarded as "prudent" by the Executive. For this purpose, your Committee have prepared and reported a resolution, which is appended to this report, and the adoption of which they respectfully recommend.

It is but justice to the Executive of the State to observe, in this connection, that his Excellency appears to have been misled, in his action upon the requisition of the United States Government, by the two letters of the Secretary of War, dated April 17, in which that gentleman informs him that "the troops to be raised in Maryland will be needed for the defence of the Capital and of the public property in that State and neighborhood." "There is no intention," the Secretary adds, "of removing them beyond these points." In conformity with this information, the Proclamation of the Governor—of which he has not furnished a copy to the General Assembly, but which is matter of public notoriety—informs his fellow citizens to the same effect, and holds out the idea that troops from this State may be furnished for the purposes indicated. Your Committee would be happy to persuade themselves that in suggesting the possibility of its being "prudent," at any time, for the Maryland quota to be furnished to the Government, his Excellency could only have contemplated their employment, in any contingency, for the limited purposes in question. But it does not become the House of Delegates to allow themselves to be deceived by any such intimations from the Government, as these which imposed upon the Governor. The Proclamation of Mr. Lincoln, under which the troops of Maryland have been called into the field, is directed (as has already been observed) against the seceded States and none other. The Militia were summoned to execute the laws and suppress unlawful combinations in South Carolina, Georgia, Florida, Alabama, Mississippi, Louisiana and Texas; and not in Maryland or the District of Columbia. The very requisition of the Secretary of war upon the Governor, is in direct and absolute contradiction to the assurance contained in his letter. The one asks for troops to be used in the South, and not at the Federal Capital, the other declares that their employment, at the Federal Capital and not in the South, is the only purpose contemplated.

One of two things, therefore, is perfectly clear. Either the Government had called out troops under the pretence of needing them for one purpose, while intending to use them for another, or it contemplated employing a portion of them at Washington, as a guard and a reserve, but in aid, at the same time, of its offensive movements to the South of the Potomac. In the one case, it can have no claim upon our confidence; in the other, we should be false to ourselves and to free institutions, if we were to hesitate about refusing it our co-operation. Whatever destiny the people of Maryland may be able or willing to shape for themselves, now or hereafter, the Committee would be pained to believe it possible, that a single citizen of the State could be forced or persuaded to take part, directly or indirectly, in the slaughter and subjugation of our Southern brethren and the overthrow of Constitutional Government by usurpation and brute force. If the Government desires to put an end to all doubts as to the safety of the Capital, it can do so at a word, by putting an end to its own purposes of coercing the South.

What the Committee have already suggested in regard to the character and purposes of the conflict, which Mr. Lincoln has inaugurated, under the pretense of enforcing the laws, is so manifestly and indisputably corroborated by his course since the Legislature was convoked, that the Committee cannot discharge their duty without alluding to that course in this connection. Reference is especially had to the Proclamation of the 3d of May, calling out over forty-two thousand additional volunteers, to serve in the militia for a period of three years, and increasing the regular force of the United States by an addition of nearly twenty-three thousand men to the army, and eighteen thousand seamen to the navy. The most unscrupulous advocate of the Administration and its policy, would be compelled to shrink from the task of pointing out any legal or Constitutional authority of any sort, for this unprecedented measure. The right of increasing the army and navy is one which belongs exclusively to Congress, and over which the President has no more Constitutional control than the humblest citizen. His right to call out the militia is expressly limited by the restriction that their use shall only continue "if necessary, until after the expiration of thirty days after the commencement of the then next session of

Congress," (Act of 1795, Sec. 2.) The Proclamation is therefore without any color whatever of right, and is as plain and bald a subversion of the letter and spirit of the Constitution and the laws, as ever was attempted by the military power, in any Government ostensibly free. The pretense of " existing exigencies " is but the shape in which military revolutions have always begun, since the prestige of free institutions has rendered it necessary, even for usurpers to make a show of apology for overthrowing them.

If ever a triumphant illustration could be given of the wisdom of our fathers, in providing by the constitution, that the government should operate upon its individual citizens through the laws, and not upon the States by military coercion, it is to be found in the fact, that the first administration daring to depart from this fundamental and consecrated principle, has rushed, in the short space of sixty days, into the assertion of absolute control over the whole military resources of the country, in open and reckless defiance of every legal and constitutional restraint. The Committee hazard nothing in saying, that there is not a citizen of Maryland, whatever be his political opinions, who must not shudder at the palpable and ominous presence of this usurpation, and who does not recognize, for the first time, in his own experience or the history of Maryland, that he is living and moving and holding his civil and political rights at the pleasure of an unrestricted military power, and subject to the arbitrary and anti-republican caprices of what is entitled " military necessity." For any man to be able to persuade himself, under such circumstances, that the policy of the administration ever meant peace and not war—the "enforcement of the laws,"—the " defence of the capital"—and not subjugation—requires a peculiarity of mental construction with which reason is at a loss how to deal. To suppose that a blockade of the whole sea coast, from the capes of the Chesapeake to the extreme borders of Texas, with a land army extraordinary of one hundred and fifty thousand men, and a naval increase of eighteen thousand, can be intended only in aid of "the ordinary course of judicial proceedings, or the powers vested in the Marshals," and is therefore within the scope of the President's civil functions, and not of the war-making power, which only Congress can exercise, implies a facility of conviction, to which nothing can be regarded as impossible.

The Committee are of course not unacquainted with the familiar doctrine laid down by the Supreme Court of the United States in the case of Martin vs. Mott, (12 Wheaton,

19,) and so often cited by those who maintained the absolute authority of the President over the whole question of calling out the militia. The Committee might readily dispose of it if they were willing to stand upon the same grounds with the Administration, by applying to it the doctrine of the inaugural of Mr. Lincoln, and might insist upon confining the ruling of the Court to the particular case and the individual parties concerned, repudiating its controlling authority, upon the one side or the other, on a question of administrative government. Believing, however, that the true and only "loyalty" of a free people consists in their reverence for the laws and Constitution, and their obedience to the tribunals by which these are expounded, the Committee assume that the people of Maryland will cheerfully bow to whatever the Supreme Court has determined, upon the question under discussion, or any other. The case of Martin *vs.* Mott was a controversy between a private of militia and one of the United States Marshals, who had seized his goods, in enforcement of a fine imposed by court-martial, for failure to enter the service upon requisition, according to law, during the war of 1812. The jurisdiction of the court-martial, and the authority of the President to issue the Proclamation under which the militia were called out to repel invasion, were both considered in the case; the question in chief, however, of course being the right of the individual citizen to judge, for himself, whether the legal occasion existed, upon which the President might rightfully summon the citizens to arms. This latter was the real and only point in controversy, and the Court decided, that under the Act of 1795, it was for the President, exclusively, to determine whether the exigency contemplated by the law had arisen, and that no soldier or officer had any choice but to obey.

The principle of military subordination upon which this adjudication is distinctly placed by the court, is too obvious to be confounded with the recognition of arbitrary and irresponsible power, to which the decision is sought to be perverted, by the supporters of the existing order of things. To determine that the President is the exclusive judge of whether an exigency has arisen, in a case to which his discretion is lawfully applicable, is one thing. To give to him the exclusive and irreversible authority to determine, not only the existence of the exigency, but the existence of the case in which it may lawfully arise, is quite another thing. The first is what the Supreme Court has done, the second is what no respectable Court, it is confidently assumed, can be persuaded or forced to do, except under the pressure of "military necessity." The one gives to the President the exercise of a discretion, in certain named and ascertained cases. The other gives him absolute power in all cases. The one endows him with a necessary executive· function. The other makes him supreme over all law, by granting him the exclusive control of its application. If the President cannot only invoke the military power at his discretion, in cases of invasion, insurrection and resistance to the laws, but can create invasion, insurrection and resistance, by merely proclaiming that they exist, whether, in fact, they do so, or not; there is not a moment of his term, at which he cannot constitutionally compass the absolute subjugation of the people, through the mere official assertion of a falsehood. Assume for a moment, for the sake of the argument, that the attitude of the United States, is not, in fact or law, a case authorizing the President to call out the militia, under the act of 1795, is it to be pretended that he makes it such a case simply by calling it such, in a proclamation? Is it to be gravely argued, under a constitutional government, that the nation is bound to acquiesce in it as a fact, against the public knowledge to the contrary, and must accept the war, indorse the bloodshed, pour out the treasure, and submit to the usurpation, with no other remedy than articles of impeachment, or the chances of the next Presidential election?

The commonest intelligence—the most superficial acquaintance with the scheme and spirit of republican institutions—revolts at conclusions so monstrous. And yet precisely such must be the conclusions to which any man must yield who supposes the Supreme Court to have decided, as has been pretended. That high tribunal never meant to decide, and never did decide, a principle so wholly irrational and despotic. It is a disrespect to its character to put such a question even in dispute. The way in which the States and the people may and ought to deal with such a usurpation is a matter apart, but that it does not cease to be a usurpation, because of the insertion of a form of words in a Proclamation, is a matter which the Committee will not disparage the manliness and sense of the House by discussing further. Indeed, in his letter of May 4th, 1861, to the U. S. Minister at Paris, which has appeared during the preparation of this report, the Secretary of State does not hesitate to throw aside all the masks and pretenses of the Proclamation, and to admit that it is no longer a simulated question of "enforcing the laws" and "defending the Capital," but a downright case of "civil war"—of "open, flagrant, deadly war," which the United States have "accepted." Such a confession—nay, such a bold and defiant annunciation—that the President has assumed upon himself the power of peace and war, in glaring and indisputable subversion of the Constitution, leaves to the people of Maryland nothing further to consider, in this connection, but the fact, that they are face to face with a military despotism, whose only law is its will.

If the Committee are justified, by what has been said, in their view of the constitutional position of the Federal Government, and especially if the admissions now made by it, without disguise, show but the consummation of an original and persistent illegal scheme on the part of the Administration, it follows, as a matter of necessity, that the troops called out by the President were and are an unauthorized body of men, passing across our territory for illegal and unconstitutional purposes, and carrying with them none of the constitutional safeguards, which would undoubtedly accompany any force of the United States exercising the right of transit for lawful and justifiable ends. They were, in fact, not United States soldiers, but "Northern troops," as they were properly designated by the Governor in his correspondence, and "Northern troops," too, whose presence in Maryland, without the consent of her constituted authorities, was indubitably an aggression upon her dignity, her safety and tranquility. Your Committee, of course, admit, without question, that only the authorities of the State were competent to deal with such a case, and that it could only have been dealt with properly, even by them, in distinct recognition of the fact, that Maryland is still a State of the Union, with all the obligations which that relation imposes upon her.

But they cannot shut their eyes to the other fact, equally indisputable, that it was primarily the fault of those who marched the Massachusetts soldiery through Baltimore, upon an unconstitutional and illegal errand, if the popular passions were unfortunately stimulated by their presence, into a lawless outbreak, too sudden and too violent to be restrained, for the moment, by the ordinary appliances of a free government. The Committee, therefore, cannot but commend the repeated efforts of the Governor to induce the President to forego his purpose of passing troops across our soil, both before and after the fatal occurrence of the 19th of April. They can only regret that the indignant feeling manifested by his Excellency in regard to the misdeeds of the "rebellious element" at home, was not testified, with equal vigor of remonstrance against the illegality and wrong, involved in the proceedings of the Government.

The events which have occurred since the period referred to, the Committee do not feel themselves called upon to discuss in any detail. They have taken occasion to allude, in a previous report, to the humiliating facts which are disclosed by the present position of Maryland. A State of the Union, held to the obligations of that relation, and having never through her constituted authorities pretended to repudiate or abjure them, she is treated as a conquered enemy. Her soil is occupied; her property and that of her citizens are sequestered; her public highways are seized and obstructed; her laws are suspended; her capital is converted into a military post; her Legislature is compelled, in the language of her Executive, to consult its "safety" by holding its sessions at a distance from her offices and archives; troops are quartered around the peaceful homesteads of her people; her citizens are subjected to the illegal and arbitrary violence of military arrest and confinement; her very freedom, in fine, all that distinguished her from a Neapolitan province, before Naples was liberated, is under the armed heel of the Government. That such a fate is imposed upon her, without constitutional authority; that indeed no respect to the constitution is even pretended in her regard; the frank admission of the Federal authorities to the Commissioners recently accredited to them by this Legislature, renders a mortifying and almost intolerable certainty.

The State of Maryland is under military rule. Partly for military convenience, and partly for chastisement, her free institutions have been temporarily suspended by the War Department, and her name blotted out, for the time, from the list of free governments. It is not the desire of the Committee to aggravate by comment the humiliation which is inseparable from these facts in their simplest statement. It is not their disposition to provoke a review of the unhappy policy, in her own councils, which has contributed to plunge the State into so hopeless and helpless a condition. They wish to deal only with the practical questions it suggests for present determination; and this brings them to consider the recommendations of the message transmitted by the Governor.

The Committee understand his Excellency as recommending, in general terms, a policy of peace. So far as that naked proposition goes, they give to it their warmest and heartiest concurrence, but they are not sure that they exactly apprehend the mode, in which the Governor proposes that the policy he so favors should be carried out.— His language is as follows: "I honestly and most earnestly entertain the conviction that the only safety of Maryland lies in preserving a neutral position between our brethren of the North and South." He then enters into a consideration of the part which Maryland has taken in the sectional contest that has been waged, and adds: "Entertaining these views, I cannot counsel Maryland to take sides against the Federal Government, until it shall commit outrages upon us which would justify us in resisting its authority." What class of outrages would furnish such justification for resistance he does not announce, but proceeds to say: "As a consequence, I can give no other counsel than that we shall array ourselves for union and peace, and thus preserve our soil from being polluted with the blood of brethren. Thus, if war must be between the North and the South, we may force the contending parties to transfer the field of battle from our soil, so that our lives and property may be secure."

The Committee confess their difficulty in perceiving how, consistently with a policy purely pacific, these counsels can possibly be made available. No matter how decidedly and enthusiastically we "array ourselves for union and peace," it is altogether impossible for us to preserve our soil from the pollution of fraternal blood, unless we possess the means and assert the power to force back the tide of war, if it comes surging across our borders. And that we should consolidate and employ such power, to the extent which the exigency may demand, is obviously the counsel of the Governor, for he proceeds to tell us, that by the action he advises, we may be able, "if war must be," to "*force the contending parties to transfer the field of battle from our soil*, so that our lives and property may be secure." Surely we cannot "force" belligerent armies from our midst, without employing force of our own. It is out of the question that we can prevent them from making our homes their battle-field, unless we have the strength to repel them, and are willing and prepared to use it.

No peaceful "array" whatever—no legislative protest— no executive remonstrance—from Maryland, can stay the strife of contending squadrons. A deputation from the Peace Society would have been as effectual in arresting a charge at Solferino. If, then, the "neutrality" of the

Governor means any thing, (speaking with all respect) it must mean a neutrality armed and resolute—prepared to assert its policy, and able to vindicate it on the field. Otherwise it would be nothing and would come to nothing. It would only irritate both parties and stay the arm of neither.

And yet although this is the result and the only practical result of the recommendation of the Message, it is difficult to reconcile such a conclusion with the other views which the Governor announces. Upon the authority of "our most learned and intelligent citizens," he admits the right of the Government to transport its troops across our soil. He recognizes the unbroken relation and the continuing loyalty of Maryland to the Union. He does not impeach the constitutionality of the action of the Federal authorities. His protests against the landing of the troops, and the seizure of the railroad at Annapolis, are based upon no denial of the right. They amount to remonstrance and advice, but to nothing more.

His theory is, and he has always steadfastly maintained it, that nothing has occurred to alter the reciprocal rights and obligations of this State and the General Government. The Constitution he believes is still over both, and the old bonds still unite them together. If all this be true, then the State of Maryland can hold no neutrality when the Union is at war. She is part of the Union ; at war when it wars ; at peace when it is peaceful. She "takes sides " against it the instant that she fails to take sides with it. Neutrality, in such a case, is nullification pure and simple, and an armed neutrality is merely rebellion and not union or peace. The position of his Excellency in the premises is, therefore, in the judgment of the Committee, wholly untenable, and it is not surprising that it should have placed him at so obvious a disadvantage, in the correspondence which he has furnished the House between himself and the astute officers of the Government. Differing from the Governor in opinion as to the course and rights of the Federal authorities, to the wide extent herein before indicated, the Committee have no hesitation in asserting and maintaining the right of the State, and its duty, to protest against the unconstitutional action of the Administration, and refuse obedience to its unconstitutional demands. Recognizing, however, to the same extent as the Governor, the fact that Maryland is still a State of the Union, the Committee cannot counsel this honorable body or the people whom it represents, to assume, under the guise of " neurality," a hostile relation to the Government, or attempt by any policy whatever, to "force" it from the position in which it is entrenched. If no better argument existed against such a project, a sufficient one would be found in its hopeless futility.

The present—and the only possible present attitude of the State towards the Federal Government is, in the judgment of the Committee, an attitude of submission—voluntary and cheerful submission on the part of those who can persuade themselves that the Constitution remains inviolate and the Union unbroken, or that the Union can survive the Constitution—unwilling and galling submission on the part of those who think and feel differently; but still, peaceful submission upon both sides. It is not for the Committee to ignore this state of things, because of the humiliation which comes with it. They feel it their duty to confess the inexorable logic of facts, and leave the future to be shaped by the people of Maryland, to whom, exclusively, that prerogative belongs, and who, doubtless, will exercise it in their own way and at their own good time.

This expression of the views of your Committee, at so much necessary length, leaves very obvious the recommendations which they ask leave to report, upon the two leading subjects submitted to their deliberation: the calling of a Sovereign Convention of the people, and the re-organization and arming of the militia of the State.

At the time when the Legislature was called together, there was certainly but little difference of opinion among its members, of all parties, as to the propriety of speedily adopting measures to secure both the objects referred to.—Since that time, the rapid and extraordinary development of events, and of the warlike purposes of the Administration; the concentration of large bodies of troops in our midst and upon our borders, and the actual and threatened military occupation of the State; have naturally enough produced great changes of opinion and feeling among our citizens. The members of the Committee, judging from their own correspondence and that of their fellow members, of all shades of opinion, as well as from the memorials and other expressions of the public will, which have reached the House, have no hesitation in expressing their belief, that there is an almost unanimous feeling in the State against calling a Convention at the present time. The reasons for this conclusion are doubtless various, in different portions of the State, and the opinions of individuals as to the probable result of the deliberations of a Convention, at this moment, are of course very wide apart. To the Committee, the single fact of the military occupation of our soil by the Northern troops in the service of the government, against the wishes of our people, and the solemn protest of the State Executive, is a sufficient and conclusive reason for postponing the subject, to a period when the Federal ban shall be no longer upon us. It does not become the dignity of the State of Maryland to attempt the performance of an act of sovereignty, absolute or qualified, at a moment when not only her sovereignty but her Federal equality is subordinated to the law of the drum-head. No election, held at such a time and with such surroundings, could by possibility be fair or free. No result which could be reached by it would command the confidence or secure the willing obedience of the people. The Committee therefore feel it their duty to recommend the postponement of the subject for the present.

For reasons almost identical, the Committee take leave to report against the arming of the State, and the organization of our military defenses at this time. If the holding of a Sovereign Convention were not regarded as a hostile movement by the Federal government, the re-establishment of the military force of the State, in a condition of present efficiency, certainly would be, however unjustly. It avails nothing to say that the arming and organization of a suitable militia, are declared by the Constitution of the United States to be "necessary to the security of a free State," and therefore especially guaranteed to us as peaceful and fundamental rights. The Constitution is silenced by the bayonets which surround us, and it is not worth while for us to fancy ourselves beneath its aegis. It would be criminal as well as foolish for us to shut our eyes to the fact that we will not be permitted to organize and arm our citizens, let our rights and the Constitution be what they may.— The interview of our Commissioners with the President sets that point at rest. It is not easy for free men to realize such a state of things ; but it is not our fault that we are helpless, nor our shame that our helplessness is abused. ·

The Committee respectfully recommend that no action be taken towards the re-organization of the militia at this time, or the doing of any act which might be construed into hostility to the Government, and that, if any purchase of arms be indispensable, it be confined, at the farthest, to such reasonable quantity as may be manufactured in our own State, for local purposes, and may aid in the equipment of the militia, when a plan for their proper enrolment and distribution shall be matured at some future day. The purchase of such a quantity can give no just ground for complaint in any quarter, as the slightest inquiry will show that the total disuse of the militia system, for many years past, has left us almost wholly defenceless in many parts of the State, and renders some such arrangement indispensable as a measure of domestic police.

The Committee regard it as within their province further to suggest to this honorable body the propriety of adjourning over to some named day, as soon as its present and pressing duties are discharged. In their opinion, the exigencies of the present crisis do not permit a final adjournment, with any proper regard to the responsibilities and dangers which may, at any moment, be precipitated on the State.

Finally, the Committee respectfully submit to the House the following resolutions, and pray to be discharged from the further consideration of the matters before them.

> S. T. WALLIS,
> J. H. GORDON,
> G. W. GOLDSBOROUGH,
> JAMES T. BRISCOE,
> BARNES COMPTON.

Whereas, in the judgment of the General Assembly of Maryland, the war now waged by the Government of the United States upon the people of the Confederate States, is unconstitutional in its origin, purposes and conduct; repugnant to civilization and sound policy; subversive of the free principles upon which the Federal Union was founded, and certain to result in the hopeless and bloody overthrow our of existing institutions ; and

Whereas, the people of Maryland, while recognizing the obligation of their State, as a member of the Union, to submit in good faith to the exercise of all the legal and constitutional powers of the General Government, and to join as one man in fighting its authorized battles, do reverence, nevertheless, the great American principle of self-government, and sympathize deeply with their Southern brethren in their noble and manly determination to uphold and defend the same ; and

Whereas, not merely on their own account and to turn away from their own soil the calamities of civil war, but for the blessed sake of humanity, and to avoid the wanton shedding of fraternal blood, in a miserable contest which can bring nothing with it but sorrow, shame and desolation, the people of Maryland are enlisted, with their whole hearts, on the side of reconciliation and peace : now, therefore, it is hereby

Resolved by the General Assembly of Maryland, That the State of Maryland owes it to her own self-respect and her respect for the Constitution, not less than to her deepest and most honorable sympathies, to register this her solemn protest against the war which the Federal Government has declared upon the Confederate States of the South, and our sister and neighbor Virginia, and to announce her resolute determination to have no part or lot, directly or indirectly, in its prosecution.

Resolved, That the State of Maryland earnestly and anxiously desires the restoration of peace between the belligerent sections of the country, and the President, authorities, and people of the Confederate States, having, over and over again, officially and unofficially, declared that they seek only peace and self-defence, and to be let alone, and that they are willing to throw down the sword, the instant that the sword now drawn against them shall be sheathed, the Senators and Delegates of Maryland do beseech and implore the President of the United States to accept the olive branch which is thus held out to him ; and in the name of God and humanity to cease this unholy and most wretched and unprofitable strife, at least until the assembling of Congress in Washington shall have given time for the prevalence of cooler and better counsels.

Resolved, That the State of Maryland desires the peaceful and immediate recognition of the independence of the Confederate States, and hereby gives her cordial assent thereunto, as a member of the Union : entertaining the profound conviction that the willing return of the Southern people to their former Federal relations is a thing beyond hope, and that the attempt to coerce them will only add slaughter and hate to impossibility.

Resolved, That the present military occupation of Maryland, being for purposes, in the opinion of this Legislature, in flagrant violation of the Constitution, the General Assembly of the State, in the name of her people, does hereby protest against the same, and against the oppressive restrictions and illegalities with which it is attended ; calling upon all good citizens, at the same time, in the most earnest and authoritative manner, to abstain from all violent and unlawful interference, of every sort, with the troops in transit through our territory or quartered among us, and patiently and peacefully to leave to time and reason the ultimate and certain re-establishment and vindication of the right.

Resolved, That under existing circumstances, it is inexpedient to call a Sovereign Convention of the State at this time, or to take any measure for the immediate organization or arming of the militia.

Resolved, That when the Legislature adjourn, it adjourn to meet at ———, on the ——— day of ——— next.

[Document G.]

BY THE HOUSE OF DELEGATES.

MAY 10, 1861.

Read, and 2000 copies ordered to be printed.

COMMUNICATION

FROM THE

𝕸𝖆𝖞𝖔𝖗 𝖔𝖋 𝕭𝖆𝖑𝖙𝖎𝖒𝖔𝖗𝖊,

WITH THE

MAYOR AND BOARD OF POLICE OF BALTIMORE CITY.

FREDERICK:

ELIHU S. RILEY.

1861.

COMMUNICATION.

To the Honorable,

The General Assembly of Maryland:

In the report recently made to your honorable body by the
Board of Police Commissioners of the city of Baltimore, it is
stated that in the great emergency which existed in this city
on the 19th ult., it was suggested that the most feasible, if
not the only practicable mode, of stopping for a time the approach of troops to Baltimore, was to obstruct the Philadelphia, Wilmington and Baltimore, and the Northern Central
Rail Roads, by disabling some of the bridges on both roads.
And it is added that—" his honor, the Mayor, stated to the
Board that his Excellency, the Governor, with whom he had
a few minutes before been in consultation, in the presence of
several citizens, concurred in these views."

As this concurrence has since been explicitly denied by his
Excellency, Governor Hicks, in an official communication
addressed to the Senate of Maryland on the 4th inst., which
I have just seen, it is due to myself that I should lay before
you the grounds on which the statement was made to the
Board of Police; on which they, as well as myself, acted. I
seriously regret that so grave a misunderstanding exists between the Governor and myself on so important a subject.

On the evening of the 19th ult., and after the collision had
taken place, I mentioned to Governor Hicks that I had begun
to fear it might be necessary to burn the Rail Road bridges,
but I did not then, in consequence of intelligence which had
been received, think it would be. To which he replied that
he had no autority to give such an order.

At about 11 o'clock P. M., of the same day, the Hon. H.
Lenox Bond, George W. Dobbin, and John C. Brune, Esqrs.,
were requested by Gov. Hicks and myself, to go to Washington in a special train, which was provided for the purpose, to
explain in person the condition of things in Baltimore, and to
bear the following communications from Governor Hicks and
myself, which were addressed to the President:

Sir:—This will be presented to you by the Hon. H. Lenox Bond, George W. Dobbin and John C. Brune, Esqrs., who will proceed to Washington by an express train at my request, in order to explain fully the fearful condition of affairs in this city. The people are exasperated to the highest degree by the passage of troops, and the citizens are universally decided in the opinion that no more should be ordered to come.

The authorities of the City did their best to-day to protect both strangers and citizens, and to prevent a collision, but in vain, and but for their great efforts a fearful slaughter would have occurred.

Under these circumstances, it is my solemn duty to inform you that it is not possible for more soldiers to pass through Baltimore unless they fight their way at every step.

I therefore hope and trust, and most earnestly request, that no more troops be permitted or ordered by the government to pass through the City. If they should attempt it, the responsibility for the bloodshed will not rest upon me.

With great respect, your ob't serv't,

GEO. WM. BROWN, Mayor.

The following from Governor Hicks was appended to my communication:

To His Excellency,

ABRAHAM LINCOLN,

President of the United States:

I have been in Baltimore City since Tuesday evening last, and co-operated with Mayor G. W. Brown, in his untiring efforts to allay and prevent the excitement and suppress the fearful outbreak as indicated above, and I fully concur in all that is said by him in the above communication.

Very respectfully, your ob't serv't,

THOMAS H. HICKS,
Governor of Maryland.

4

Baltimore, May 9th, 1861.

At about 12 o'clock P. M., the Hon. E. Louis Lowe and Marshal George P. Kane called at my house, where Governor Hicks was passing the night, and Marshal Kane informed me that a telegram had been received that other troops were to come to Baltimore over the Northern Central Rail Road. There was also a report that troops were on their way who, it was thought, might even then be at Perryville on their route to Baltimore. Mr. Lowe, Marshal Kane, my brother John Cumming Brown, and myself went immediately to the chamber of Gov. Hicks, and laid the matter before him. The point was pressed that if troops were suddenly to come to Baltimore with a determination to pass through, a terrible collision and bloodshed would take place, and the consequences to Baltimore would be fearful, and that the only way to avert the calamity was to destroy the bridges. To this the Governor replied—"it seems to be necessary," or words to that effect.

He was then asked by me whether he gave his consent to the destruction of the bridges, and he distinctly, although apparently with great reluctance, replied in the affirmative. I do not assert that I have given the precise language used by Governor Hicks, but I am very clear that I have stated it with substantial correctness, and that his assent was unequivocal, and in answer to a question by me which elicited a distinct affirmative reply.

After this, but before the interview was over, two gentlemen came into the room, both of them strangers to me, but one was introduced as a brother of Governor Hicks, and I am confident that the assent of the Governor to the burning of the bridges was repeated in the presence of those gentlemen.

I went immediately from the chamber of the Governor to the office of the Marshal of Police, where Charles Howard, Esq., the President of the Board of Police, was waiting, and reported to him the assent of the Governor to the destruction of the bridges.

Mr. Howard, or some one else, made a further inquiry as to what had been said by the Governor, whereupon Mr. Lowe, Marshal Kane, and my brother, John C. Brown, all declared that they were present at the interview, and heard Governor Hicks gave his assent.

The order to destroy the bridges was accordingly given, and carried out in the manner already reported to your honorable body.

I refer to the accompanying statements of Col. Kane and Mr. J. C. Brown, in confirmation of the correctness of my

recollection of what occurred at the interview with Governor
Hicks.
With great respect, your ob't serv't,

GEO. WM. BROWN, Mayor.

Baltimore, May 9, 1861.

About twelve o'clock, on the night of Friday, 19th April
last, I was present when a conversation took place between
Gov. Hicks and my brother, the Mayor of Baltimore, in
reference to the best course to be pursued, by which a repetition of the troubles which had occurred on that day could
be prevented·
It was represented to them by Marshal Kane that troops
from the North were on their way to Baltimore, and might
by the following morning reach the city.
The destruction of the bridges on the Northern Centrals
and the Philadelphia, Wilmington and Baltimore railroad,
was, in the opinion of my brother, the best and most effectual method to obstruct their progress. In this opinion
Gov. Hicks fully concurred. When asked by my brother,
whether or not he gave his consent to the measure, the Governor expressed a desire for time for reflection. Being reminded by those present of the lateness of the hour, and the
necessity for prompt action, my brother again earnestly appealed to Gov. Hicks, and asked him for his consent. Gov.
Hicks' answer was, in substance, although I may not use his
exact words,—"I see nothing else to be done." "But sir,"
said my brother, "I cannot act without your consent, do you
give it ?" The Governor's reply was distinctly given in
the affirmative.

J. CUMMING BROWN.

POLICE DEPARTMENT.

OFFICE OF THE MARSHAL,

Baltimore, May 9, 1861.

Near the hour of 12 P. M. of Friday, the 19th April, the
day on which the collision with the Massachusetts troops occurred, I received intelligence that the President of the

Pennsylvania Central Railroad Company had sent a dispatch to a gentleman here, that additional troops would pass through Baltimore on their way to the Capitol.

I immediately sent to the President of the Police Board the intelligence referred to, and called at the residence of his Honor, Mayor Brown, to whom I, also, communicated the information which I had received.

The Mayor immediately had an interview with the Governor, who was then staying at his (Mayor's) house, and afterwards invited me to accompany him to the chamber of his Excellency, to whom I also communicated the information of the purposed coming of the troops.

A general conversation then ensued, in which it was agreed to by all present, that any attempt to pass troops through the city, in the then excited condition of the public mind, would lead to the most fearful consequences, and that any such passage must be prevented or delayed. The Governor fully accorded in these views.

The conversation resulted in the Governor's distinctly and unequivocally consenting, in response to the direct question put to him by the Mayor, that the bridges on the roads by which the troops were expected to come, should be distroyed as the only means of averting the consequences referred to, of their coming at that time.

GEO. P. KANE, Marshal.

FREDERICK, MD., May 10, 1861.

Hon. John C. Brune:

Dear Sir: As reference has been made by his Honor, the Mayor of Baltimore city, to my knowledge of the facts connected with the interview between him and the Governor of Maryland, on the night of the 19th ultimo, it gives me pleasure to furnish the desired statement.

I was present between 11 and 12 o'clock, P. M., on Friday, the 19th of April, at the residence of a prominent citizen of Baltimore, when Marshal Kane, who was one of the company, received information by one of his officers that a telegram had been sent by the President of the railroad company at Philadelphia, announcing the approach of troops to

Baltimore. It was the spontaneous opinion of all present that, in the terribly excited condition of the public mind, an attempt to pass troops through the city would inevitably lead to a bloody collision, and perhaps to other very serious consequences. It was, therefore, proposed to repair at once to the office of the Marshal of Police, and to send immediately for the Mayor and Governor. It was supposed at the time that Gov. Hicks was stopping at the Fountain Hotel. Marshal Kane asked me to accompany him to Mayor Brown's house; and the other gentlemen proceeded to the Marshal's office. Marshal Kane and I accordingly went to the Mayor's residence, and were admitted by his brother, who said that the Mayor had retired. In a few moments the Mayor came down to the parlor, when Marshal Kane stated to him the substance of the information received, and reminded him of the excited condition of the city, which rendered it imperatively necessary to adopt some prompt and efficient measure to delay the advent of the troops, so as to give time for the Federal Government to be correctly apprised of the state of affairs, and to arrest the threatened danger. For that purpose the partial destruction of the bridges was suggested: Mayor Brown immediately assented to the suggestion as one of absolute necessity; but said that as Mayor of the city his jurisdiction terminated with its corporate limits, and that consequently he could not assume to exercise powers beyond those limits. The Mayor added—"the Governor, however, is here, and I will go up and see him." In a few moments he returned and said that Gov. Hicks was not well and would, therefore, receive us in his room. Immediately upon entering the room, Mayor Brown and Marshal Kane gave to Gov. Hicks a full statement of the matter, and solicited his authority to destroy the bridges. Gov. Hicks replied that it was a serious affair to undertake to destroy the bridges, and he expressed some doubt as to his authority to give such an order. It was urged in reply that it was a case of absolute self-preservation, that in three or four hours time a large body of troops would probably be in the city inflamed with passionate resentment against the people of Baltimore for the assault made on their comrades in the Pratt street encounter; and that, as the city was filled with hundreds of excited men, armed to the teeth, and determined to resist the passage of troops, a fearful slaughter must necessarily ensue, and the safety of the city itself be put in peril, unless by the destruction of the bridges time could be gained to avoid the difficulty by peaceable arrangement of some sort. Governor Hicks fully and most distinctly assented to all this, and said, "well, I suppose it must be done," or words of precisely that import; to which the Mayor replied, substantially—"Governor, I have no authority to act beyond the city limits, and can do nothing in this matter except by your direction; shall the bridges be destroyed?" Gov. Hicks emphatically and distinctly replied in the affirmative. It is absolutely impossible for any misapprehension to exist on this point.

The Mayor, Marshall Kane and I, then proceeded to the Marshal's office, where we found several highly respectable citizens gathered, to whom the Mayor and Marshal gave a statement of their interview with the Governor. The Mayor then issued written orders for the destruction of the bridges. The next morning I learned by the newspaper extras that the orders had been carried into effect.

Respectfully, yours, &c.

E. LOUIS LOWE.

[Document H.]

BY THE HOUSE OF DELEGATES.

JUNE 11, 1861.

Read, and 2000 copies ordered to be printed.

By order, M. Y. KIDD, Chief Clerk.

REPORT

OF THE

COMMITTEE ON FEDERAL RELATIONS

UPON THE

MESSAGES OF THE GOVERNOR,

IN REGARD TO THE

ARBITRARY PROCEEDINGS OF THE UNITED STATES AUTHORITIES,
AND THE GOVERNOR'S CORRESPONDENCE WITH THE
UNITED STATES GOVERNMENT.

FREDERICK:

ELIHU S. RILEY.

1861.

REPORT.

To the Honorable,

the Speaker of the House of Delegates:

The committee on Federal Relations, to whom were referred the two communications from His Excellency, the Governor, bearing date the 5th inst., having duly considered the same, respectfully ask leave to make the following report:

In one of the messages in question, the Governor informs the House, in reply to its respectful enquiry, that "as a matter of course" he has taken no action "to protect the citizens of the State, in their persons and property," from illegal arrest, outrage and injury, on the part of the military authorities of the Federal Government now exercising forcible jurisdiction over our people; for the reason that he has "received no official information of the arrest spoken of" in the order of the House, "nor has any complaint or demand for his interference been made to him, by any person claiming to have been arrested in the manner alleged" therein. As the House is unhappily aware, the outrages referred to are of a character so flagrant and notorious, as to have attracted the attention and comment of the whole press of the State and country, and to have filled with the deepest indignation and anxiety, not only the reflecting people of Maryland, but all good citizens, throughout the land, who are not willing to sacrifice its free institutions, forever, to the mad excitements and usurpations of the hour. It is safe to say that the Governor cannot have opened a newspaper, nor have taken part in a public conversation, since the adjournment of the General Assembly, last month, without having had his attention attracted to the engrossing subject which he now officially ignores.

4

In the case of Mr. John Merryman, a respected fellow-citizen of the Governor and of ourselves, an open conflict of authority has taken place between the highest judicial functionary of the Republic, upon the one hand,—asserting and maintaining, as became him, the freedom of the citizen and the supremacy of the laws and Constitution—and the Federal Executive, upon the other hand, assuming a sovereign discretion and prerogative to over-ride the Constitution and tread the laws beneath his feet. No case of such absorbing interest has excited the public mind, since the Union was established—none is likely to occupy so prominent a place in the judicial annals of the country, as a monument of public liberty assaulted, and manfully, though unsuccessfully, defended. Mr. Merryman still lies a prisoner at Fort McHenry, the victim of military lawlessness and arbitrary power—the great remedial writ of *habeas corpus*, and all the guaranties of freedom which it embodies, having been stricken down, at one blow, for his oppression. Of facts so startling and so universally known—perhaps the most conspicuous of that series of extraordinary events which have crowded into a few short weeks, more than the history of half an ordinary century—your committee cannot sufficiently express their astonishment that the Governor of the State in the midst of which they have occurred, should require "official information," to suggest the discharge of his imperative official duties in the premises. Of such facts the simple occurrence is notice to all the world—notice, which amounts to knowledge, where men honestly desire to know—notice which at all events makes enquiry an official obligation, wherever a proper sense of such obligation exists. The members of the House cannot forget—for it is matter, not only of public notoriety, but of official record—how diligently, a little while ago, his Excellency gave ear to every whispered rumor of conspiracies, and plots, and plans, to seize upon the National Capitol and lay violent hands upon high functionaries of the Government. How little he was then disposed to stickle for "official" or any other sort of legitimate "information," his own recorded testimony before the Congressional Committee of Enquiry will sufficiently certify. How zealously and with what solicitude he dedicated his talents and valuable time to the accumulation and encouragement of the empty gossip referred to, and how much undeserved reproach he brought upon the State and her commercial metropolis, by the importance which his official endorsement conferred on it, are matters too recent to have escaped any one's memory. So far as this committee are aware, there was then no "official complaint or demand for" his Excellency's "interference," from any quarter. It might, therefore, in the opinion of the committee, have been fairly presumed, and the House, in adopting its order of June 5th, had not only the manifest right, but was bound to presume, that occurrences so momentous to the people of Maryland, as the suspension of the *habeas corpus* and the substitution of military authority for a government of laws, had attracted the Governor's official attention, and had suggested to him the propriety and obligation of some official interposition on his part. Indeed the fact that his Excellency's own official proclamation of May 15th, calling out a portion of the militia of the State, in *quasi* obedience to the demand of the Federal Executive, and in gross violation of the policy announced by this General Assembly, for the State of Maryland, but the day before—was contemptuously "countermanded," the day after, without more ado, through the newspapers, by a recuiting captain of the U. S. army—might of itself have been deemed sufficient to furnish to his Excellency a reasonable official intimation, that the institutions and established government of the State were not exactly in their normal condition. When it is further considered, however, that the Governor himself was personally present, as this whole Honorable body is aware, when a venerable and prominent citizen, a useful and respected member of this House, proceeding to his home from the discharge of his official duties here, was arrested by military force, without color of lawful authority, and hurried into illegal imprisonment within the walls of a Federal fortress, your committee are at a loss to conceive the extent of the evidence which his Excellency might require, to give him "official information" of any fact whatsoever. They cannot hope that any demonstration which it is in the power of this House to furnish, could add strength to the testimony of his Excellency's own bodily senses. But believing that no government is faithful to its trusts, which does not feel and resent the oppression of a single and the humblest citizen, as a wrong done to the State and to every man within its borders; and believing too, that the Executive of Maryland, clothed with all necessary powers, and bound by his oath "to take care that the laws be faithfully executed," is of all others (and especially in the absence of the Legislature) the person upon whom the duty of vinditing the independence of the commonwealth and the supremacy of its laws, to the best of his ability, devolves; your committee are constrained to regard the silence and inaction of the Governor, under the circumstances in question, as a grave and inexplicable dereliction of public duty.

In his other message, the Governor responds to the thrice-repeated and respectful solicitation of this honorable body, that he would be pleased to furnish it with copies of his correspondence, since the 4th of March last, with officers of the Federal Government. As the House will remember, his Excellency was respectfully requested in its last order of June 5th, to communicate his reasons for withholding such correspondence, should he decline to transmit it. His response is as follows; neither more nor less:

"I have already furnished your honorable body with copies of all correspondence between myself and officers of the general government which I deem it necessary to lay before you." The Committee are compelled to presume, that in his elevated and honorable position, rendering doubly obligatory, in official intercourse, the observance of those courtesies which are an instinct among private gentlemen, his Excellency could not have so far forgotten himself, as to have used the curt language which has been quoted, with any purpose of intentional disrespect. They therefore pass, without further comment, to a consideration of the substance of the message.

The 28th section of the III. Article of the Constitution expressly provides, that the House of Delegates "may call for all public or official papers and records, and send for persons whom they may judge necessary, in the course of their enquiries concerning affairs relating to the public interest." If, in response to such a call, the Governor or any other public officer can set up his judgment, as to the propriety of the requisition, against the judgment of the House, and can refuse to obey the call, because he does not "deem it necessary" to furnish, what the House "may judge necessary" to demand, it is quite obvious that the constitutional provision just quoted is a nullity, and the powers of the House, as "the grand inquest of the State," are altogether at an end. This honorable body cannot, of course, tolerate, from any quarter, so manifest an insubordination to its plain constitutional authority, and the undersigned accordingly recommend the appointment of a special committee to inspect the Executive records in the custody of the Secretary of State, or elsewhere, with power to institute such enquiries, and send for such persons and papers, as may be necessary, to place the House in possession of all needful information, in regard to the official relations between the general government and the Executive of the State since the 4th of March last, or since the commencement of our unhappy national troubles. The undersigned assume, from the tenor of the Governor's message, that such correspondence as this House has enquired for, has in fact taken place. Were it otherwise, his Excellency would of course have so stated, and would not have intimated the contrary, for the sake of making, what, in such case, would be a purely gratuitous issue, with the legislative department of the government. Should such correspondence have been had, the Executive records will of course disclose it, if, as your committee are bound to suppose, the constitutional duty of recording "all official acts and proceedings" has been faithfully discharged.

Your committee recommend the adoption of the following order and resolutions in conformity with the views above expressed.

S. T. WALLIS,
J. H. GORDON,
JAMES T. BRISCOE,
G. W. GOLDSBOROUGH,
BARNES COMPTON.

Ordered, That a committee of three be appointed by the Speaker, with instructions to examine the Executive records and call for such persons and papers as they may deem necessary, to enable them to ascertain and report to the House, without delay, the precise character of the relations established by the Executive of this State with the federal government since the commencement of our existing national troubles.

Whereas, Ross Winans, a member of the House of Delegates of Maryland, from the city of Baltimore, on his way to his home from the discharge of his official duties, on the 14th of May last, was arbitrarily and illegally arrested, on a public highway, in the presence of the Governor of this State, by an armed force under the orders of the Federal Government, and was forcibly imprisoned and held in custody, thereafter, at Annapolis and Fort McHenry, without color of lawful process or right, by the command and at the arbitrary will and pleasure of the President of the United States; and

Whereas, sundry other citizens of Maryland have been unlawfully dealt with, in the same despotic and oppressive manner, by the same usurped authority, and some of them have in fact been removed by force beyond the limits of the State of Maryland and the jurisdiction of her tribunals, in utter violation of their rights, as citizens, and of the rights of the State, as a member of the Federal Union: and

Whereas, the unconstitutional and arbitrary proceedings of the Federal Executive, have not been confined to the violation of the personal rights and liberties of the citizens of Maryland, but have been extended into every department of oppressive illegality, so that the property of no man is safe;

the sanctity of no dwelling is respected; and the sacredness of private correspondence no longer exists; and

WHEREAS, the Senate and House of Delegates of Maryland, recognizing the obligation of the State, as far as in her lies, to protect and defend her people against usurped and arbitrary power—however difficult the fulfillment of that high obligation may be rendered by disastrous circumstances—feel it due to her dignity and independence, that history should not record the overthrow of public freedom, for an instant, within her borders, without recording, likewise, the indignant expression of her resentment and remonstrance; now therefore be it

Resolved, That the Senate and House of Deiegates of Maryland, in the name and on behalf of the good people of the State, do accordingly register this their earnest and unqualified protest against the oppressive and tyrannical assertion and exercise of military jurisdiction, within the limits of Maryland, over the persons and property of her citizens, by the Government of the United States, and do solemnly declare the same to be subversive of the most sacred guaranties of the Constitution and in flagrant violation of the fundamental and most cherished principles of American free government.

Resolved, further, That these resolutions be communicated, by the President of the Senate and the Speaker of the House, to the Hon. James Alfred Pearce and the Hon. Anthony Kennedy, Senators of Maryland in the Senate of the United States, with the request that they present the same to the Senate, to be recorded among its proceedings, in vindication of the right and in perpetual memory of the solemn remonstrance of this State against the manifold usurpations and oppressions of the Federal Government.

[Document I.]

BY THE HOUSE OF DELGATES,

Read and ordered to be printed.

JUNE 12, 1861.

By order,   M. Y. KIDD, Chief Clerk.

REPORT

OF THE

COMMITTEE ON MILITARY AFFAIRS

IN REGARD TO THE

$70,000 APPROPRIATION.

REPORT.

The committee on Military Affairs, to whom was referred the communications of the Governor and Adjutant General in response to an order of the House adopted April 19th, calling upon them to report to this House at the earliest moment practicable, what amount of the $70,000 appropriated at the last session of the Legislature to arm the State, has been expended, and by whom expended, and whether any agent has been appointed by the Governor and Adjt. General to disburse the said $70,000, or any part thereof, either directly or indirectly, or to procure samples of arms, and if so, whether said agent was employed at the expense of the State, and if so, what compensation he is to be paid, and whether such appointment is authorized by the Constitution or any law of this State, and who such agent is, what number, kind and quality of arms have been purchased under said appropriation, of whom purchased and at what prices, and where they were deposited, and whether they were inspected, if so, by whom inspected, and by whom distributed, to what counties, the number and kind to each county, whether any of said arms have been seized or stolen by any individual or individuals, what number, kind and quality of the arms purchased from the $70,000 appropriated now remain on hand, and where deposited; whether any of said arms have been condemned by the inspector or inspectors, what number, kind and quality so condemned, and what disposition has been made or will be made of the same; ask leave to report that they have had the same under consideration, and submit the following report:

The Adjt. General states in his report that of the $70,000, the amount appropriated in the bill, under the provisions of

which the transaction under consideration was conducted,
$64,415.05 have been expended, leaving in the State treasury
a balance of $5,584.85, and that the proper vouchers for
these expenditures are now on file in the Executive
Chamber.

Accompanying the report of the Adjt. General and Governor, among other papers, the committee find two documents
—one containing proposals from Eli Whitney, of New Haven,
Conn., to furnish the State of Maryland with 2000 rifled
muskets of the Minnie pattern, and 1000 army or navy revolvers with the necessary accoutrements for each description
of arms: the other proposal by the Ames manufacturing
company to furnish the State with 1000 sabres. The terms
upon which Whitney offers to furnish the arms and accoutrements named in his contract are as follows: "2000 Minnie long range muskets, equal to the samples furnished by
said Whitney, and then at Annapolis, the calibre of said
muskets being fifty-eight-one-hundredth of an inch in diameter, to be packed in cases and delivered in Baltimore, (cost of
cases and packing and cost of transportation to be paid by
said Whitney,) at his risk, subject to the order of the Governor and Adjt. General. The appendages to be as follows:
4 Minnie bullet moulds and 2 cone wrenches to every case of
20 guns, 1 screw driver and wiper to each gun, the price of
the gun and appendages as above ($15.00) per gun."
"Said Whitney also agrees to furnish and deliver in Baltimore, at his risk and expense, 1000 medium army or navy
revolving pistols, like and equal to the samples furnished by
said Whitney, and then at Annapolis, at $16.20 cents each,
appendages included." "The above arms to be inspected at
the factory by H. C. Hicks, and packed under his direction."

The proposals by the Ames manufacturing company
are as follows: "One thousand light cavalry sabres of the
last model, issued by the U. S. Government for $7.00 each,
to be tested, &c., and subject to the inspection of H. C.
Hicks, to be well packed, and delivered at the port of Baltimore, at the expense of the Ames manufacturing company."

The committee find by an estimate of the cost of the above
described arms at the price stated by the contracting parties
the aggregate amount to be $53,200. This amount deducted
from the sum $64,415, the amount reported by the Adjt.
General, as having been expended, leaves the sum of $11,215
unaccounted for in the report.

The Adjt. General reports that they (the Governor and
himself,) had no agent for the purchase of the arms, but that
H. C. Hicks was employed to procure samples, the contracts

being made by himself and the Governor. He further reports that after the contracts had been entered into, and the arms purchased, the Governor and himself concluded that it would be attended with less expense and more facility of transportation to the different companies throughout the State, to have the arms deposited in a warehouse in the city of Baltimore; and in furtherance of their object procured the services of H. C. Hicks, to act as agent to inspect the arms, and to forward them under orders from the Adjt. General to the different companies, and to pay the cost of transportation. For these services H. C. Hicks was to receive the sum of $500.

The Adjt. General does not state, but your committee are brought necessarily to the inference, that this sum of $500 has been appropriated to the use indicated, from the amount appropriated by the State for the purchase of arms. Your committee think the report of the Governor and Adjt. General, not only an incomplete and unsatisfactory response to the order of the House, failing as it does, to give an account of all the money expended, but as clearly exhibiting an unwarrantable use of the public money entrusted to their care, by appropriating a portion of the same to a use for which it was not designed, and a deliberate violation of the law under which they acted, by entrusting the disbursement of a portion of the money, and the inspection of the arms, to a party not legally bound to them, or the State, and whose agency under the law they were not authorized to make or employ.

Further, in the adoption of a warehouse in the city of Baltimore as a place of deposit, when they were expressly required by the law to deposit the arms in the armories of the State, the result of which has been the loss to the State of 370 infantry arms and accoutrement, and 16 cavalry arms and accoutrements, the balance remaining on hand, not distributed. Your committee, therefore, recommend, in view of these facts, as an act of justice to the people of the State, as well as to the authorities concerned, a thorough investigation of this whole matter, by a committee appointed for that purpose, and that said committee have power to send for persons and papers.

BARNES COMPTON, Ch'n.
B. MILLS,
ROSS WINANS,
THOS. C. WORTHINGTON.

BY THE HOUSE OF DELEGATES,

JUNE 18, 1861.

Read and 1000 copies ordered to be printed.

By order,   M. Y. KIDD, Chief Clerk.

PETITION

OF

RICHARD B. CARMICHAEL

AND OTHERS,

AGAINST THE ADJOURNMENT OF THE LEGISLATURE SINE DIE.

PETITION.

To the General Assembly of Maryland:

The undersigned, citizens of Queene Anne's county, make this petition to the General Assembly of Maryland, in consequence of reported applications, by others professing to be citizens, who assume to advise the Legislature to adjourn *"sine die."* The undersigned ask a counter hearing, and pray, and, so far as is consistent with perfect respect, insist, that the high trust committed to your honorable bodies, by the good people of the State, be maintained in your own keeping, until your successors shall have been chosen.

The plain and obvious object of those who originate petitions for your final adjournment, is to put the State back into their own keeping, where it had remained, until a few weeks ago, to the shame and dishonor of every true citizen. Conspiring with those, who, a long time have subverted the Constitution of the United States, in their section, and who had unblushingly repealed the guaranties made by their forefathers and accepted by our own, these persons, at an early stage of the existing crisis, had obtained control of the Executive will. How they abused their power over the Governor, is disclosed in the debased and oppressed condition of Maryland, at this time.

The General Assembly of Maryland is convened at Frederick. Yet the constitution of the State provides, that the seat of government be at Annapolis, and the "Bill of Rights" that the Legislature should convene there.

The General Assembly of Maryland is in session by Executive proclamation. Yet the constitution provides that they shall be convoked by the Governor to Annapolis, unless "the presence of an enemy," or some "other cause" should render that place "unsafe for the meeting of the Legislature." An armed force—strangers to the State—occupied the seat of government, when the Executive proclamation called them

4

to Frederick. It does not belong to the object of this petition here, to designate the relation of these intruders. If
they were friends, it was not not unsafe for the Legislature
to meet at Annapolis. If they were enemies, it *was* unsafe.
How the Governor regarded them, his proclamation, calling
the Legislature elsewhere, discloses.

If they were, at the time of their intrusion, enemies, their
conduct since has made no change in that relation. If any
loyal citizen of Maryland entertained a doubt of their hostile
feeling toward those in the State, who were true in their allegiance to our laws and institutions, the daily acts of atro-
cious outrage done by them, has disabused him. They have
subverted the law of this State, and all other law that has
ever obtained here, and in its stead have set up brute force—
"the higher law"—heretofore promised by their chief.

They have seized private citizens, without warrant of law
—they have deprived them of their liberty without a hearing
before judge or jury—they have a military force within our
border without sanction of the Legislature—they have set the
military above the civil power—they have subjected persons
to martial law, who are not soldiers, nor mariners, nor ma-
rines, nor of the militia in the regular service of the State.
The *habeas corpus* has been suspended. The right of the
people to bear arms has been infringed, and the militia of
the State is being disarmed, thereby depriving us of the best
"*security of a free State.*" On the holy Sabbath last, an
armed force—strangers and aliens to the State—was marched
into a neighboring peaceful village; private citizens were
arrested, on the high road, without *imputation* of offence
against any law; and acts of outrage perpetrated by outlaws,
bearing the authority of the person who is styled "the Governor of Maryland." On yesterday a gang similarly armed,
and bearing the same authority, visited our County town,
and subjected our people to the like oppression. This day
they are traversing the county, invading the sanctity of our
homes, alarming the children and the tender sex—with Minnie rifle in one hand and the Governor's warrant in the
other.

They who ask your honorable bodies to adjourn are the
confederates of the Governor and of these out-laws. The undersigned are citizens of the State of Maryland, who hold as
their highest obligation their allegiance to the State. They
are fully conscious of the obligations, which their relation to
the Government of the United States imposes. They do not
lose sight of the fact, that they are citizens of a State, in
Union with those States, who hold the Government of the
United States. But they do not recognize any powers in

that government, except such as were delegated at its adoption and are expressed in the Constitution; and with all deference to the presence before which they come with this petition, they pronounce and denounce the exertion of power, manifested in the acts above recited, usurpation. Those who exercise it—usurpers,—and *their* aiders and abettors in the State of Maryland—traitors—traitors to Maryland, where they owe allegiance, and traitors to the United States, whose constitution they subvert with force.

It may be, that at this time, the Legislature may be unable to accomplish anything to abate the rigor of a necessity, under which the loyal men of Maryland are held in determined submission.

On this subject the Legislature has acted, and the undersigned do not mean to indulge any review. But the Legislature is the only power, through whose agency the sovereign will can exert efficient action. How soon the occasion for such action may be presented, or how long deferred, is not to be considered. The extent to which freemen may be brought to endure, by the guilty contrivance of those in authority, is undergoing a cruel test in Maryland. But the end *must* come, and come when it may, the Legislative arm will be wanted to supply the means of redress. It belongs to the people. An "extraordinary occasion" has lifted it up. Let it not relapse until the exigency has past. Let not the powers of the State be again committed to those "very learned and intelligent citizens" who, using the Executive with suple art, have prostituted them to the purposes of the parasites of power. The expense of continued or of frequent sessions, is not to be weighed, in such a crisis. Nothing is to be put in the scale, against the liberty of the people.

The subscribers will cheerfully incur their respective shares of the cost, and they believe their fellow-citizens generally in the State, who have not taken a willing part in the treason that yet reigns rampant are ready and resolved to partake. In the firm trust that the General Assembly concur in heart with the prayer herein made, and that they will act as they feel, the undersigned will ever pray, &c.

[Signed,]

RICHARD B. CARMICHAEL,

and 48 other citizens.

Document [K.]

BY THE HOUSE OF DELEGATES,
JULY 31, 1861.
Read and 1,000 copies ordered to be printed.

REPORT

AND

ACCOMPANYING DOCUMENTS

OF THE

HOUSE COMMITTEE,

APPOINTED TO EXAMINE INTO THE AFFAIRS OF THE

MARYLAND PENITENTIARY.

FREDERICK, MD.
E. S. RILEY, PRINTER,
1861.

REPORT.

The special Committee appointed under the resolution of June 11th, 1861, to examine generally into the affairs of the Maryland Penitentiary, beg leave respectfully to report that they organized in the city of Frederick on the 25th of June, and selected Mr. Thomas H. Moore as clerk, and adjourned to meet on the 1st of July, in the city of Baltimore, at the Maryland Penitentiary.

Their duties, as pointed out in the resolution and order above referred to, consisted of an investigation of the following matters :

1st. The memorial of John H. Duvall and William Howard, asking relief from losses growing out of the destruction of their property by fire.

2d. The memorial of Charles Murdock, asking relief by a modification of his contracts with the Directors of the Penitentiary and the equitable settlement of claims in dispute between them.

3d. An investigation of the manufacturing department of the Institution generally.

4th. An examination of the financial affairs and condition, and

5th. An enquiry into its general management and discipline.

Taking the points to be examined in the order they appear, the Committee commenced with the memorial of Messrs. Duvall and Howard.

The memorial states that on the 3d of October, 1859, they entered into a written contract with the Directors of the Maryland Penitentiary for the rent of certain shops and yard room, and the employment of convict labor in the manufacture of barrels, and in the prosecution of that business had invested a large amount of money in the purchase of patent rights, machinery, and the necessary stock to carry it on successfully ; that while in the prosecution of a successful business, on the 23d of December, 1860, their work shops were fired by some of the convicts, and their property almost destroyed, entailing, as they allege, a loss over and above the amount of insurance of $23,150, and avers that said fire was caused partly by the refusal of the Directors to permit them to have their own watchman on the premises on Sunday, (the fire having occurred on that day,) whereby their property was left in an unprotected state on Sundays, and partly by a want of proper discipline on the part of the officers of the Institution, by which the convicts were enabled to obtain access to the shops and commit the incendiary act; and the memorialists plead that as the loss was by no act of their own, but was indirectly caused by the officers of the State, as above stated, that the Legislature should grant them relief by reimbursing in whole, or in part, the loss sustained.

The magnitude of the claim, and the importance of it to the memorialists, who were entirely ruined by the fire, as well as to the State, whose finances are not in a condition to bear any burdens that are justly avoidable, demanded of the Committee the most careful and thorough examination of the case, it was conducted and argued by eminent counsel on both sides. Numerous witnesses were examined, whose evidence will be found in the proceedings of the Committee, pages 1 to 53, herewith submitted; and while deeply sympathising with the memorialists in the heavy loss they have sustained, the Committee have been unable to arrive at the conclusion that the case presents any just grounds for a claim on the State, the allegation that the Directors refused to permit the presence of a private watchman on Sundays, was not sustained by the evidence, and although it was proved that the shops were fired on Sunday by some of the convicts, yet it did not appear to have arisen from any lack of ordinary discipline on the part of the officers, it being utterly impossible with few officers and many prisoners, strictly to carry out the prison rules which requires a prisoner to be always under the eye of an officer, neither have the Committee been able to arrive at the conclusion that a loss by fire, even if proved to have been caused by negligence on the part of the officers, would afford just cause for a claim on the State.

The second portion of the investigation was the memorial of Charles Murdock, asking a modification of his contracts with the Directors and the arbitration of a disputed account between them.

It appears that Mr. Murdock for some ten years past has rented work shops and employed the convict labor of the Institution, principally in the manufacture of cedar ware, and at the time of his memorial, had in his employment one hundred convicts whose time would expire July 1, 1861, and fifty, whose time, under his contract, would expire January 1, 1865. Mr. Murdock deemed himself justified in asking relief from his contracts on the ground that the existing war and blockade of the Southern States had seriously embarrassed him in the prosecution of his business, the raw material that he uses being derived entirely from the South, and his manufactured goods finding an exclusive market there, thus completely shutting him out on both sides, and rendering it impossible to carry on his busines until peace should be restored.

Before the Committee proceeded to take evidence in this case, an. arrangement and settlement was happily made between the Directors and Mr. Murdock, by which the latter pays in full to the Directors the amount in dispute, and retains the labor of 50 men at 50 cents per day until January 1, 1865. This, with the rent of the shops, will give the Institution a revenue from that source of about $8,300.

The 100 men whose time with Mr. Murdock expired on the 1st of July, the Directors propose to employ in the weaving department.

The Manufacturing Department.

This department is devoted to the manufacture of plaid cottons, with a few linseys and coarse carpets, and the Committee regret to report it in a very depressed condition. At no time has it been a source of much revenue to the Instition, arising from the inability of hand loom labor to compete successfully with power looms; still, the superior quality of its manufactured goods and its wide-spread reputation has heretofore insured their immediate sale, but the embarrassment growing out of the blockade of the Southern States has produced the same results as in the case of Mr. Murdock; nearly all the yarns used are the product of Southern mills, while the manufactured goods find a market exclusively in the Slave States. The consequence is, that no sales have been made by the Directors for the past three months, and none of any consequence can be made until the Southern markets shall be re-opened. No revenue, therefore, can be expected from this department as long as the present unfortunate state of affairs continues to exist. The stock of manufactured goods now on hand amounts to $10,500, and of materials to $2,300, which, when manufactured, will increase the stock of goods to $15,000, all of which, in ordinary times, could be made available to pay the debts and expenses of the Institution.

The Committee, after a patient and thorough investigation of this branch of the subject, are satisfied that the entire system of labor at the Institution is wrong, and demands a radical change, as at present conducted, it must always be, as it has been, a heavy burden on the State. It has not been furnished by the State with the cash capital necessary to carry on successfully a manufac-

turing business; its operations are, necessarily, on a
credit basis, and the disadvantages of this system may be
illustrated by the single fact that it has paid during the
last five years the sum of $13,015 for interest alone, to say
nothing of the increased cost of supplies when purchased
on credit, and the saving of the discount which always
accompany cash payments.

A careful analysis of the operations of this department
for the past five years exhibits the fact that the nett earnings of all the convicts employed by the Institution average
but eleven cents per day, and this, without making any
allowance for cost and depreciation of machinery, while
about the same number of convicts employed by the contractors at 50 cents per day, gave a revenue of $28,800 for
labor, and $700 for rent of work shops. It is true that
the labor employed by the latter was of better quality,
but that would account for but a small portion of the difference.

The Committee would recommend the total abolition of
all manufacturing on account of the Institution, and the
substitution of a system farming the convict labor to contractors. Under this system, the Institution can be made
to support itself and the State relieved from a heavy burden, while the prisoners will be taught some useful trade,
the knowledge of which, by giving them the means of
procuring an honest livelihood, would in many instances
prevent them from relapsing into crime.

It is very true that the difficulties of the present time
will prevent this plan from being carried out at once, but
with peace will come the ordinary demand for labor, when
it can be successfully accomplished.

It will not be out of place here to illustrate the proposition by an estimate of its results.

The expenses of all kinds of maintaining the Institution, simply as a prison, may be estimated at about $37,000.
This, by a judicious economy, might be probably reduced
to $35,000. The prisoners average about 420 in number,
of which 400 are males. Suppose the sick, the infirm,
and those necessary to perform the ordinary house work
of the Institution to amount to 100, there remains 300
whose labor may be made available. These would not be
equally valuable, and may be thus classified:

200 worth 50 cents per day, - - - -			$31,300
50 " 25 " " " - - - -			3,912
50 " 12½ " " " - - - -			1,956
Producing - - - - - -			$37,168

A sum fully equal to all the expenses of the Institution. This change would not entail any expense on the State, inasmuch as the work shops now used for spinning and weaving would be sufficient and answer for any other occupation.

The Financial Condition of the Institution.

In the investigation of this branch of the inquiry every facility was afforded by the Board of Directors, and Mr. J. J. C. Dougherty, the financial clerk and book-keeper.

The Institution has been singularly fortunate in securing the services of the latter officer, whose books and accounts are kept in a manner highly creditable to himself and those who appointed him.

This examination produced the following results :
Liabilities of the Institution, over
and above cash on hand July 1st, 1861, $45,298 41.

ASSETS.

Appropriation at April session
  not yet collected, $25,000
Active debt due (good) by contractors,   6,764.65
Suspended debt,   5,414.47
Manufactured goods and mate-
  rials on hand,   12.669.29   49,848.41.

Nominal surplus, $4,550.00

The stock of manufactured goods on hand is not available for reasons before stated, and the suspended debt is in the same condition, from the same causes ; it consists of the notes of merchants, hitherto of undoubted solvency, doing business in the South, whose business is now prostrate, and whose only chance of paying their debts is in the probability of being able at some future day to collect the debts due them in the Southern States.

From this exhibit it will be seen that until peace is restored, and trade resumes its accustomed channels, the Institution must become a heavy burden on the State, and that to carry it through the next twelve months an additional appropriation of not less than $25,000 will be absolutely necessary.

The General Management and Discipline.

On this subject it affords the Committee much pleasure to speak of the faithful and efficient manner in which the Directors and officers have discharged their.duties, under the immediate management of Mr. Alfred D. Evans, the Warden, and his deputy, Mr. Isaac G. Roberts. The entire prison presents an air of neatness and cleanliness rarely met with in public buildings of the kind, and would indeed be creditable to any private house; the prisoners were well clad and cleanly in their persons, and the food sufficient in quantity and quality. The discipline, if not at all times carried out to the strict letter of the law, is as perfect as the limited number of officers and guards would admit of.

But there are some matters in this connection which humanity demands at the hands of the Legislature as early action as the finances of the State will justify. The law requires that each prisoner shall be confined in a separate cell; this from the want of necessary accommodations cannot be carried out; five, six, and sometimes as many as eight are confined in one room, subject to all the evils that arise from free intercourse between criminals; in addition to this the basement cells of the eastern dormitory (some fifty in number) are under ground and unfit for the confinement of human beings—it is true the present Warden, by flooring the brick pavement, has improved their condition somewhat, still they are not fit to be used.

A new dormitory, with not less than 150 cells, should be erected as soon as the means of the State will permit.

There is another evil that requires Legislative action—it is too much the practice of the courts throughout the State to send persons to the Penitentiary for small offenses whose proper destination would be the County Almshouse or the Insane Hospital. There are now in the Institution many of both classes, some who commit a petty theft for the sole purpose of being provided with a home, and others idiotic or insane at the time of commitment.

One case may be instanced by way of illustration; the commitment is from Calvert County and reads thus :—

"George Norfolk, presented for feloniously entering the dwelling of Wm. Ogden and taking therefrom a bottle of whiskey, a pan of milk, and some bread and meat. Verdict of the jury, *Guilty, and insane at the time of the committal of the act and insane now,* and sentenced by the Court to be confined in the Penitentiary house of the State of Maryland *until he shall recover his reason,* and be discharged by due course of law."

This is virtually an imprisonment for life for the offense of stealing something to eat, the party being idiotic and insane at the time, and the effect is to transfer his support from the county to which he belongs to the State at large.

All of which is respectfully submitted.

LAWRENCE SANGSTON,
CHARLES H. PITTS, } Committee.
JOHN THOS. FORD,

9

FREDERICK CITY, June 25, 1861.

The Committee appointed by the House of Delegates of Maryland to examine into the questions in dispute between Messrs. Duvall and Howard, and Mr. Charles Murdock and the Board of Directors of the Maryland Penitentiary, as also to inquire into the financial condition of the same, assembled this day in Frederick, at 12 o'clock, M.

Present—Messrs. Sangston, Pitts and Ford, of the Committee.

Mr. Thos. H. Moore was unanimously selected as clerk to the Committee.

After consultation, the Committee adjourned to meet in Baltimore city, on Monday, July 1st, 1861, at the office of Charles H. Pitts, Esq., at 11 o'clock, A. M.

By order,

THOMAS H. MOORE.

BALTIMORE, July 1st, 1861.

The Committe appointed to examine the questions in dispute between Messrs. Duvall and Howard, and Charles Murdock and the Board of Directors of the Maryland Penitentiary, as well as to inquire into the financial condition of said Institution, assembled this morning at the office of Charles H. Pitts, Esq., St. Paul street, pursuant to adjournment.

Present—Messrs. Sangston, Pitts and Ford, of the Committee. Thomas H. Moore, Clerk.

The Clerk was directed to notify the Board of Directors that the Committee would visit the Penitentiary on to-morrow, July 2d, for the purpose of examining into the facts connected with the contract of Messrs. Duvall and Howard.

The Committee then adjourned.

By order,

THOS. H. MOORE, Clerk.

The Committee of the Legislature of Maryland assembled this morning at the room of the Directors of the Maryland Penitentiary, at 10 o'clock, pursuant to adjournment.

Present—Messrs. Sangston and Ford, of the Committee.

Mr. John H. Duvall, George M. Gill, Esq., his counsel, and Messrs. John Hurst, John Hilbert, Wm. Chestnut, R. Middleton and Lefevre Jarrett, of the Board of Directors.

The Clerk proceeded to read the memorial of John H. Duvall and William Howard to the Legislature of Maryland.

Isaac G. Roberts, Deputy Warden, was sworn on the Holy Evangely of Almighty God.

Examined by Mr. Sangston.—Question. Were you the bearer of an order from the monthly Committee of the Board of Directors to Mr. Duvall, directing him to dispense with the services of a watchman on Sunday?

Answer. No; not that I recollect. The order was given me by the Warden to tell Messrs. Duvall and Murdock that there should be no more Sunday work, and to stop all work of that kind.

Question. Did that order extend to the services of Mr. Duvall's watchman?

Answer. They did not tell me that; they only said no more fires should be made on Sunday.

Question. Who was the watchman?

Answer. I believe his name was Gambrill.

By Mr. Gill.—Question. You gave the same directions to Mr. Murdock?

Answer. I do not recollect whether I gave him or Mr. Kimball the directions. I know that Mr. Duvall's man was at work on Sundays.

By Mr. Duvall.—Question. Did you not deliver the order to me in this way, " Your men must not be about here on Sundays?"

Answer. No, sir; the order was, that Sunday work should be stopped throughout. The order I received from the Warden was general.

By Mr. Gill.—Question. Did you tell Mr. Murdock, or his man either, that they should not have a watchman on Sunday?

Answer. The prisoners attended to Mr. Murdock's work; he did not have a watchman on Sunday in daytime.

Question. Do you recollect any conversation had with Mr. Murdock, or did you tell Mr. Murdock that you had told Mr. Duvall the watchman should not be there on Sunday?

Answer. I do not recollect such conversation. The directions given to Mr. Duvall was some time before the 23d December, 1860. The man employed by Mr. Duvall was attending to the dry-houses, who was also night watchman. The fire took place after dinner on Sunday, between 2 and 3 o'clock; before 3 o'clock, 23d December, 1860.

Question. Did you investigate into the causes of the fire?

Answer. I did, and was under the impression that Samuel Green, Edward Perry, John Butler and Joe Wheatley, all colored, committed the act. The men could very easily get from the church to the shop—about sixty yards.

Question. Were they permitted to go about without an officer under the proper discipline of the establishment?

Answer. It is customary to go about without an officer. The officers on the wall are constantly on the look out, with arms in their hands. If they had attended to their duty, the prisoners could not enter the shop of Mr. Duvall except at one point in the rear ; Mr. Murdock's dry-house obscured the view from the officer's box, leaving a space of three or four feet a prisoner could enter. The dormitories are cleaned between 10 and 12 o'clock. The fire took place about fifteen minutes of 3 o'clock. I ascertained from investigation, that three of the parties were guilty, and one was present. Wheatley said that Green had a box with yellow cotton in it ; Green set the cotton on fire in the dormitory. Green and Perry went to Duvall's shop together, when they built the fire. Wheatley said the whole four were connected ; that he, Wheatley, set the fire, but the others assisted. Yellow cotton is an article used in the manufacturing department, and makes a very good slow-match. A piece three feet long would burn two hours.

Question. How far is the dormitory where the cotton was. set on fire from Duvall's shop?

Answer. About seventy-five yards.

Cross-examined by Mr. Hurst.—*Question.* Did the Court rule your testimony out?

Answer. It did upon the second trial, because the information I derived was through stratagem.

By Mr. Jarrett.—*Question.* How long have you been connected with the Penitentiary?

Answer. Three years under William Johnson Waden, one year under I. M. Denson, and upwards of three years under A. D. Evans.

Question.—Are the present officers as great in number as those of former administrations?

Answer. There are four more than under the late Warden, Mr. Merryman.

Question. How does the discipline of this Institution as at present, compare with that of former wardens?

Answer. I think it might be more strict ; my own orders are to carry out the strictest discipline, and I have endeavored to do so.

Question. Has not Mr. Duvall been notified that the condition of his shops prevented the officers from having a strict supervision over the same?

Answer. I have notified him several times that the quantity of barrels prevented the officers from having a full view of the entire shop during work hours.

By Mr. Sangston.—Question. Who was the watchman on duty nearest the shop of Mr. Duvall?

Answer. Mr. Suter was the guard.

Question. Was any action taken by the Board in relation to the negligence of the guard?

Answer. Yes. Mr. Suter was discharged.

James Gambrell, sworn.

By Mr. Gill.—Question. You recollect the fire at Mr. Duvall's shop, 23d December, 1860?

Answer. Yes. I do.

Question. How long prior to that fire had you been employed by Mr. Duvall?

Answer. Seven months and nineteen nights and days. I commenced about the 4th May, 1860.

Question. What was your duty?

Answer. Watch out for fires ; put out all fires used in shop after prisoners had left ; not to permit any fires after Saturday night, 12 o'clock.

Question. When you first attended, what did you do on Sundays?

Answer. The first two Sundays I was not admitted to the yard of the Institution until my hour for duty arrived.

Question. What did you do for the subsequent time on Sundays?

Answer. On and after the third Sunday, I cleaned out the boilers of the engine, and watched for anything that might be wrong until Mr. Duvall's foreman or sons arrived, which continued until three or five Sundays before the fire, when I stopped coming to the Institution until my hour arrived for night duty, about sun-down. I stopped then by Mr. Duvall's directions. I understood from him that the Directors were not satisfied with his men coming upon the premises on Sunday ; after which notice I did not watch on Sundays.

Question. Was any work done on Sundays after you entered Mr. Duvall's employment?

Answer. Nothing was done except cleaning the boilers, which was done by me until stopped, as before mentioned, by Mr. Duvall.

Cross-examined by Mr. Jarrett.—Question. When Mr. Duvall told you that your services on Sunday were dispensed with, no work was then required of you?

Answer. I had the same watching to do.

By Mr. Ford.—Question. Did you understand from any person connected with the Institution that objection was raised against your being there as watchman simply?

Answer. I had no information on the subject.

Cross-examined by Mr. Jarrett.—Question. Did the officer in charge of Mr. Duvall's shop complain in your hearing of the condition of the shop?

Answer. I did hear him complain, and have seen him take Mr. Duvall's men and remove the cause of complaint.

Question. Have you seen Mr. Evans, the Warden, pass through at late hours of the night and examine Mr. Duvall's shop?

Answer. I have.

Question. Did the Warden sometimes previous to the fire express to you his apprehensions that because of the non-employment of the convicts, and the unsafe condition of Mr. Duvall's shop, a fire would result therefrom?

Answer. I do not think the convicts were referred to, but he did complain of the condition of the shop, and requested me to keep a bright look out.

Direct examination resumed by Mr. Gill.—Question. If you had continued up to the time of the fire, would you not have been able to prevent the fire?

Answer. I think I would.

Question. Could the regular watch of the Institution prevent the convicts from going into Mr. Duvall's shop?

Answer. I think they could.

Mr. Charles Murdock, sworn for Complainant.

Examined by Mr. Gill.—Question. Prior to the fire, was a watchman on duty on Sunday in Mr. Duvall's shop?

Answer. I have seen one on duty, presuming he was from what I have seen him do, the impression on my mind being that both Mr. Lamb and Mr. Gambrell have attended to the fires on Sunday, although I am not sure of the same.

Question. Had you any conversation with Mr. Roberts prior to or subsequent to the fire in relation to the direction he had given Mr. Duvall as to the watchman being there on Sunday?

Answer. After the fire Mr. Roberts admitted to me that he had given the order to Mr. Duvall forbidding his watchman on Sundays. The order to stop the watchmen was given one or two months prior to the fire.

By A. D. Evans. I understood Mr. Roberts to say that the watchman was stopped from doing whatever he had been previously doing?

By Mr. Jarrett.—Question.—Have you heard any objections from any Director to a watchman being employed by a contractor?

Answer. No, sir; because I have had to employ no watchman.

By Mr. Ford.—Question. Did you understand the order as forbidding all persons employed by contractors coming upon the premises?

Answer. I did so understand the order.

By Mr. Hurst.—Question. After the order was given, did you not see persons at work on Sunday in the shop of Mr. Duvall?

Answer. I cannot say.

By Mr. Jarrett.—Question. Have you ever expressed any apprehensions from fire because of the condition of Mr. Duvall's shop.

Answer. I believe I have.

Mr. Gambrill, recalled by Complainant.

By Mr. Gill.—Question. Did you know of any work being done on Sunday while you were acting as watchman?

Answer. I do not know of any.

Michael Conner, sworn by Complainant.

Examined by Mr. Gill.—Question. You were the foreman of Mr. Duvall in the manufacturing department?

Answer. Yes, sir, from the 28th February, 1860. I had no knowledge of any order being given, except that no prisoners should be worked on Sundays, and no fires be permitted in the dry houses on that day.

The Committee then adjourned until to-morrow, Wednesday morning, at 10 o'clock.

———

WEDNESDAY, July 3d, 1861.

The Committee met pursuant to adjournment. Present, Messrs. Sangston and Ford.

Mr. Murdock, recalled by Complainant.

Examined by Mr. Gill.—Question. If the rules and regulations of the Penitentiary, as laid down in the Code and printed orders, had been followed on the day when the shop of Mr. Duvall was fired, would not such fire have been prevented in your opinion?

Answer. I understand that under such rules an officer should have had the supervision of the prisoners, and if this had been so, it would be impossible, in my judgment, for the fire to have occurred. It would be difficult among so large a number of convicts to have *at all times* an officer with each convict. When the rules and regulations were made, the number of shops were less, and the prisoners were not so scattered, although no difference existed on Sundays.

Question. Is there, or not, more danger on Sundays from fire by the convicts than on other days? If so, state the reasons?

Answer. On Sundays there is less danger from accidents; but more danger from incendiaries, because on Sunday if the prisoners are allowed in the shops the fire would not be so readily discovered, there being so few persons about.

Question. How long have you been employed in the Penitentiary?

Answer. The best part of ten years, with very few intervals.

Cross-examined by Mr. Hurst.—Question. Were the prisoners allowed to go into the shops of Mr. Duvall, or any of them, on Sundays?

Answer. I do not know that they were, except by special permission, although I have seen them in the shops on Sunday, and I understood from Mr. Roberts that it would not be permitted for the future. I never supposed that they were permitted to enter unless they had business.

By Mr. Jarrett.—Question. So far as you know, have not the rules and regulations, as far as practicable, been carried out?

Answer. I have no knowledge of what the rules and regulations are, unless as printed; in many respects they have not been carried out as printed, in others they have.

Question. What is your opinion of the general discipline of the Institution for the past three years?

Answer. In some respects I have considered the discipline has been very good, the difference between the present and former administrations exists in the fact, that I have been enabled to compel my men to work under the present administration, when they were disposed to object; I have had more control over the men; a great portion of the discipline of the Institution I have no means of knowing anything about, as it does not come under my supervision or observation. The discipline in the shops under my control has been somewhat better than under former administrations; I have thought that the rules were defective in not placing the watchman on Sundays on duty at noon instead of at night.

Question. Is it not an utter impossibility for the officers to have their eyes on every prisoner during work hours?

Answer. I believe it is.

Question. Was your shop ever burnt out by fire?

Answer. Several times; in 1857 by a very heavy fire; I lost all my machinery.

Question. Did you ever make a claim against the State for damages resulting from fire?

Answer. No. I did not. At the fire of 1857 the Directors gave me the labor of a considerable number of men, free of charge, until my shops were re-built.

Question. Was the same routine in regard to the enforcement of the rules and regulations on Sundays carried out then as now?

Answer. I do not know, not being present on Sundays.

Question. Has not a disposition been manifested always by the Board of Directors and officers to give your property every protection and security against loss by fire?

Answer. As far as I know, it has.

Cross-examined by A. D. Evans, Warden.—Question. Do you remember of there ever being a watchman in the yard on Sundays previous to the fire of Mr. Duvall's shop?

Answer. I had supposed so until I ascertained much to my surprise about three years ago, that the watchman did not go on duty until Sunday night. I refer to the watchman of the Institution. I do not know whether I ascertained this fact prior to, or since the present administration.

Cross-examined by Mr. Jarrett.—Question. Have you not considered that Mr. Duvall kept his fires at too great a degree of heat in the dry houses, and thereby endangered the premises?

Answer. I considered that at times he did keep the fires hotter than I deemed prudent to keep mine, but I had no knowledge of the degree of heat, except from what I heard from others.

By Mr. Evans.—Question. What degree of heat do you deem proper and safe?

Answer. I think it dangerous to go above 125 degrees; the material used by me, however, being lighter than that used by Mr. Duvall.

The testimony for complainant here closed for the present.

Mr. A. D. Evans, Warden of Penitentiary, sworn for Directors.

Examined by Mr. Jarrett.—Question. Has the same protection been given to Mr. Duvall's property as has been given to Mr. Murdock's and the property of the State?

Answer. Yes, sir, fully as much, no complaint of want of protection has ever been made to me by either Mr. Duvall or Mr. Murdock.

Question. Has any extra advantages or favors been extended to Mr. Duvall in the prosecution of his business?

Answer. In the selection of good workmen, in the increase of the hours of labor, when other contractors did not desire it; an extra officer placed in the wagon yard to facilitate the delivery of the barrels; and giving the convicts their breakfasts earlier, so that the time of labor was increased, for the space of three days, which was changed at Mr. Duvall's request.

Question. Did not Mr. Duvall keep his shop in an unsafe condition, and did you not notify him of the same?

Answer. The shop was in a very unsafe condition for a long period of time, so much so, that it was constantly complained of by the officer, Mr. Lefevre, that he could not perform his duties as he would like. I told Mr. Duvall the Directors thought his shop was in an unsafe condition, and I thought so too, and that the shop must be cleared; Mr. Duvall said he could not do it, because he had no other place for his stuff, and that the Directors had no authority or control over his shop, as the contract did not mention anything of that character.

Question. Was not the State deprived of the services of convicts from accidents occurring in Mr. Duvall's shop?

Answer. Yes, of a large number.

Question. Did you make it your duty or practice to go through Mr. Duvall's shop during the week and on Sundays more than through other shops?

Answer. Some six or eight weeks prior to the fire, I did visit his shop more than any other, because the shop was lumbered more than formerly, and in a dangerous condition, and I feared it might be fired either by accident or design.

Question. While Mr. Duvall's shop was in such a condition, was he not absent a great part of the time?

Answer. Yes, a week at a time.

William A. Wisong, sworn.

Examined by Mr. Hurst—Question. Have you not had frequent opportunities to witness the operation of the Institution, and what is your opinion of the general discipline of the same?

Answer. I have, and I believe the discipline to be as good as that of any other of the kind, and a good deal better than some. I have been connected with the Penitentiary, as agent of the Prison Association, for two years past, and believe that the rules are fully enforced.

Cross-examined by Mr. Gill.—Question. Did you ever go into the shops on Sunday?

Answer. I never did. I visited only the chapel and hospital on Sundays.

The Committee adjourned to meet on Friday morning, at 10 o'clock.   By order,

THOS. H. MOORE, Clerk.

2

BALTIMORE, July 5, 1861.

The Committee met. Present Messrs. Ford and Sangston.

Mr. John H. Duvall, sworn and examined.

By Mr. Gill.—Question. What was the first direction and
order received by you in relation to the employment on
Sundays of any persons acting for you, and when and by
whom? What was the second order, and from whom and
when? And what was done after each of these orders?

Answer. Some time prior to the accident by which I was
shot, on the 21st of April, 1861, I received an order from
Mr. Evans, the Warden of the Penitentiary, that no more
work should be done in my shops on Sunday, at the Penitentiary, such as firing the dry houses, &c. Some time
prior to the fire, I do not know how long, the Deputy, Mr.
Roberts, told me he was instructed by the Committee to
say to me that any watchman or any of my men must not
be about there on Sundays. I directed the firing of dry
houses to be discontinued on Sundays. It was discontinued. After the second order from Mr. Roberts, I directed
the watchman, Mr. Gambrill, not to be there on Sundays
until the hour of going on duty at evening, which was
obeyed to the best of my knowledge.

Question. Did you employ a watchman to take care of the
property in the shops carried on by you in the Penitentiary, and especially on Sundays, and when did he cease to
do that duty, and why?

Answer. I did employ a watchman; the first one, Mr.
Lamb, who continued until about the first of May, 1860,
when the fire of Mr. Murdock's shops occurred; that one of
the Directors, Mr. Bryson, I think, sent by Mr. Howard
when I was confined to bed, that Mr. Lamb ought to be discharged; he was accordingly discharged, and Mr. Gambrill
appointed in his stead, at the solicitation of Mr. Bryson.
Gambrill continued in my employment until the 23d of December, 1860, when the fire took place, it may have been a
little later. Gambrill's duty was to watch the place at night
and on Sundays, and attend to the dry houses. The duty
was performed until the order was given herein before
stated, as given by Mr. Roberts· After which order Gambrill ceased to be there on Sunday in the day time.

Question. At what time on Sunday, the 23d of December,
did the fire at your shop occur, and to what cause do you
attribute the same, and if your watchman had been on duty
as before the order was given by Mr. Roberts, would or
would not the fire have been prevented in your judgment?

Answer. The fire occurred on Sunday, 23d December,
about half-past two to three o'clock, the cause I attribute

to the act of incendiary convicts. If my watchman had been on duty as previously to the order of Mr. Roberts, the fire could not have occurred in my judgment.

Question. Are you acquainted with the rules and regulations of the Maryland Penitentiary, and especially in relation to convicts, and the course pursued to them on Sundays, and state what they were? Also state if such rules and regulations had been pursued on Sunday, the 23d December, 1860. Would or would not, in your judgment, the fire at your shop on that day have been prevented?

Answer. I know of no rules and regulations except the published ones, a copy of which was handed me soon after my contract. I have no information in regard to the management of prisons on Sundays, except from what I have derived from observation. It is usual for a portion of the negro convicts, some fifteen or twenty in number, to be employed in cleansing the dormitories and carrying off the filth to the pen; in doing which they have to pass through a large portion of the yard and around most of the shops. If properly supervised by an officer, they could not enter the shops without the knowledge of the officer. I think the fire would have been prevented if the rules and regulations had been enforced.

The Committee here adjourned until to-morrow morning at 10 o'clock.

BALTIMORE, JULY 6, 1861.
The Committee met pursuant to adjournment. Present, Messrs. Sangston and Ford.

The examination of Mr. Duvall resumed.

By Mr. Gill.—The particular rule to which I refer, which, if observed, would have prevented the fire, is to be found in the Code of General Laws, Art. 73, Sec. 82: "The Warden must not permit any prisoners to be together at any time without the proper supervision of an officer."

. *Question.* Were there or not any fires in and about your shop at the Maryland Penitentiary immediately prior to the fire of the 23d December, 1860, or on the premises connected therewith? How did the fire which destroyed your property occur as you have been advised, and what were the circumstances thereof? State all of them? What precautions might have been and ought to have been taken to prevent the convicts from getting into your shop on that day, and if taken, what would probably have been the effect thereof?

Answer. We were running our engine the day before (Saturday) with the usual fire, and on the same day some fire may have been in other stoves, as it is usual to have them at that season; all of which were extinguished, to my knowledge, about 5 o'clock, P. M., of that day, (Saturday.) In the usual course of business there would be no fires during the whole day of Sunday, and as far as I know there was no fire on that Sunday; but I was not there until after the fire.

From what I have learned from the Deputy Warden, the fire was the act of incendiary convicts, as he had ascertained by their confessions, accomplished by the use of slow-matches and powdered sulphur and rosin. That they had applied the matches in the early part of the day, probably about 11 o'clock.

After Mr. Roberts had ascertained these facts, in company with some of the officers in the Warden's Lodge, an experiment was tried with the yellow cotton yarn, which the convicts confessed to have used as matches. The experiment proved that the yarn made a good slow-match, and that it would have been easy to have communicated the fire by such matches.

The convicts who cleaned the dormitories are engaged on Sundays at this work about 10½ A. M., or later, while religious services are performed.

The distance from the door of the dormitory to the pen is, say 150 to 200 yards, this route would pass my shop, and would also pass two of Mr. Murdock's shops and dry-houses, the State dry-house and smoke-house, and also Mr. Murdock's broom corn shed. Convicts passing those shops, if properly supervised by an officer or officers, could not have obtained access to them.

Question. Who were interested in the business carried on by you at the Maryland Penitentiary?

Answer. My son-in-law, William Howard, and myself were interested in the business referred to.

Question. What was the amount of loss sustained from the fire of the 23d December, 1860, by you and your partner; state the details, and show how such loss is made up.

Answer. According to an estimate made by Mr. Conner and myself:

Materials prepared in the shop, &c., destroyed, would have made up 82,500 barrels. The barrels were sold for 35 cents a piece. Hoops and labor 9 cents—26 cents—
amounting to $21,450.00
Besides on hand 1200 barrels, at 36 cents,   432.00
Loss in machinery, dry houses, cost $9,500 worth, 7,100.00
                                                  _____
                                                   $28,982.00

Less insurance money received,   5,600.00
                                                  ─────────
My claim being $23,382.00

Question. What amount did you pay the Directors of the
Maryland Penitentiary for the hire of convicts prior to the
fire, and what did you pay after the fire, and under what
circumstances did you make such payment after the fire?

Answer. During the contract, and before the fire, I paid
$7,031.07 to the Directors for labor, &c.

After the fire I paid $1,075.59 to the Directors, accord-
ing to an account which I produce with my answer and
file as part of it, (marked A.) The fire ruined my business, soon after which the Directors desired to know of me
what was my intention about going on with the contract.
I informed them that our misfortunes at the fire had destroyed our business, and I was unable to do it. I was
asked the question by one of the Directors, if I was aware
that I could be required to build the shop, and pay for the
prisoners, while it was going on. This induced me to consult my counsel, Mr. Gill, who informed me that under the
contract I could be so held. My counsel, therefore, advised
me to make the best settlement I could with the Directors,
and I accordingly did so, as the paper alluded to, marked
A, shows.

(A)

BALTIMORE, December 31, 1860.

Messrs. John H. Duvall & Sons,
            In account with Maryland Penitentiary.

Work done in smithing, October, 1860, - - - $ 3.22
Water rent from July 1 to Nov. 1, 1860, $240, - 80.00
Work done in smithing, November, 1860, - - -   4.57
Rent from August 31 to Nov. 30, 1860, $200, - - 50.00
Hire, November, 1860, - - - - - - - - -   180.05
 "   from Dec. 1, 1860, to 22d, inclusive, - - ⎫
 "   1,157¾ days, at 60 cents, - - - - ⎬ 694.65
 "   19   "   at 25 " - - - - - -   4.75
Work done, December, 1860, - - - - - - -   1.68
Rent from Nov. 30 to Dec. 31, 1860, - - - - -   16.67
 "   Water " 1 "   "   " - - - - - -   40.00
                                               ─────────
                                               $1,075.59
                       CR.
By 101 lbs. tobacco, at 20 cents, - - - - - -   20.20
                                               ─────────
                                               $1,055.39

CR.

1861. January 30, By cash, - - - - - - - 140.00

$915.39

CR.

By R. Norris, Jr's., note, dated January 31, 1861,
   at 3 mos., for $800, less interest 3 mos., $12,   788.00

$127.39

Received balance by check, January 31, 1861.

JNO. J. C. DOUGHERTY, Clerk.

After we had agreed on the terms of settlement, I informed the Directors that my only means of payment was the property then on hand, and not destroyed. I asked permission to remove some of it, and dispose of it for that purpose. This permission was refused, and they would not allow me to do so until the settlement was made.

To make the settlement I had to encounter great inconvenience and difficulty, in consequence of the misfortune of the fire.

Mr. Gill, in his opinion, also advised that no suit could be maintained against the State or the Directors as such. If they could have been sued, he would have advised me to bring suit.

Cross-examined by Mr. Brune.—Question. What work was done on Sundays, before the order which you say was given by Mr. Evans?

Answer. There was no general work done on Sundays, except making fires in dry houses. There was occasionally other work done. It was not the practice to do work on Sundays, except from necessity. The orders given by Mr. Evans were followed, and the fires discontinued, so far as I know, after such order had been given.

Question. Who was your watchman at the time of this order from Mr. Evans, and when precisely was this order given?

Answer. Mr. Lamb was the watchman when the order was given by Mr. Evans. I cannot state more specifically than I have done in my direct answer, the time when Mr. Evans gave the order referred to.

Question. Why was Mr. Lamb discharged, and was there or not a fire or fires at the Penitentiary while he was your watchman?

Answer. I do not know why Mr. Lamb was discharged, except as already stated. There was only one fire of importance while Mr. Lamb was my watchman. That was at one of the dry houses, and in January, 1860. There was nothing that destroyed anything. On one occasion, while at work at shop, some boards took fire, and they were immediately put out. Mr. Lamb was not then present; beside these there was the fire on Mr. Murdock's premises in May, 1860, and which led to Lamb's discharge.

Question. Who were the Monthly Committee at the time the order of Roberts, spoken of by you in answer to the first direct question, was given, and was such order *in writing*, through Mr. Roberts?

Answer. I do not know who constituted the Monthly Committee of the Penitentiary when the order given to me by Roberts was received. The order from Roberts was verbal.

Question. Did you, after this order was given to you by Roberts, make any application to the Monthly Committee or to any of the Directors in relation thereto, and if you did state to whom you so applied?

Answer. I did not. I obeyed the order without making any complaint about it or seeing any of the parties.

Question. Did you, or your sons, or your foreman of machinery, Mr. Murdock, ever go into the shops on Sunday after this order?

Answer. I do not know that any one but myself did go over to the Penitentiary on Sunday after the order from Roberts; I did sometimes go over on Sunday in the morning, and sometimes in the afternoon.

Question. Have you any recollection of Mr. Murdock's covering a pully with wood on a Sunday?

Answer. I recollect that a pully was covered with wood on Sunday by Mr. Murdock, but I think it was done prior to the order from Mr. Roberts.

Question. Before the order which you state came from Mr. Roberts, was it the habit of Mr. Gambrill to make a fire on Saturday night and keep it up during Sunday? If not, when was the fire made on Sunday before and after said order, and what time was the watchman expected to come on duty every day and go off, and who watched while he was off duty?

Answer. Before the order from Roberts it was not the habit of Mr. Gambrill, the watchman, to make up the fires on Saturday night and keep them up on Sunday. After the order from Mr. Evans they stopped firing at 12 o'clock on Saturday, and began again at 12 o'clock on Sunday night. Some time after this I got permission from Mr. Hilbert to make the fires at dark on Sunday night, and to stop them at *daylight*. The watchman usually came on about supper time during the week, he would be there on Saturday night, and was relieved on Sunday morning at about 10 o'clock, when witness would sometimes relieve him, and would return at about 12 or 1 o'clock, and sometimes later, to resume his duties; this was before the order given by Mr. Roberts, afterwards he quit when the state watchman would go away in the morning, and not return again. When not relieved by witness, the watchman would go for his meals during Sunday from the premises—before the order from Roberts.

Question. Why did you extinguish the fires on Saturday, the 22d of December, at 5 P. M., if you had under Mr. Hilbert's permission right to continue them until Sunday at daylight?

Answer. We had no fires on Saturday, the 22d, or for some days prior to that time in the dry houses. They had been unable for some weeks, say six weeks, to procure a supply of hoops, and during that time had not finished barrels. There was an intermission of that particular kind of work. There was a good deal of other work done, such as cutting and drying timber. They had kept on at that until every place was full where they could put it in the shop or dry houses.

Question. Did Mr. Gambrill remain all night of Saturday, the 22d of December? Do you know when he left in the morning of Sunday?

Answer. Mr. Gambrill did remain all night, so far as I know on Saturday night, the 22d of December, 1860. I do not know when he left on Sunday morning, the 23d of December, 1860.

Question. Can you say from your own knowledge or observation that the negro convicts in cleaning the domitories on Sunday, the 23d of December, were not properly supervised?

Answer. On that day I was not present at the Penitentiary until after the fire broke out. I cannot say.

Question. With what Committee or Directors was the agreement (A) made?

Answer. The agreement was made at a Board meeting. Mr. Hurst was present, and Mr. Jarrett, and three or four others.

Question. At the time this agreement for settlement with the Board was made, did you complain of the orders of Messrs. Evans and Roberts, or either of them, or set up any claim on your part against the Directors or the State of Maryland?

Answer. I do not recollect that anything was said about the orders of Mr. Evans or Mr. Roberts at the time of the agreement for settlement, nor did I then complain of such orders or either of them, and at that meeting I did not set up any claim against the State or the Directors. I did not mean to speak of that and did not.

Question. Did you not express to the Board or to some members of it, at that meeting or subsequently, that you thought they were dealing liberally with you, or words to that effect?

Answer. When the settlement was made, I thanked the Board for the settlement because I was glad to make it to enable me to get some of my property out of the place to live upon.

(Copy of Bond filed.)

Question. Did you not, subsequently to the agreement for a settlement, obtain premission from the Directors that your goods might remain on the premises for some time, and did you not verbally or in writing propose to the Board to renew your contract on certain terms?

Answer. At the time of the settlement I did get permission to permit goods to remain until they wished to re-build. Subsequently I received notice that the rent would be $25 per week for the premises burnt. I asked the Board if they would make a contract with me on certain terms, which they declined.

Question. Where was your property insured, and was the insurance money paid, and why was it not insured for a larger amount?

Answer. The property was insured at the Lynchburg Office and the Valley Insurance Company at Virginia, and it was not insured for a large amount, for the reason that it was difficult to procure good insurance. Application was made and declined by several offices, because the risk was too great.

The Committee adjourned to Monday morning next, at 10 o'clock.

By order,

THOMAS H. MOORE, Clerk.

MONDAY, July 8th, 1861.

The Committee met pursuant to adjournment. Present, Messrs. Sangston and Ford.

The cross-examination of J. H. Duvall continued by Mr. Brune.

A letter marked (B,) now exhibited and filed.

(B)

BALTIMORE, March 21, 1861.

To the Directors of the Maryland Penitentiary:

GENTLEMEN :—

With the view of arranging so as to enable me to make another contract with you, I propose to ask you the following questions, viz:

1st. Would you rebuild the shop so as to afford the largest possible amount of yard room, and enable me thereby to dispense with a portion of the dry houses; building say 25 or 26 feet wide, two stories, one end of it for the accommodation of machinery, &c., say 40 or 50 feet square, with celler under such portion of it as might be wanted, and shed for boiler and engine?

2d. Would you buy my boiler and engine at fair price, say $2,000, to be put and kept in order by me, and to be paid for as may be agreed by the labor of the prisoners for which I may contract?

3d. Would you contract for, say thirty-five first class prisoners, as far as you may have them, the same as worked for me before—that I may select, at fifty cents per day, and ten to fifteen second class at twenty-five cents—this latter class to be healthy and strong, but say short term, and such as you always have, that cannot be employed to better advantage, either by the State or a contractor, the fifty cent men at all times to be first class; and if upon trial of, say one month, any such shall be found not to answer the purposes for which they were taken, to be exchanged. All to work for three months, as they are taken to learn at twenty-five cents per day—I to take such portion of them from time to time as I may require them—and take all by a day to be agreed upon; and have the privilege of increasing from time to time, as I may want them—the fifty cent men, say to the number of sixty, and the twenty-five cent men to the number of twenty-five; and to have such labor as may be wanted in fitting up the shop for commencement without charge?

4th. What will you charge for the rent of the shop, and boiler and engine, including water rent?

Which I respectfully sumbit.

Very truly,
Your obedient servant,
JOHN H. DUVALL.

Question. Look at paper B, now presented to you, and say whether it is in your hand-writing.
Answer. It is.

Question. Were you here on Sundays, so as yourself to
see the way in which the dormitories were cleaned by the
negroes, as spoken of in your examination in chief?

Answer. I have been present on Sundays and witnessed
the manner in which the negroes carried off the filth from
the dormitories to the filth pens.

Question. Did you ever complain to the Warden or Directors, or any of them, and if so, when and how; that the
negroes thus engaged were without the proper supervision
of officers?

Answer. I have no recollection that I ever did.

J. G. Roberts, recalled by Directors.

By Mr. Brune.—Question. In your previous examination
you stated, in answer to a question in regard to the present discipline of the Institution—"I think it might be
more strict; my own orders are, to carry out the strictest
discipline, and I have endeavored to do so." Will you
explain the apparent discrepancy in portions of your said
answer?

Answer. I meant to say that the discipline was as good
as it could be under existing circumstances; by existing
circumstances I mean the contract system as it now prevails; the contract system has prevailed for the last three
years to my knowledge. I was assistant Warden nine
years before the present term; when I was first here no
contract system prevailed.

Cross-examined by Mr. Gill.—Question. You were not
present when the fire took place?

Answer. No, sir.

Question. You were then Deputy Warden?

Answer. Yes, sir.

Question. How long had you been absent before the fire?

Answer. About two weeks.

Question. Why were you absent so long?

Answer. I had been confined for a long time and obtained
leave of absence from the Board for two weeks.

Question. Who was appointed in your absence?

Answer. I believe Mr. Sparks discharged my duty.

Question. Do you know who filled your position on the
day of the fire?

Answer. I do not know.

Question. Have you ever said to Mr. Charles Murdock,
that if you had been present on the day of the fire, the
same would not have occurred?

Answer. I might have said so, I do not recollect it; I have
had frequent conversations with him on the subject of the
fire.

Question. Have you not said to Mr. Murdock that during your absence from the Penitentiary, there was a want of discipline therein, and that you attributed the fire to such want of discipline, and state what you did say to Mr. Murdock in reference to the discipline of the Penitentiary, and the effect thereof in producing the fire at Mr. Duvall's shop?

Answer. If I did say so, it was in assent to a remark from him.

Mr. Charles Murdock, recalled.

By Mr. Gill.—Question. Had you any conversation with Mr. Roberts after the fire, relating to his absence at the time of the fire at Mr. Duvall's shop, and the effect thereof in his judgment, if so, state it?

Answer. I have had conversation with Mr. Roberts.

Question. Did Mr. Roberts say to you, that if he had been present, in his opinion, the fire would not have occurred?

Answer. I have heard Mr. Roberts express his opinion, that if he had been here, the fire would not have occurred. I understood him to mean if he had been on duty. I never heard him say specifically why the fire would not have occurred, if he had been present.

Mr. Gill here exhibits and filed a printed copy of the rules and regulations for the government of the Maryland Penitentiary, 1853.

(C)

The officers are required to preserve harmony and kind feelings among themselves, to the end that a desirable official intercourse may obtain. They must, therefore, be respectful in their intercourse and communications with each other, and indulge in no undue liberties.

The Deputy Keepers must yield that ready obedience to their superior officers, so necessary to secure the beneficial results of effective co-operation and good government.

Whenever a Deputy Keeper may be absent from sickness, or other *necessary cause*, the Warden shall designate one of the approved supernumeraries to take his place, at such Deputy Keeper's expense.

Mr. Conner recalled and cross-examined by Mr. Brune.—Question. What were Mr. Gambrill's duties as watchman after he came and down to the time of the fire; was he a day or night watchman, and what were his hours for going on and coming off duty?

Answer. I understood the duties of Mr. Gambrill, during the time that staves were in the dry houses, to keep up fires and to get steam on the steam boxes in the morning, so that the men could get to work. On Saturday evening or Sunday morning, after the boiler was "blown off," he cleaned the boiler out, no change took place in the duty that I am aware of down to the time of the fire. I never considered him a day watchman, he would generally go on duty about the time the men would leave off work, about supper time. I was never present when he came off duty in the morning.

Question. At what time did you come on duty in the morning?

Answer. I generally came on at 6½ to 7 o'clock in the morning.

Question. Was Gambrill generally gone when you came on duty?

Answer. He was, every day excepting when Mr. Murdock was away; this does not apply to Sundays. It was very rarely I came on Sundays.

Question. Did you make any examination of the property manufactured and the machinery remaining after the fire. If so, state for what purpose, and was it carefully done and in connection with Mr. Duvall?

Answer. I made an examination of the loss in stock at Mr. Duvall's request, for the Insurance Company; it was carefully done.

Question. Will you be so good as to state to the Committee. as well as you now can, the result of such inquiry and the statement of loss to the stock?

Answer. The statement prepared for Insurance Company made the amount of stock in the main shop to be one million of pieces, from what I could understand from Mr. Duvall and his sons, we estimated these pieces to be $7 per thousand pieces, were dried and ready, the greater portion to put in barrels. We estimated either 90 or 95 thousand pieces were not damaged, there were four dry houses, two were destroyed entirely and two damaged, one damaged to the extent of one-half. In two of the houses I considered a total loss had occurred; I considered the loss to be 200,000 pieces, at $7 per thousand, $14,000. For the other two houses I considered the loss to be one half, making $700 of loss. 1,200 barrels fully completed were ready for delivery, with the exception of a few hoops, the value of each barrel I believed to be 35 to 36 cents per barrel. I did not make an examination of the loss to the machinery, that was done by Messrs. Denmead and Pool.

Question. Was the property remaining or any part of it sold, and if so, to whom, and for about what amount?

Answer. Yes, sir, the barrels on hand, those not burnt entirely through were sold to Mr. Everitt at 12½ cents per barrel; I think between 500 or 600 were sold him; they were sold for about $60. I understood from Mr. Duvall that he sold all the leavings or remnants for $100 ; the cost of the labor of cleaning up the remains of the fire would have been much more than he received from the sale.

Examination resumed by Mr. Gill.

Question. How many barrels would the stuff destroyed by the fire have made ?

Answer. According to the estimate made for the Insurance Company, about 46,154 barrels.

Question. Did that estimate include the whole quantity destroyed ?

Answer. It did not, because Mr. Duvall said that the amount of loss was so far above the insurance, it was unnecessary for me to go fully into the examination.

Question. Was or not, in your judgment, a much larger amount of stuff destroyed than covered by estimate of ·insurance, and how much more ?

Answer. I believe there was more, but how much more I am unable to say.

Question. Do you recollect having any conversation with Mr. Duvall shortly prior to his application to the Legislature, in relation to the amount of stuff lost by the fire, as compared with estimate made to Insurance Company, and what amount of barrels you stated to him the stuff would have made up.

Answer. I remember having a conversation with Mr. Duvall upon the subject, and in that interview he exhibited some papers, among which was the estimate that had been made to the Insurance Company, another was an estimate to prove to the Legislature Committee, and by whom the amount of stuff he had on hand, and the number of barrels he could have made. I do not remember to have expressed any opinion as to the number of barrels that could have been made. Before and subsequent to the fire it was commonly observed among us, that we had stuff enough to make 100,000 barrels, but it was not my opinion ; I do not believe it would have made one-half of that number, if that. Mr. Duvall had contracted to sell the barrels to two parties at 36 cents, and to one other party at 35 cents per barrel. I estimate the cost of finishing each barrel about 9 to 10 cents. I have no knowledge of the agreement by which Mr. Duvall employed Mr. Gambrill. I am now a substitute officer in the employment of the Penitentiary.

John R. Hynson, sworn.

Question. Are you now an officer of the Maryland Penitentiary, what office do you hold, and how long have you held it?

Answer. I am an officer of the Maryland Penitentiary, and have been watchman of the yard since May, 1860.

Question. Did you know Mr. Gambrill, who was formerly in the employ of Mr. Duvall? If so, will you state when he was in the habit of going on and coming off duty; state particularly when he went on on Saturday evening, and when he went off on Sunday mornings?

Answer. Yes, sir; he would go on duty usually about the time of locking up in the evening, and he came off when Mr. Duvall's hands went to work. On Saturday evening he would go on about the usual time; on Sunday morning he would go off duty some time before I did. I went off on Sunday morning at 7 o'clock; I was a night watchman.

Question. Was Mr. Gambrill in the habit at any time, while he was in the employ of Mr. Duvall, of coming to the Institution on Sundays after he left in the morning, before the evenings when you came?

Answer. I never saw him at the Penitentiary on Sunday mornings, as I was not here myself; although I have heard him say he had attended and cleaned the boilers, we would frequently come together when about to go on duty for the night.

Question. Where did he get his meals on Sundays; and is it not necessary for a night watchman to get rest during each day?

Answer. As far as I know he did not get them in the Institution on Sunday. It is necessary for a night watchman to get rest during the day.

By Mr. Sangston.—I do not think that I ever came to the Institution on Sundays.

Mr. A. D. Evans, Warden, recalled.

Question. What time did Mr. Gambrill leave the Institution usually on Sunday mornings? Where did he get his meals, and when did he usually return, and state your means of knowledge?

Answer. Mr. Gambrill would leave the Institution in the morning about 7 o'clock, and would leave about the same time on Sundays as on week days. He did not get his meals at the Institution. He usually returned a little before dusk, although I have seen him here somewhat earlier. My means of knowledge are derived from personal observation.

Question. Had you ever any knowledge that Messrs. Lamb and Gambrill were day watchmen for Mr. Duvall?

Answer. I never knew it; I did know that they were night watchmen.

Wm. J. Bryson, a Director, sworn.

Question. Had you ever notice in any way from Mr. Duvall, or did you know in any way that Mr. Gambrill or Mr. Lamb had been appointed day watchmen by him, or that it was part of their duty to watch the premises occupied by Mr. Duvall during the day time on Sundays?

Answer. I never did; I was here a great deal on Sundays, and I never saw Mr. Gambrill on Sundays, with one or two exceptions. I solicited the appointment of Mr. Gambrill as a watchman, and I always supposed his position to be a night watchman.

John Hilbert, a Director, sworn.

Question. Had you ever notice in any way from Mr. Duvall, or did you know in any way that Mr. Gambrill or Mr. Lamb had been appointed day watchmen by him, or that it was part of their duty to watch the premises occupied by Mr. Duvall during the day time on Sundays?

Answer. I never had notice of such fact; I am seldom absent on Sundays, and never yet saw Mr. Gambrill on duty on Sundays. I visit the Institution generally between 9 and 10 o'clock in the morning, and leave between 12 and 1 o'clock. I have frequently visited Mr. Duvall's shop on Sundays, and complained of the hands doing work on that day; it was on account of this work a resolution passed the Board instructing the Monthly Committee to notify the Warden to stop all work of convicts on Sunday. I cannot fix the time of the resolution.

Cross-examined by Mr. Gill.—The directions given by the Board was, that no convicts could be worked on Sundays, and that no fire should be allowed in the dry houses; the resolution referred to was passed 29th of March, 1860, upon reference to the proceedings of the Board of that day, and reads as follows:

"*Resolved*, That on and after this date there be no fire allowed either in the State's or any other dry houses on the Sabbath day; nor shall the prisoners be allowed to work on the Sabbath."

Question. Was any other resolution passed restricting the said work except the one of 29th of March, 1860?

Answer. None that I am aware of.

33

Lefevre Jarrett, a Director, sworn.

Examined by Wm. Brune.—Had you ever notice in any way from Mr. Duvall, or did you know in any way that Mr. Gambrill or Mr. Lamb had been appointed day watchmen by him, or that it was part of their duty to watch the the premises occupied by Mr. Duvall during the day time on Sundays?

Answer. I had no notice of such fact. I always regarded the appointment of Mr. Gambrill as a night watchman.

Question. Was any other resolution passed by the Board restricting the work on Sundays except the one of 29th of March, 1860?

Answer. None that I am aware of.

Mr. Richard Middleton, a Director, sworn.

Question. Had you ever notice in any way from Mr. Duvall, or did you know in any way that Mr. Gambrill or Mr. Lamb had been appointed day watchmen by him, or that it was part of their duty to watch the premises occupied by Mr. Duvall during the day time on Sundays?

Answer. I had no notice of such fact. I always supposed they were night watchmen.

Question. Was any other resolution passed by the Board restricting the work on Sundays, except the one of 29th of March, 1860?

Answer. None that I am aware of.

Mr. Hilbert recalled by Mr. Brune.

Question. Please state as to the regulation on Sundays in regard to watching the wall and yard, and particularly during the religious services at the Institution? State when the prisoners are locked up on Sundays?

Answer. The watch goes on the wall the same on Sundays as during the week; some of the prisoners attending Sunday School are let out of the dormitories sooner than those who do not; the religious services commence at quarter past 10 o'clock, A. M., where all are required to be, with the exception of those engaged in cleaning the dormitory and old buildings. All at Sunday School and at church are under the supervision of officers. The prisoners go direct from church to the refectory for dinner, and after dinner to their cells, where they are locked up.

Cross-examined by Mr. Gill.—Question. Were you present on the day of the fire?

Answer. Yes, sir. I was there until nearly 1 o'clock. I do not know what officer was present or had charge of the convicts who were employed on that day in cleaning

3

the dormitories. I do not recollect seeing any officers. Mr. Sparks acted as Deputy Warden during Mr. Roberts' absence.

Question. Is it not the rule that all persons cleaning the dormitories are placed in the charge of an officer? Have you any doubt that an officer was so employed on the day of the fire?

Answer. It is the rule, and I have no doubt that an officer was so employed on the day of the fire.

Question. If the officer in charge had accompanied the convicts engaged in cleaning the same from the dormitory to the filth pen, could those convicts thus employed have entered Mr. Duvall's shop and set it on fire without his knowledge?

Answer. I cannot answer, because I do not know whether the convicts set the shop on fire or how it originated.

Mr. Hurst, a Director, sworn.

By Mr. Brune.—Question. Had you ever notice in any way from Mr. Duvall, or did you know in any way that Mr. Gambrill or Mr. Lamb had been appointed day watchmen by him, or that it was part of their duty to watch the premises occupied by Mr. Duvall during the day time on Sunday?

Answer. I never had such notice or knowledge.

Question. Were you not one of the Committee, and personally engaged•in making the agreement of settlement between Mr. Duvall and the Board, and had you not frequent interviews with Mr. Duvall in relation to said agreement, and did he to you or to the Board up to the time of such settlement complain of the action of the Board in connection with his loss by the fire? State all that you think important in relation to such agreement of settlement?

Answer. I was appointed by the Board of Directors to effect a settlement or compromise with Mr. Duvall, subject to the ratification of the Board; I had frequent interviews with him, he never complained to me of the action of the Board, but thanked me and the Board, through me, for our liberality in settling with him, and I never knew that he set up any claim against the Board or the State until I saw the application in the newspapers.

Question. Were you on the Committee to investigate the cause of the fire on Mr. Duvall's premises, of which a report was made to the Board on the 17th of January, 1861? If so, state whether any and what specific charges of neglect of duty were proved to the Committee in reference to officers Mills and Suter?

Answer. I was on the Committee; it is the duty of the wall guard to be on duty when ever the prisoners are not in their cells, and it is not expected that the officer who has charge of the men cleaning the dormitory to follow every man as he goes to the filth pen, but that they are under the supervision of the wall guards. That although there was no proof against the guard named Wills, I thought proper to suspend him for three days. Mr. Suter was a substitute, acting as a wall guard, at the time of the fire. I dismissed him, believing it would increase the efficiency of the officers.

Mr. Gill here files an extract from the proceedings of the Board of January 17, 1861, marked (D.)

(D)

Copy from Proceedings of the Board,

January 17th, 1861.

Your Committee ordered a thorough examination into the cause of the fire, and placed the examination in the hands of the Warden and Deputy-Warden, which was conducted in a manner so skilful as to meet our warm approbation, and resulted in the fact, that the place was set on fire by four prisoners, all colored, viz: Joseph Wheatly, John Madison, —— Butler, Samuel Green and E. Perry, who have all acknowledged their guilt. We are indebted to prisoners Burkhiser and Offutt for valuable information.

In this connection, we have suspended officers Wills and dismissed substitute Suter for inattention and neglect of duty while on the wall the morning of the fire.

In connection with Col. Chesnut, appointed by the Board, and with the assistance of Messrs. Middleton and Hilbert, we have settled all differences existing between the State and Messrs. Murdock and Duvalls by first calling to our aid the professional advice and assistance of F. W. Brune, Esq., of the firm of Brown & Brune, Attorneys-at-Law. With Mr. Murdock we have agreed to terminate his old contract of one hundred men, and to make a new one for the same number of hands from the 1st January, 1861, for four years, giving Mr. Murdock power to terminate the same on the 1st of July, 1861, or the 1st of January, 1862, by his giving us the three months' notice of the same.

We have made two propositions to Mr. J. H. Duvall, to which he promptly accorded, but he has not yet informed us which one he would select; we to terminate the contract of Mr. Duvall upon his paying the rent of his shop, the hire of his men and water rent to January 1st, 1861, or to surrender to the State the bricks in his dry house, and to pay his hire of prisoners up to the date of the fire, to wit: the 23d December, 1860, and water rent of shop to 1st January, 1861.

The sixty hands that has been returned to the State upon the termination of the above contract we are placing on the looms as fast as circumstances will permit.

Question. Will you state to the Committee the value to the State of Maryland, in a financial point of view, of the contract system in the management of the Maryland Penitentiary, and how long such system has continued here, and state also how the sums realized by the Institution under the contracts made by the present administration, until the commercial and political troubles of the country arose, will compare with the amounts received under previous administrations?

Answer. I consider the contract system has been a benefit, in a financial point of view. It went into operation a short time before the present Board came into power. The Institution under the contract system, which we increased more than double after we came here, came nearer paying the expenses of the same than formerly. I did not consider the contract with Mr. Duvall as profitable, for many reasons. From the nature of the employment, extra clothing was required by the convicts, and they were subject to casualties.

Cross-examined by Mr. Gill.—Question. In the conversation you had with Mr. Duvall prior to or at the time of the settlement testified to by you, was anything said in relation to the cause of the fire at Mr. Duvall's shop?

Answer. I think not.

Question. Were you not aware that, owing to the loss Mr. Duvall sustained by fire, that he had no other means to rebuild and carry out the first contract?

Answer. I had no knowledge of Mr. Duvall's means, any further than that I heard him say that his all was invested in the business.

To the General Assembly of the State of Maryland:

The Memorial of Charles Murdock, of the City of Baltimore, respectfully represents that he has been for some years engaged in the business of manufacturing brooms and wood-ware, and to enable him to conduct this business, he has heretofore made various contracts with the Directors of the Maryland Penitentiary for the rent of shops of the Penitentiary and ground belonging to the Penitentiary, on which your memorialist built shops, and for the hire of convicts in the said Penitentiary, to be employed in the said manufacture; that your memorialist commenced the said business in the year 1850 on the said Penitentiary grounds, and has continued ever since, under various written contracts, which he is prepared to present at the proper time and place, and is still so engaged; that various questions have arisen between your memorialist and the Directors of the Maryland Penitentiary, about which your memorialist, although believing himself to be in the right, has yet been compelled to submit to the decision of that body, having no tribunal or third party to whom he could appeal.

Your memorialist further states, that he has invested a large sum of money in the Penitentiary grounds, in buildings, machinery, &c., and has paid annually large sums of money to the Directors of the said Penitentiary, and for the last year nearly the entire income thereof has been derived from the payments made by your memorialist, arising from the rent of buildings and employment of convicts by him; the amount paid by your memorialist from April, 1860, to April, 1861, being $21,811.43.

Your memorialist further states, that at the present time a difference exists between your memorialist and the said Directors in relation to the present indebtedness by your memorialist to them; that your memorialist has offered to pay all he now owes, but this has been refused, and a large amount claimed, which is denied to be due by your memorialist; and the Directors of the said Penitentiary have refused to permit your memorialist to remove any of his manufactured articles from the said Penitentiary until he pays an amount which he believes not to be due, and which the Directors have, in his view, no right to exact or claim; and that thereby his business has been seriously injured.

Your memorialist further states, that owing to the change of times which, as is well known, has effected all kinds of business and the value of all property, your memorialist has found himself unable to conduct the business at the

Penitentiary, and to employ, according to the terms of his contract, the number of convicts agreed upon and as regularly as agreed upon; that your memorialist has been unable to obtain the necessary supply of materials for manufacturing purposes, owing to the fact that, by the existence of war and the blockade of ports, this supply has been cut off, and that even if this difficulty were removed, it would be found to be impossible, or nearly so, to dispose of the articles when manufactured, because the usual and customary markets are closed against their reception.

Your memorialist, finding himsef thus deprived of the power to continue the manufacture of goods at the Maryland Penitentiary according to his contracts, has applied to the Directors thereof for a modification of his contracts, but in vain; they insist upon a literal compliance therewith, even if by so doing your memorialist will be ruined; that finding no relief can be had from the Directors, your memorialist has appealed, as he now does, to your Honorable Body for relief in the premises; and he now prays that such a settlement shall be made as to you may seem just, and that such modifications and alterations in his contracts may be made as will do justice to both parties, and at the same time secure to the State such income and revenue as can be obtained from the Maryland Penitentiary in the existing circumstances and condition of the country.

Your memorialist would further state, that owing to causes already set forth, he will be compelled, unless some material change be made in his arrangements with the Directors of the Maryland Penitentiary, or some unexpected change should take place in the affairs of the country, to discontinue his manufacturing business at the Penitentiary, in which event there will necessarily be a large loss in the revenues heretofore derived from that Institution.

CHARLES MURDOCK.

To the General Assembly of the State of Maryland:

The Memorial of John H. Duvall and William Howard respectfully states, that on the fourth day of October, in the year of our Lord, one thousand eight hundred and fifty-nine, one of your memorialists—viz., John H. Duvall—entered into an agreement with the Directors of the Maryland Penitentiary to rent the blacksmith's shop at the Penitentiary grounds, in the city of Baltimore, and certain yard room for the storage of wood, and for hiring of thirty male convict prisoners, to be employed in the man-

ufacturing of barrels, with the privilege of increasing the
number of convicts, the particulars of which agreement
will appear by the written agreement entered into, a copy
of which is hereto annexed, and the original of which
will be produced whenever called for.

Your memorialists further state that, after making the
said agreement, the said John H. Duvall became connected
in the business of manufactoring barrels with the said
William Howard, who furnished capital to carry on the
same—that your memorialists invested at the said Penitentiary, in machinery, buildings and fixtures necessary for
their business, more than eight thousand dollars in addition to the value of patent rights and materials for manufacturing—that they continued to perform the agreement
entered into by John H. Duvall until the 23d December,
1860, and paid from the time of making the said agreement
and the said 23d December, 1860, for the labor of the prisoners employed by them the sum of $7,031.07—that on
Sunday, the 23d December, 1860, their shops were fired
by incendiary convicts and their contents nearly destroyed,
and that the loss sustained by your memorialists amounts
to $23,150.

Your memoralists further state, that after making the
said agreement by the said John H. Duvall, your memoralists, believing it to be proper to do so, employed a watchman to guard their property at the Penitentiary during
the night, and on Sundays during the day time, that while
this watchman remained in charge and on duty no damage
was done, but that prior to the fire, which occurred, as
aforesaid, notice was given to your memorialists through
the Deputy Warden, Isaac G. Roberts, by the monthly
Committee of the Penitentiary, that their watchman would
not be permitted to be at their shop in the Penitentiary
on Sundays, and your memorialists were thereby required
to withdraw their watchman on Sundays, which they accordingly did, being compelled to obey such order—that
their property was fired and burned on Sunday, 23d December, 1860, by a portion of the convicts at the said Penitentiary, which would have doubtless been prevented if
their watchman had been at his post and on duty as he
had been prior to the time of giving the aforesaid order,
not to be on duty on Sundays.

Your memorialists further represent, that after they had
been prevented by the order of the Monthly Committee of
the Penitentiary from having their private watchman on
the premises on Sundays, they had a right to expect, and
did expect and believe that the vigilance and activity of
the officers of the Penitentiary in guarding and taking

care of their property at the Penitentiary on Sundays would be increased, but on the contrary, when on Sunday, the 23d December, 1860, the fire took place, there was no proper or sufficient care taken; and it was owing to the gross remissness and negligence of these officers that these convicts at the Penitentiary obtained access to the work shops, and thus were able to set fire to them and reduce them to ashes.

Your memorialists further state, that the rules and regulations prescribed for the government of the Penitentiary would, if faithfully carried out on the Sunday when the fire took place, have prevented the loss which then took place, but it can be made to appear beyond all doubt that these rules and regulations were disregarded and not maintained. Your memorialists, who were not permitted to maintain a proper guard over their property, which they had done until ordered to discontinue it, have been subjected to heavy loss by the conduct, omission and negligence of the officers of this State.

Your memorialists further state, that after the heavy loss they had sustained by the fire, and under the circumstances hereinbefore mentioned, they were required to settle for the rest of the property and hire of convicts up to the 31st December, 1860, and to pay to the Directors of the Maryland Penitentiary the sum of $1,075.59 from the payment of which they ought, as they insisted, when making said payment, and still insist, to have been excused and relieved.

Your memorialists further state, that they have been advised that if they had made an agreement with individuals, or a body corporate, liable to be sued, that they might have maintained an action at law, and recovered, under the circumstances, the amount of their loss; but that, inasmuch as no suit can be maintained against the Directors of the Maryland Penitentiary, and none against the State of Maryland, they have no redress except by application to your Honorable Body.

Your memorialists, finding that their only redress, under the circumstances in which they have been placed, must come from your Honorable Body, which has the power to grant full and adequate relief, have made this application in the hope and belief that you will cause a full and complete examination into all the circumstances of this transaction to be made, and do what is just, proper and equitable; and they therefore pray that you will make good their loss and grant full relief to them, &c.

JOHN H. DUVALL,
WILLIAM HOWARD.

June 10, 1861.

41

These articles of agreement made and concluded between the Directors of the Maryland Penitentiary on the one part, and John H. Duvall, of the city of Baltimore, on the other part, witnesseth, that the said Directors on their part do covenant and agree with the said John H. Duvall.

1st. To rent unto him the blacksmith shop now vacant at the Penitentiary, with all the rooms and conveniences thereunto attached, except the carpenter shop, the engine and boiler, one of the blacksmith furnaces, to be placed in the south-west corner of the shop for the use of the Institution, to be worked at no time by more than two hands, for the remaining portion of the year eighteen hundred and fifty-nine, and for five years thereafter, for the annual rent of two hundred dollars, with the privilege of removing the present engine and boiler, and of erecting others of more power, and also of erecting steam boxes and dry houses, and removing a portion of the fire places and chimneys, and of making such other changes and additions, without injury to the premises, as may be necessary for the convenience of manufacturing barrels by machinery, and also for the use of yard room for the storage of one hundred cords of wood; all said changes and additions to be at the cost of John H. Duvall, and to be made under the supervision and directions of the Directors and Warden.

2nd. That the said Directors agree to hire unto the said John H. Duvall thirty of the male convict prisoners, such as they have or may have best adapted for his purposes, to be employed by him in the manufacturing of barrels, for the term of five years from the first day of January, eighteen hundred and sixty, and to grant him the privilege of increasing the number, if they be required by him, from time to time, (any increase of prisoners at any time to be kept by John H. Duvall to the end of the term of this agreement,) to the number of seventy-five. The hire of all said prisoners to be at the rate of twenty-five cents per day for the first three months, as they enter his employment, and sixty cents per day thereafter, with the privilege of receiving as many of the prisoners as he may require at any time during the remainder of the year eighteen hundred and fifty-nine.

3rd. That the said Directors grant unto the said John H. Duvall the right to remove at the expiration of this contract all his machinery and building materials, and effects of every kind, he having first discharged to said Directors his debts and obligations under this contract.

These articles of agreement witnesseth, on the second part, that the said John H. Duvall doth agree on his part, and hereby binds himself, to employ the thirty convict prisoners, as provided for above, and to make payment for the same weekly in current funds of the State of Maryland, and to pay for the shop, yard room, &c., herein before specified, at the end of each quarter, in current funds of the State of Maryland, and also that all agents and superintendents of the shops occupied by him, which he may employ at his own expense, shall be subject to the rules and regulations of the prison.

2nd. That the said John H. Duvall agrees to make payment to the Institution monthly for all over work made by the prisoners in his employ, and to permit the Directors and Warden to regulate the tasks of said prisoners, said prisoners tasks to correspond, as can be made practicable, with the tasks exacted of the prisoners in the other shops of the establishment.

3rd. That the said John H. Duvall agrees, and hereby binds himself, to a faithful observance of the terms of this contract for the period herein named, under the penalty of one thousand dollars for its violation, and to let his buildings and fixtures remain as security for the fulfilment of his obligations until they are fully discharged.

And lastly, it is understood and agreed upon by and between the Directors of the Maryland Penitentiary and said John H. Duvall, that if either of the parties to this cantract shall desire to terminate the same at the end thereof, it shall be the duty of the party desiring such termination to give notice in writing to the other three months before the expiration of the time for which this contract is now made.

In witness whereof, Wm. J. Bryson, John Hurst, John Hilbert and R. Middleton, Monthly Committee acting for the Board of Directors of Maryland Penitentiary, in behalf of said Board of Directors and said John H. Duvall, have interchangeably set their hand and seals this fourth day of October, eighteen hundred and fifty-nine.

JOHN H. DUVALL, [SEAL.]

Committee. { WM. J. BRYSON, [SEAL.]
JOHN HURST, [SEAL.]
JOHN HILBERT, [SEAL.]
R. MIDDLETON, [SEAL.]

TEST:

JNO. J. C. DOUGHERTY.

[Document L.]

BY THE HOUSE OF DELEGATES,

AUGUST 1, 1861.

Read and ordered to be printed.

By order,   M. Y. KIDD, Chief Clerk.

REPORT

OF THE

𝔓𝔬𝔩𝔦𝔠𝔢 𝔠𝔬𝔪𝔪𝔦𝔰𝔰𝔦𝔬𝔫𝔢𝔯𝔰

OF BALTIMORE CITY,

WITH ACCOMPANYING DOCUMENTS.

MAYOR'S OFFICE,
CITY HALL,
Baltimore, July 30, 1861.

To the Honorable,
    the General Assemly of the State of Maryland:

Gentlemen:—

I respectfully submit for the information of your Honorable Body a memorial of the Mayor and city Council of Baltimore with accompanying documents, which was recently laid before the Senate and House of Representatives of the United States.

Very respectfully, your obd't servant,

GEO. WILLIAM BROWN,
Mayor.

REPORT.

To the Honorable,

the General Assembly of Maryland:

The undersigned Commissioners of Police of the city of Baltimore, have the honor, respectfully to report—

That from the date of their report made to your Honorable Body in May last, they continued faithfully to discharge the duties imposed on them by the laws of the State, until Thursday morning, the 27th of June. At an early hour on that day Col. George P. Kane, the Marshal of Police, was arrested at his residence, by a body of military, acting under an order of Major General Banks, in the service of the United States, and was taken to Fort McHenry, where he is still confined. A few hours afterwards, the Board were called on by Col. Kenly, who read to them an order of Gen. Banks appointing him Provost Marshal, and a proclamation by the same officer, announcing to the citizens of Baltimore, that the Marshal of Police had been arrested, and that the official authority of the Board of Police was "superseded."

The Commissioners of Police having maturely considered their duties and obligations under the law by which they held their appointments, could not avoid the conclusion, that such action, on the part of an officer of the General Government, who in point of fact held at the time military possession of the city of Baltimore, at once suspended the active operation of the Police law, and put for the time off duty, all the officers and men, who could not without directly violating both the letter and spirit of the law, recognize the authority or be subject to the control of any other head than the Board of Police. Accordingly the Board unanimously adopted a resolution to that effect.

On the following Monday morning, the first of July, about the hour of 3 o'clock, all the members of the Board with the exception of the Mayor were arrested in like manner by order of Gen. Banks, at their respective residences and taken to Fort McHenry. One of them Mr. C. D. Hinks, was after a few days confinement allowed to return to his own house on parole, upon the representations of his physicians, that owing to his state of ill health his life would be seriously endangered by a continuance of his imprisonment. The other Commissioners, Messrs. Howard, Gatchell and Davis, constituting a majority of the whole Board have ever since been confined in Fort McHenry, but they have this morning been officially notified that they are to be removed on the steamer Adelaide, to some other place at 6 o'clock this evening.

The undersigned, Charles Howard, William H. Gatchell and John W. Davis, further respectfully report, that being deprived of their liberty without legal process, and the Courts of Justice, as well of the United States as of the State of Maryl and, being prevented by the military power of the former from affording them any relief; they addressed to the Congress of the United States a memorial, asking that any charges made against them might be speedily investigated, and that the grievances of which they complain might be properly redressed.

To that memorial were appended copies of the two proclamations issued by Gen. Banks, in reference to the Board of Police, and of the preamble and resolutions adopted by the Board in reference to the first of said proclamations.

The undersigned respectfully ask leave to submit herewith, as a part of this report copies of the above mentioned memorial to Congress, and to refer to the same and to the documents appended thereto, for more full information in reference to their proceedings, and to the views by which they have deen governed.

All of which is respectfully submitted,

CHARLES HOWARD,
WM. H. GATCHELL,
JOHN W. DAVIS,

GEO. WM. BROWN, Mayor

And ex-officio member of the Board of Police,

Fort McHenry, July 29th, 1861.

MEMORIAL

OF

Charles Howard, Wm. H. Gatchell, John W.
Davis, Police Commissioners of the City of
Baltimore, to the Senate and House of Rep-
resentatives of the United States.

_____

To the Honorable

the Senate and House of Representatives

of the United States:

The Memorial of CHAS. HOWARD, WM. H. GATCHELL, *and*
JNO. W. DAVIS, *citizens of Baltimore, in the State of Mary-*
land, respectfully represents:

That between two and three o'clock, on the morning of the
1st of July instant, they were severally aroused from sleep,
at their respective dwellings, by large bodies of soldiers of
the army of the United States, quartered in or about this
City, and were removed, by force and against their will, from
their homes and families, to Fort McHenry, where they have
ever since been confined as prisoners, and now are.

Your memorialists, at the time, received no further information as to the cause of their arrest, than that the same
was made by order of Major General Banks, commanding this
Military Department, nor have they since been informed of
any charges whatever against them, further than those contained in a proclamation of General Banks issued later in the
same day, a copy of which, taken from one of the newspapers of the City, they append hereto.

By reference to the said proclamation, your Honorable Bodies will perceive that the arrest of your memorialists is alleged to have been made "in pursuance of orders issued from the headquarters of the army at Washington, for the preservation of the public peace in this department;" and is attempted to be justified by the refusal of your memorialists, as members of the Board of Police of Baltimore, to acquiesce in the legality and effect of a previous proclamation of General Banks, declaring their official authority superseded. The proclamation in question goes on to charge, that your memorialists, after such attempted suspension of their functions, had continued to hold sessions daily; that "upon a forced and unwarrantable construction" of the previous proclamation referred to, they had declared the Police Law to be suspended and their police force to be off of duty, "intending to leave the city without any police protection whatever;" and that they had moreover refused to recognize, as policemen, certain persons selected by a Provost Marshal, under General Banks, to act in that capacity. There is a further allegation that the "head quarters under the charge of the Board, when abandoned by the officers, resembled in some respects a concealed arsenal."

Your memorialists respectfully represent, that together with their colleague Charles D. Hinks, Esq., who was arrested with them, (but has since been discharged, upon his parole, because of ill health,) and the Mayor of the city who has not been arrested, they constitute the Board of Police, a *quasi*-corporation created by the Legislature of Maryland, and having exclusive police jurisdiction in the city of Baltimore. The nature and extent of their functions and duties will be made known to your Honorable Bodies, by an examination of the Code of Public Local Laws of the State of Maryland, (Art. IV, Sect. 806 to 822 and Sect. 199 to 228 inclusive. It will there be seen that their powers are of the amplest character, and that they not only have control of the whole Police Department of the State, within the city limits, but are likewise charged with the appointment of all Judges of Election, and the conduct of all elections, whether Federal, State or Municipal, to be held in the city; so that every such election is, by special enactment, declared invalid and of no effect, unless held by the Board, and under its control and supervision. It will further appear, by the explicit terms of the law, that no police force can lawfully exist in Baltimore, unless appointed and governed by the Police Board, and that neither officers nor men, when appointed, have any official authority or jurisdiction, independently of or apart from the Board; but that all of them are merely employed, in pursuance of the express provisions of the law,

" to enable the Board to discharge the duties imposed on them." By section 819 of the article of the Code already referred to, heavy pecuniary penalties are imposed upon any person who shall forcibly resist or obstruct the execution or enforcement of any of the provisions of the law, in the premises, or disburse any money in violation thereof, and it is made the duty of the Board to enforce such penalties by civil action, leaving the parties who may have violated the law, still subject to indictment for any criminal offence committed by them in the course of such violation. Your memorialists, with their colleague, Mr. Hinks, were duly appointed by the Legislature of Maryland, at its January Session, 1860, to carry out the provisions of the police system, of which they have thus indicated the leading features, and they duly took the oath to do so, which is prescribed by the law. The term of office of Messrs. Howard and Davis does not expire until the 10th of March, 1862, and that of Messrs. Gatchell and Hinks extends for still two years longer. None of them are subject to removal, except by the Legislature of Maryland, from which they derive their authority and functions. All the provisions of the Police Law were fully tested by legal proceedings instituted in the Superior court of Baltimore city shortly after its enactment, and carried, on appeal, to the Court of last resort in the State. The result was an unqualified recognition by all the Judges, of the conformity of the law, in all particulars, with the Constitution of Maryland and that of the United States.

Such being the official tenure and lawful and constitutional powers and duties of your memorialists, they were astonished on the 27th of June last, to be visited, without previous notice, by Col. Kenly, of the Maryland Volunteers, then encamped near Baltimore, and to be informed by that officer, that he was instructed by Major General Banks, to read them a proclamation declaring their official authority superseded, and appointing Col. Kenly Provost Marshal to administer the Police Law of the State in their stead. Of that proclamation a copy is appended to this memorial, by which it will be seen, that although various causes are alleged for the arrest of Col. GEORGE P. KANE, Marshal of Police, and for superseding his official authority likewise, no ground of complaint whatever is pretended to exist against the Board of Police, and no excuse is vouchsafed for the overthrow of the constitutional authority of the State of Maryland, vested in your memorialists, and of course incapable of being constitutionally or lawfully divested, by any federal authority, civil or military.

2

The City of Baltimore being entirely commanded by large bodies of federal troops stationed around it, and it being wholly impossible for your memorialists to offer any effective resistance to the illegal proceedings of General Banks, they had no alternative but to submit to force, and to vindicate as far as practicable, the authority of the State of Maryland, and their own personal and official rights and self respect, by protesting against such proceeding as an arbitrary and unconstitutional exercise of military power. They accordingly adopted the preamble and resolutions likewise hereto appended. It is in this act and in their continuing their sessions, under and in pursuance of the law, that Gen'l. Banks, in his proclamation issued on the day of their arrest, professes to find justification for his unwarrantable and unlawful violation of their personal liberty. It is no part of the intention of your memorialists to enter into any discussion of the allegations of that proclamation, further than to say, that is wholly untrue, as therein alleged, that they continued to hold the Police force of the State of Maryland in the city of Baltimore, subject to their orders, for any purpose inconsistent with the peace or security of the Government. They declared the active operation of the Police Law to be suspended, for the obvious and unanswerable reason, that the forcible suspension of the functions of the Board which alone had authority to administer the law, necessarily paralized the law also. They declared the Police force appointed by them to be still an existent body, because the law creating the force forbids the dismissal of the men, except for cause, and then by the Board of Police alone, after trial had. They declared it to be still subject to their orders, for so long as the force exists it cannot be subject, under the law, to any other. They refused, as a matter of obvious duty, to recognize as policemen the parties named by Col. Kenly to act as such, for they assumed it, as they still consider it, to be beyond dispute, that Col. Kenly could have no lawful right to appoint policemen, under the laws of Maryland, whatever his authority may have been as a military officer, (which they do not propose to consider,) to appoint military subordinates in the stead of policemen, outside of those laws or in derogation of them. The attempt by Col. Kenly to enforce such Police appointments, and all efforts of his nominees to act thereunder were moreover punishable offences under the Police law, the penalties of which it was the sworn duty of your memorialists to enforce, and in the violation of which it was impossible that they could acquiesce. But your memorialists distinctly and emphatically deny that they had any other purpose in their official protest and action, than to

fulfil their manifest and sworn obligations, and to maintain
the dignity and assert the authority of the laws of Maryland
which were entrusted to their hands for execution, but which
they were precluded by force from executing. They solemnly
declare, that if they had been permitted to continue in the
exercise of their functions, after the arrest and imprisonment
of the Marshal of Police, on the 27th of June, they would
have continued to discharge their duties, as they had discharged them, theretofore, in all respects faithfully, impartially, and to the best of their ability, in obedience to the laws
and the constitution, and they asseverate, and will maintain,
that the imputation of any other intention or purpose on
their part is wholly destitute of foundation in fact. The
statement in regard to the "concealed arsenal" at the Marshal's Office, they do not deem it necessary to allude to, further than to say, that it is perfectly notorious and has been
fully shown by the Message of the Mayor to the City Council
of Baltimore, that the arms in question were the lawful property of the city; that they were insignificant in quantity,
constituting but little more than the customary armament of
the force, for its public duties, and were lawfully concealed,
to prevent unlawful seizure. Your memorialists therefore
respectfully represent that the grounds set up by General
Banks in his proclamation give to their arrest and imprisonment no color of justification or necessity.

And as to the proclamation of General Banks issued on
the 27th of June, announcing the arrest of the Marshal of
Police and declaring his official authority to have been superseded, these memorialists respectfully say, that the charges
against that officer, contained therein, are equally without
foundation, so far as they believe or have any reason to suspect. They have personal knowledge of the fact, which is
equally well known to all impartial citizens of Baltimore,
that the official duties of Col. Kane have been discharged,
throughout, with singular ability, integrity and courage,
and never more conspicuously, or in better faith, or at more
imminent risk of his own life, than in the protection of the
troops of the Federal Government, on the 19th of April. Of
the police force, placed under his command by these memorialists, and selected wholly without reference to their political opinions (as the law and the official oath of your memorialists require) your memorialists can say, without exaggera-
tion, that they do not believe a body of men can be found,
any where, more entirely devoted to the conscientious discharge of official duty, or less justly liable to the accusation
of entering into unlawful combinations themselves, or encouraging or permitting such combinations by others. Down to

the moment of the suspension of the active duties of the force, by General Banks, these memorialists have pride in asserting that no community ever acknowledged, more universally than the citizens of Baltimore, and none ever had better reason to acknowledge, the successful operation of a police system, in securing the strictest enforcement of the laws, the amplest protection of private rights and the most rigid maintenance of public order. Your memorialists further say, that with every opportunity afforded by their official position and every energy stimulated by their sense of duty, to ascertain the existence of all unlawful combinations or associations within their jurisdiction, they have no reason whatever to suspect that any such combinations did in fact exist, as alleged by General Banks in his proclamation of June 27th, and they confidently assert their conviction, that his allegation to the contrary was founded upon false information, communicated to him by designing persons, and cannot be sustained or countenanced by credible evidence of any sort. But even if your memorialists were and are altogether mistaken in these particulars: if the Marshal of Police had been faithless to his obligations as charged, and had been willing or able to seduce the men under his command from theirs also: it was still only necessary for General Banks to furnish the Board of Police with the slightest evidence to that effect, and your memorialists would have given to his suggestions the most prompt and respectful consideration. They would have suspended or removed the Marshal, if such action had been proper, and would have placed beyond question their own disposition and ability to discharge the whole of their duty in the premises. If General Banks, even without advising them, had seen fit to arrest the Marshal of Police, upon any charge which might have been deemed sufficient to justify such a step, your memorialists would have taken care to govern the police force, efficiently and properly, during his confinement. The legality of such arrest would have been a question for Col Kane and not your memorialists to consider, but either of the courses suggested would have fulfilled the purposes and have met the exigency announced in the proclamation. General Banks, acting doubtless in conformity with his orders, adopted neither the one course nor the other, but assuming jurisdiction not only over the person of an alleged offender, but over his official functions likewise, saw fit not only to arrest and imprison him, but to dismiss him from his place as a public officer of this State, (which only your memorialists could lawfully do,) and to supersede the lawful authority of your memorialists besides. Knowing that such a proceeding could not, by possibility, be justified, by any thing in the Laws or Constitution of Maryland or the United States, your memorialists were compelled, by every consideration of sworn duty, to treat the same as an arbitrary act of force and usurpation, no matter by whose orders it might have been committed, or under what pretexts it was sought to be excused. No construction which it was possible for them to give to the proclamation of the 27th of June could have brought them to any other conclusion than that it was their bounden duty to enter their protest against it.

They therefore deny that the construction which they adopted was either "forced" or "unwarrantable," as charged in the proclamotion of July 1, and they emphatically protest against the truth of the further allegation contained in the latter document, to the effect that their official course upon the occasion was dictated by a purpose to "leave the City without any police protection whatever." If indeed they had entertained such a purpose, they respectfully suggest that it was not a matter with which any officer of the Federal Government had any rightful concern, how much soever it would have furnished their fellow citizens, with just cause of complaint. But they entertained no such purpose. On the contrary they aver and are prepared to show, that when General Banks, by his proclamation of June 27th, interrupted the exercise of their lawful authority, the City was thorougly protected, in all particulars, by your memorialists and the force under their command; that its tranquility was perfect; its peace was neither disturbed nor threatened; the rights of person and property, of all men, were inviolate: the civil authorities of the State and city were in the beneficial and effective exercise of all their functions, and the laws were supreme, except in so far as interfered with by the military power. If therefore the City was left without protection, on the 27th of June, it was the fault, and upon the responsibility, not of your memorialists, but altogether of that Department of the General Government, by which the constituted authorities of the State were superseded, and the protective provisions of its laws deprived of their vitality. If General Banks himself were unlawfully superseded by force, he surely would not regard it as just, in his captors, to accuse him of leaving his Department without protection, because he refused, as a man of courage and honor, to acquiesce in their violent suspension and assumption of his functions. Your memorialists claim to be judged, officially and personally, by no lower standard of dignity, responsibility or honor. As public officers, and men of ordinary integrity, it must be obvious to your Honorable Bodies that they could not lend themselves, in any way, to what they knew to be a palpable violation of the law they had sworn to support. They could not transfer, or acquiesce in the transfer to General Banks or Col. Kenly of an authority which the law commanded them to exercise exclusively themselves. They could not authorize their police force to serve under any command or control but their own, in the face of the express provisions of the law to the contrary. They could not expose their officers and men to civil and criminal responsibility by leaving them on duty, under unlawful orders, which could afford them no protection before the tribunals of justice. Your memorialists had no choice therefore but to protest as they did; to declare their force off duty, and leave the military authority to deal, on its own responsibility, with the exigency it had seen fit to create.

In entering, thus at large, into a discussion of the grounds set up by General Banks in justification of their arrest, your memorialists have been governed, altogether, by a desire to vindicate their official and personal character and conduct from unfounded and disparaging imputations, and to demonstrate the gratuitous character of the injustice, against which they appeal to Congress for relief. They are in no wise to be considered as thereby recognising, for an instant, the right of the War Department, or of any officer acting thereunder, to proceed against them in the mode adopted, even if the accusations which they have repelled were perfectly well founded. The State of Maryland is one of the States of the Union. She is at peace with the Government. Her people are disarmed, and her territory is occupied by an overwhelming military force. Martial law has not been proclaimed among her people, but on the contrary all intention to set it up or enforce it is disavowed, in the most explicit way, in the proclamation of June 27th. The Federal Courts, and those of the State are in full and undisturbed operation, so far as citizens not belonging to the military force are concerned, and process is served, without obstruction, and is obeyed without resistance by all except those in military authority. If, therefore, your memorialists were charged with any offence known to the law, there was and is nothing to prevent their arrest and detention by the civil arm, in due course, and upon proper and lawful warrant supported by oath, as prescribed and required by the Constitution. But they respectfully submit, that in the proclamation by which their arrest is sought to be justified, there is no allegation of any matter or thing which, if sworn to in proper form of law, would authorize the issuing of process against them, by any judicial tribunal. If they were so unfortunate as to place an erroneous construction upon the first proclamation of General Banks, as he alleges, they are not aware of any statute of the United States which renders such a mistake a penal offence. If it be a crime, on their part, to regard as illegal and wholly null, the attempted suspension, by a federal officer, of their functions as constituted authorities of the State of Maryland, they have been unable to learn by what provisions of the Constitution and laws such an offence is created or defined. If they are lawfully punishable for holding, subject to their orders, a police force which the laws of Maryland made it their duty so to hold, and for refusing to recognize as public officers of Maryland, the appointees of General Banks, whom they are bound under the laws of Maryland to prosecute as offenders, for attempting to exercise police functions, they are at loss to conceive under what head of the penal law such criminality on their part exists. They mean no improper reflection when they assert their belief, that no law officer of the government would venture to ask for a warrant, upon an affidavit of the facts recited in the proclamation of July 1st, and that no competent tribunal would hesitate to quash such a warrant if issued. They know no principle of criminal jurisprudence, under free institutions, which would authorize even the Courts of recognized jurisdiction to sanction the arrest and confinement of a citizen, upon the indefinite allegation of his entertaining "some purpose, not known to the Government," but still alleged to be "inconsistent with its peace or security."

But be this as it may, these memorialists respectfully insist, that if they are charged with any offence which is known to the laws, it is their constitutional right, as citizens of the United States, to be dealt with according to law. If they are charged with no offence, it is equally their constitutional right to have the fact recognized, and to enjoy their personal liberty. They have, through their counsel, respectfully asked of General Banks a statement of the grounds of their imprisonment, and have challenged an investigation of any and all charges affecting either their personal or official integrity or their fidelity to the laws and the constitution. No such statement has been made to them; no such investigation has been granted and no hope has been held out to them of any speedy relief from the unjust and unlawful imprisonment under which they are suffering. In the meantime, they are withdrawn from their homes and separated from their families; their public duties are unlawfully committed to other hands; their private interests are exposed to detriment and perhaps ruin, and they themselves are held as malefactors before the country, and are compelled by force to endure mortification and obloquy. The arbitrary suspension of the writ of

Habeas Corpus has of course deprived them of the means provided by law for their deliverance, and unless your Honorable Bodies should see fit to relieve them, they are wholly without means of present redress. They therefore most respectfully and earnestly invoke the immediate interposition of Congress in their behalf. They repeat that they have administered their public trust faithfully, impartially and to the best of their ability, and have not used the police force under their control, nor have they permitted it nor contemplated permitting it be used for any other purpose, than the legitimate and faithful discharge of its duties, as prescribed by law. As private citizens, they invite scrutiny, likewise, into their conduct, in every respect in which it may be lawfully impugned, and they assert their readiness to meet, without a moment's delay, any charge which may be responsibly laid against their individual or official proceedings. As citizens of the United States, they therefore appeal to your Honorable Bodies for relief from oppression and unconstitutional wrong. As public officers of the State of Maryland, they protest against the usurpation of their official authority by an officer of the United States army and they protest the more strongly, because the usurpation against which they remonstrate is not an irresponsible proceeding of the officer in question, but the advised and deliberate act of the War Department itself. They are aware that the President of the United States has called upon Congress to sanction the suspension of the Habeas Corpus, and other acts which have been done by the Executive Department, upon its responsibility, without previous sanction of law. But the President has not asserted, in his message, any right on the part of the Federal Government to depose and appoint State officers, or annul laws of the States constitutionally enacted, nor has he suggested any power in Congress to clothe him with any such authority. He has asserted no right to do wrong to individuals, nor has he asked the interposition of Congress to such an end. But whatever may be the claims of the Executive, your memorialists respectfully insist that the demands of the constitution and of individual right and public liberty are very far above them, and they throw themselves therefore for redress and deliverance upon the justice and authority of the representatives of the people. They have no other recourse against arbitrary power and military force, and they demand, as matter of right, that their case be investigated by Congress or remitted to the tribunals of justice to be lawfully heard and detemined.

CHARLES HOWARD,
WILLIAM H. GATCHELL,
JOHN W. DAVIS.

Fort McHenry.

APPENDIX.

General Banks' Proclamation of June 27th.

PROCLAMATION TO THE PEOPLE OF THE CITY OF BALTIMORE.

Headquarters Department of Annapolis,

June 27th, 1861.

By virtue of authority vested in me, and in obedience to orders, as Commanding General of the Military Department of Annapolis, I have arrested, and do now detain in custody, Mr. George P. Kane, Chief of Police of the city of Baltimore. I deem it proper at this the moment of arrest to make formal and public declaration of the motive by which I have been governed in this proceeding.

It is not my purpose, neither is it in consonance with my instructions, to interfere in any manner with the legitimate government of the people of Baltimore or Maryland. I desire to support the public authorities in all appropriate duties; in preserving peace, protecting property and the rights of persons, in obeying and upholding every municipal regulation and statute, consistent with the laws of the United States and of Maryland.

But unlawful combinations of men, organized for resistance to such laws, that provide hidden deposits of arms and ammunition, encourage contraband traffic with men at war with the government, and while enjoying its protection and privileges, stealthily wait opportunity to combine their means and forces with those in rebellion against its authority, are not among the recognized or legal rights of any class of men,

3

and cannot be permitted under any form of government
whatever. Such combinations are well known to exist in this
department.

The mass of citizens of Baltimore and of Maryland, loyal
to the Coustitution and the Union, are neither parties to nor
responsible for them. But the Chief of Police is not only
believed to be cognizant of these facts, but in contravention
of his duty, and in violation of law, he is, by direction or
indirection, both witness and protector to the transactions
and the parties engaged therein. Under such circumstances
the government cannot regard him otherwise than at the head
of an armed force, hostile to its authority and acting in concert with its avowed enemies.

For this reason, superseding his official authority and that
of the Commissioners of Police, I have arrested and do now
detain him in custody of the United States; and in further
pursuance of my instructions, I have appointed for the time
being Col. Kenly, of the first regiment of Maryland Volunteers, *Provost Marshal,* in and for the city of Baltimore, "to
superintend and cause to be executed the Police Laws provided by the Legislature of Maryland," with the aid and assistance of the subordinate officers of the Police Department.
And he will be respected accordingly.

Whenever a loyal citizen shall be otherwise named for the
performance of this duty, who will execute these laws impartially and in good faith to the government of the United
States, the military force of this department will render to
him that instant and willing obedience which is due from
every good citizen to his government.

NATH. P. BANKS,

Maj. Gen. Com'g Dep't of Annapolis.

Preamble and Resolutions adopted by the
Board of Police, on June 27th.

Whereas the laws of the State of Maryland give the whole and exclusive control of the police force of the city to the Board of Police, organized and appointed by the General Assembly; and not only are the said Board bound to exercise the powers in, and to discharge the duties imposed upon them, but all other persons are positively prohibited, under heavy penalties, from interfering with them in so doing; and

Whereas there is no power given to the Board to transfer the control over any portion of the police force to any person or persons whomsoever, other than the officers of police appointed by them, in pursuance of the express provisions of the law, and acting under their orders; and

Whereas by the orders of Major General Banks, an officer of the United States Army, commanding in this city, the Marshal of Police has been arrested—the Board of Police superseded, and an officer of the army has been appointed provost marshal, and directed to assume the command and control of the police force of the city; therefore be it

Resolved, That this Board do solemnly protest against the orders and proceedings above referred to of Major General Banks as an arbitrary exercise of military power, not warranted by any provision of the constitution or laws of the United States, or of the State of Maryland, but in derogation of all of them.

Resolved, That whilst the Board, yielding to the force of circumstances, will do nothing to increase the present excitement, or obstruct the execution of such measures as Major General Banks may deem proper to take on his own responsibility for the preservation of the peace of the city, and of public order, they cannot, consistently with their views of official duty and of the obligations of their oaths of office, recognize the right of any of the officers and men of the police force, as such, to receive orders or directions from any other authority than from this Board.

Resolved. That in the opinion of the Board, the forcible suspension of their functions suspends at the same time the active operation of the Police Law, and puts the officers and men off duty for the present, leaving them subject, however, to the rules and regulations of the service as to their personal conduct and deportment, and to the orders which this Board may see fit hereafter to issue when the present illegal suspension of their functions shall be removed.

CHARLES HOWARD, Prest,

WM. H. GATCHELL,

CHAS. D. HINKS,

JOHN W. DAVIS,

GEO. WM. BROWN, Mayor

And ex-officio member of the Board of Police.

TO THE PUBLIC.

Headquarters Dep't., of Annapolis,
Fort McHenry, July 1.

In pursuance of orders issued from the Headquarters of the Army at Washington, for the preservation of the Public Peace in this Department, I have arrested and do now detain in custody of the United States the late Members of the Board of Police—Messrs. Charles Howard, William H. Gatchell, Charles D. Hinks and John W. Davis. The incidents of the past week afforded full justification for this order. The Headquarters, under the charge of the Board, when abandoned by the Officers, resembled in some respects a concealed Arsenal. After public recognition and protest against the "suspension of their functions," they continued their sessions daily. Upon a forced and unwarrantable construction of my Proclamation of the 27th ultimo, they declared that the Police Law was suspended, and the police officers and men put off duty for the present, intending to leave the city without any police protection whatever. They refused to recognize the officers or men necessarily selected by the Provost Marshal for its protection, and hold subject to their orders, now and hereafter, the old Police force, a large body of armed men, for some purpose, not known to the Government, and inconsistent with its peace or security. To anticipate any intentions or orders on their part, I have placed temporarily a portion of the force under my command within the city. I disclaim on the part of the Government I represent all desire, intention and purpose to interfere in any manner whatever with the ordinary Municipal affairs of the City of Baltimore. Whenever a loyal citizen can be named who will execute its Police laws with impartiality and in good faith to the United States, the military force will be with-drawn from the central parts of the municipality at once. No soldier will be permitted in the city except under regulations satisfactory to the Marshal; and if any so admitted violate the municipal law, they shall be punished according to the civil law, by the civil tribunals.

NATHANIEL P. BANKS,

Major General Commanding.

MEMORIAL

MAYOR AND CITY COUNCIL OF BALTIMORE.

To the Honorable

the Senate and House of Representatives

of the United States:

The Mayor and City Council of Baltimore respectfully present this their memorial :

The recent suspension of the functions of the Board of Police of this city, makes it the duty of your memorialists to call your attention to certain consquences of that action which affect every citizen in this community. The memorial of the Board of Police already presented to your Honorable Bodies, has given you full information of the nature and extent of their powers. A brief reference to certain leading features of the law of Maryland under which they hold office, and with whose execution they are charged, will enable you to appreciate the embarrassments which now affect the due administration of the Government of Baltimore. The Board of Police is, under the laws of Maryland, the sole Police authority of the city. It alone is competent to provide for the preservation of peace and order within our limits; to appoint subordinate police officers, to appoint judges of elections and provide for the execution of the laws regulating elections, to enforce all ordinances of the Mayor and City Council of Baltimore for the preservation of health and the maintenance of peace and order. By other provisions of the laws for the Police government of this city, the organization of any permanent police force other than that organized by and acting under the orders of the Board of Police, is distinctly prohibited.

To the due execution of the laws of their State for their local government, by legally constituted officers, the free citizens of Baltimore have an unquestioned constitutional right. The manner in which that right has been respected will appear from the facts which we now recite:

The Major General commanding in the military department of which this city forms a part, issued a proclamation dated June 27th, announcing the arrest of the Marshal of Police. With professions of respect for every municipal regulation and public statute, the proclamation further announces to the public that the official authority of the Marshal of Police and the Board of Police is superseded, and a "Provost Marshal," an officer unknown to the civil law of Maryland, is appointed. No charge is preferred against the members of the Board of Police, nor is any reason assigned for superseding them and depriving the citizens of Baltimore of their only legal Police authority.

The Board of Police, yielding to the force which prevented their execution of the laws of this State, submitted to the practical suspension of their functions, and neither offered nor permitted any resistance to such action as the General in command saw fit to adopt.

The Provost Marshal appointed by the General in command to execute the police laws of Maryland for the government of the city of Baltimore, took possession of the offices belonging to the city, and removed certain officials not appointed by the Board but by the Mayor and City Council of Baltimore, appointing others in their place.

The memorial of the Board of Police has presented at length the considerations of official duty which made it impossible for them either themselves to aid, or to permit the officers under their command to aid in violations of the law under which they hold office. A comparison of the reasons assigned by them, with the provisions of the police law, to which they direct your attention, will prove the correctness of their conclusions. Under date of July 1st appeared a third proclamation of the General in command, announcing the arrest of the members of the Board of Police. Again disclaiming for those under whose authority he acts, any intention to interfere with the municipal affairs of Baltimore, he assigns certain reasons for the summary arrest of these gentlemen, whom without complaint on oath or civil process he arrested, and now holds in custody. Examined in connection with the law under which they were appointed, the pretended offences charged against them, amount together to the simple performance of their official duty. Had they aided or acquiesced in the establishment of any police authority other than their own, they would have plainly violated the law under which they hold office.

By a fourth proclamation, dated July 10th, the Major General in command informs the public that he has removed the "provost marshal," and has appointed a "marshal of police," "in all respects to administer every department of the police law in full freedom for the peace and prosperity of the city, and the honor and perpetuity of the United States." This officer now affects to administer the law for the police government of Baltimore, by means of a force organized under and acting by his direction.

Whatever professions of regard for our laws accompany these transactions the facts are too plain to be concealed. The local laws of the State of Maryland, for the police government of the city of Baltimore, to which all officers of the federal government are bound to yield obedience within our limits, have been set aside. The only officers competent to administer those laws have been superseded, and then imprisoned. The General in command, professing to act under instructions from the federal government, has marched large bodies of armed men into the city, planted cannon in the principal streets and public squares, and, by the law and authority of superior force, has established the present acting police force, has enabled its officers to take possession of the offices and buildings belonging to the city of Baltimore, to eject officers appointed by the Mayor & City Council, & to assume the function of executing laws whose fundamental provisions they daily violate by the exercise of police authority. Your memorialists need not dwell on the embarrassments which must certainly result from thus disorganizing the civil government of a city, nor on the sense of insecurity which affects citizens who reflect that the present police acts without legal warrant or authority. A community thus deprived of its lawful government is entitled to demand that those who assume so grave a responsibility shall furnish some sufficient reason for their action. It is impossible to believe that the federal authorities have wantonly disturbed the peace and good government of the city. No doubt statements have been made to which credit has been given, and on the faith of which the government has acted. The proclamation of the General in command, issued immediately after the arrest of the members of the Board of Police, vaguely charges that the Board "hold, subject to their orders, now and hereafter, the old police force, a large body of armed men for some purpose unknown to the government, and inconsistent with its peace and security."

4

Your memorialists are left in doubt as to the precise nature of the purpose referred to, but the suspension of their authority, and the subsequent imprisonment of the Board of Police, seems to have been the result of a belief that their authority would be used to the injury of the government of the United States.

That this opinion has any foundation in facts, your memorialists deny, and appeal to the history of the official acts of the Police authority of this city.

For a detailed account of the unhappy occurrences of the 19th April, you are referred to the statement of the Mayor of the city, which is herewith submitted. No evidence of failure of duty on the part of the police authority on that day can be produced. The Mayor, ex-efficio a member of the Board, shared the dangers to which the troops were exposed, and both he and the Marshal of Police risked their lives for their protection. The great excitemsnt which ensued, and which was intensified by the wanton killing of a citizen, at a distance from the scene of the riot, and who was shot from the window of the cars as the train passed out of the city, was represented to the President by the Mayor of the city. The President and his cabinet recognized the necessity of temporarily avoiding a passage through Baltimore, and gave repeated assurances that troops should not be brought through the city. Unauthorized persons declaringly openly their intention to cut their way through Baltimore with or without the orders of the government, the authorities of Baltimore, as well the Police Board as your memorialists, called their people to arms, procured such weapons as could be hastily gathered, and did all in their power to provide for the defence of their city from the threatened danger. This they did and this they justify. In the then excited condition of the people, a portion of our population may have entertained designs of active hostility to the government. If such designs existed, they were frustrated by the precautions of the Board of Police. Fort McHenry, believed to be without either a sufficient garrison or armament, was nightly guarded by the military of the city, acting under the orders of the Board of Police. Other government property received especial protection. Arms supposed to belong to the United States and found in the hands of individuals were taken possession of and preserved by the Board of Police, who gave notice to the government agents of their action. The persons and property of all citizens received equal and sufficient protection. Whatever charges malice may suggest, the preservation of peace in the city, the prevention of conflict between citizens divided in opinion, the protection of life, limb and property, during a period of great popular excitement, is a monument to the zeal and good faith of our police authorities. When there no longer seemed any necessity for a military array, the arms placed in the hands of the people were recalled, and the city resumed its ordinary condition of quiet. So Baltimore remained until May 14th, when it being ascertained that the people were disarmed, and that the movement could be made without serious danger, the General then in command in this department occupied a portion of the city with certain troops under his command. His arrival was announced by proclamation, and in the afternoon of May 14th he sent a detachment of troops into the city, who sezed and carried off arms belonging to and in the custody of the authorities of the city of Baltimore. No resistance was offered or permitted by the authorities of the city. Two of our citizens, one of them a member of the Legislature of Maryland, were by the orders of the same military officer summarily arrested, and after an imprisonment of a few days, were released because their existed no sufficient cause for either arrest or detention.

Since the middle of May, many thousand United States soldiers have passed through this city. There has been no single instance of opposition to their progress, nor any failure on the part of the city authorities to take proper precautions for their protection as well as for preserving the peace of the city. The Courts of the United States are and have been unimpeded in the performance of their duties, save when in a memorable instance, the Marshal of the U. States was not permitted to enter Fort McHenry, or to serve process issued by the highest judicial officer of the United States. The order of the city has been preserved. No resistance of any kind has been made, even to illegal and unconstitutional acts of military officers. No arrest that has been made by mere military authority, but that could have been made by civil officers. Thus without the extence is of a single fact to justify an appeal to a supposed authority growing out of military necessity, citizens have been seized and imprisoned, their homes invaded and searched without warrant, or complaint, on oath, as required by law. The protection afforded by constitutional guarantees of the liberty of the citizen and constitutional restraints imposed on the power of the executive, has been denied.— Obedience to the Courts is refused when they interfere for the protection of the citizen. Arms belonging to the city of Baltimore and rightfully in the custody of its authorities have been taken. The buildings of the city have been given into the custody of officers not known to its laws.—

Its Court House has been occupied by troops. Its civil authority has been disregarded, and a revolutionary government established by mere force of arms and against law.

Against these manifold wrongs your memorialists for themselves and the free community which they represent do most solemnly protest. The State of Maryland has been and is subject to the Constitution and laws of the United States, and her citizens are of right entitled to the protection of that Constitution and of those laws. The civil authorities of this city have heretofore and do now render fitting obedience to the requirements of both. If disaffection is believed to exist, from which danger is apprehended, the guns of Fort McHenry turned on the homes of the women and children of an unarmed city—the Federal troops encamped around its limits would seem an adequate protection to the Government. Whether that disaffection is weakened by depriving a whole community of the protection of its laws—whether the risk of disorder is diminished by establishing a police government which fails to command the respect accorded to undoubted lawful authority, you, in your wisdom, will determine.

But your memorialists respectfully, yet most earnestly demand, as a matter of right, that their city may be governed according to the Constitution and laws of the United States, and, of the State of Maryland. They demand, as a matter of right, that citizens may be secure in their persons, houses, papers and effects against unreasonable searches and seizures, and that they be not deprived of life, liberty, or property, without due process of law. They demand, as a matter of right, that the military render obedience to the civil authority, that our municipal laws be respected, that officers be released from imprisonment, and restored to the lawful exercise of their functions, that the police government established by law, be no longer impeded by armed force to the injury of peace and order.

These, their rightful demands, your memorialists submit for the consideration of your honorable bodies.

MAYOR'S MESSAGE.

To the Honorable the Members of the

First and Second Branches of the City Council:

GENTLEMEN :

A great object of the Reform movement was to separate municipal affairs entirely from national politics, and in accordance with this principle, I have heretofore, in all my communications to the City Council, carefully refrained from any allusion to national affairs. I shall not now depart from this rule further than is rendered absolutely necessary by the unprecedented condition of things at present existing in this city.

On the 19th of April last an attack was made by a mob in the streets of Baltimore on several companies of a regiment of Massachusetts troops, who were on their way to the city of Washington in pursuance of a call for 75,000 men made by the President of the United States.

On the day previous, troops had been safely passed through the city under the escort of the police. In the afternoon of the same day (18th,) the regiments from Massachusetts were expected, and provision was made by the police for their reception, but they did not arrive, and the Board of Police could not ascertain when they would come, although two of the members of the Board went in person to the station of the Philadelphia Railroad Company to obtain the necessary information. On the morning of the 19th, about ten o'clock, I was at my law office engaged in the performance of professional business, when three members of the City Council came to me with a message from Marshal Kane to the effect that he had just learned that the troops were about to arrive, and that he apprehended some disturbance. I immediately hastened to the office of the Board of Police and gave notice. George M. Gill, Esq., Counsellor of the city, and myself, got into a carriage and drove rapily to the Camden station, and the Police Commissioners followed without delay. On reaching Camden station we found Marshal Kane in attendance and the police coming in squads to the spot. The plan of the agents of the Railroad Companies was that the troops which were to arrive in the cars at the President street station, should in the same way be conveyed through the city, and be transferred to the cars for Washington at the Camden street station. Accordingly the police were requested by the agent of the road to be in attendance at the latter station. After considerable delay, the troops began to arrive and were transferred under the direction of the police to the Washington cars as rapidly as possible. There was a good deal of excitement, and a large and angry crowd assembled, but the transfer was safely effected. No one could tell whether more troops were expected or not. At this time an alarm was given that a mob was about to tear up the rails in advance of the train on the Washington road, and Marshal Kane ordered some of his men to go out the road as far as the Relay House, if necessary, to protect the track. Soon afterwards, and when I was about to leave the station, supposing all danger to be over, news was brought to Commissioner Davis and myself, who were standing together, that other troops were left at the President street station, and that the mob was tearing up the track on Pratt street. Mr. Davis immediately ran to summon a body of police to be sent to Pratt street, while I hastened alone down Pratt street, towards President street station. On arriving at the head of Smith's wharf I found that anchors had been piled on the track, so as to obstruct it, and Sergeant McComas, and a few policemen who were with him, were not allowed by the mob to remove the obstruction. I at once ordered the anchors to be removed, and my authority was not resisted. On approaching Pratt street bridge I saw several companies of Massachusetts troops, who had left the cars, moving in column rapidly towards me. An attack on them had begun, and the noise and excitement were great. I ran at once to the head of the column—some persons in the crowd shouting as I approached, "Here comes the Mayor." I shook hands with the officer in command, saying as I did so, "I am the Mayor of Baltimore." I then placed myself by his side and marched with him, as far as the head of Light street wharf, doing what I could by my presence and personal efforts to allay the tumult. The mob grew bolder, and the attack became more violent. Various persons were killed and wounded on both sides. The troops had sometime previously begun to fire in self defence; and the firing as the attack increased in violence, became more general.

At last when I found that my presence was of no use, either in preventing the contest or saving life, I left the head of the column, but immediately after I did so Marshal Kane, with about fifty policemen from the direction of the Camden station, rushed to the rear of the troops, forming a line across the street, and with drawn revolvers checking and keeping off the mob. The movement, which I saw myself, was perfectly successful, and gallantly performed. I submit herewith Marshal Kane's account of the affair, published on the 4th of May last, which substantially agrees with my own.

It is doing bare justice to say that the Board of Police, the Marshall of Police, and the men under his command, exerted themselves bravely, efficiently, skillfully and in good faith to preserve the peace and protect life. If proper notice had been given of the arrival of the troops, and of the number expected, the outbreak might have been prevented entirely, and but for the timely arrival of Marshal Kane with his force, as I have described, the bloodshed would have been great. The wounded among the troops received the best care and medical attention, at the expense of the city, and the bodies of the killed were carefully and respectfully returned to their friends. The facts which I witnessed myself, and all that I have since heard, satisfy me that the attack was the result of a sudden impulse, and not of a premeditated scheme.

But the effect on our citizens was, for a time, uncontrollable. In the intense excitement which ensued, which lasted for many days, and which was shared by men of all parties, and by our volunteer soldiers, as well as citizens, it would have been impossible to convey more troops from the North through the city without a severe fight and bloodshed. Such an occurrence would have been fatal to the city, and accordingly, to prevent it, the bridges on the Northern Central Railroad, and on the Philadelphia, Wilmington and Baltimore Railroad, were, with the consent of the Governor, and by my order, with the co-operation of the Board of Police, (except Mr. Chas. D. Hinks, who was absent from the city,) partially disabled and burned, so as to prevent the immediate approach of troops to the city, but with no purpose of hostility to the Federal Government. This act, with the motive which prompted it, has been reported by the Board of Police to the Legislature of the State, and approved by that body, and was also immediately communicated by me, in person, to the President of the United States and his Cabinet. I enclose a copy of the report made by the Board of Police to the Legislature on the third of May last. On the evening of the 19th of April, a portion of the military of the city were called out. On the 20th of April, your honorable body by a unanimous vote, placed at my disposal the sum of $500,000 for the defence of the city, and the banks, with great patriotism and unanimity, voluntarily offered to advance the money through a committee of their Presidents, consisting of Messrs. Columbus O'Donnel, Johns Hopkins, and John Clark, who notified me, in person, of the fact on the morning of the 20th of April at the Mayor's office. A number of citizens, in all the wards, volunteered for the purpose of defence, and were enrolled under the direction of the Board of Police; and for their use arms were partially provided. The Commander-in-Chief of the forces of the United States, with the approbation of the President, in view of the condition of affairs then existing in the city, on the earnest application of the Governor of the State, of prominent citizens and myself, ordered that thereafter the troops should not be brought through Baltimore, and they were accordingly transported to Washington by way of Annapolis.

But great danger existed to Baltimore from large bodies of unauthorized men at the North, who threatened to cut their way through the city, and visit upon it terrible vengeance for the acts of the 19th of April.

As soon as this danger had passed away, and the excitement among our own citizens had sufficiently subsided, the military were dismissed, and the citizens who enrolled were disbanded by order of the Board of Police. The peace of the city had been preserved, and its safety and the persons and property of men of all parties, protected under the circumstances of great peril, and the most intense excitement, and it was hoped that affairs would be allowed to return as nearly as possible to their previous condition. To this end my efforts, and those of the Board were devoted. Large bodies of troops from the North have ever since passed through the city without molestation, and every proper precaution to accomplish that object was taken by the Board of Police and carried out by the force.

But civil war had begun on the immediate border of our State. A great division of opinion in regard to it existed among the people, and the events which had occurred in the city, and their consequences, seems to have made an indelible impression on the minds of the authorities at Washington, that the police force of the city of Baltimore was prepared to engage in hostility against the General Government whenever an opportunity should occur.

The result has been very unfortunate. On the ground of military necessity, of the existence of which, and of the measures required of it, the Federal officers claim to be the sole judges, our city has been occupied by large bodies of troops in its central points; picket guards have been stationed along many of our streets; the arms provided by the city for its defense and those left by private individuals with the authorities for safe-keeping, the station-houses and other property of the city have been seized, operators in the Police and Fire Alarm Telegraph Office have been displaced and others substituted in their stead; the Marshal of Police and the Board of Police, with the exception of myself, have been arrested and are now imprisoned in Fort McHenry, one only, who is in bad health, has been released on his parole; the writ of *habeas corpus* has been suspended; the police force, established under a law of the State, has been set aside by superseding the only power which could lawfully control it; a new police, without authority of law, has been established under the control of a Marshal appointed by the commanding General, and all power to hold elections in the city has been for the present set aside by suspending the functions of the Board under which alone elections can lawfully be held.

The grounds taken by Major General Banks as a justification for these proceedings, and the position assumed by the Board of Police, respectively, will be found in the proclamations of the General and the protest of the Board, which I enclose.

The hidden deposits of arms and ammunition referred to in the proclamation of June 27th, are, I suppose, those found in the City Hall, in reference to which a few words of explanation may be made. The arms consisted in part of muskets, which belonged to the old police established under the administration of Mr. Swann; of revolvers procured for the police, and of some rifles, carbines, &c., lately procured in part for the use of the police and in part for the defense of the city. The Board of Police considered it proper that there should be a sufficient number of efficient weapons to arm the entire police force in case of an emergency. There were not enough in the City Hall for that purpose. An allegation has been made that some of the arms and ammunition belonged to the Massachusetts troops; but I am informed that this is not the case, except perhaps as to two muskets which were taken by the police from the hands of the mob. The ammunition at the Hall which was purchased for the defence of the city, was more than was entirely safe. Of this I was well aware, and should have ordered it to be removed if the city had had any proper place of deposit; but I apprehended that any attempt at removal at this time would only lead to a seizure on the part of the officers of the General

5

Government, and to unfounded rumors and suspicions; for all the rest of the arms and ammunition belonging to the city, and all the arms left with the city authorities for safe keeping, which were placed in depositories procured expressly for the purpose, and in no way concealed, had been previously seized by the authorities of the United States, under circumstances very mortifying to the pride of the people. That some of the arms and ammunition were concealed about the building, is sufficiently explained by the fact that the officers in charge desired to secure them from seizure, but such concealment was made without my knowledge.

The proclamation charges the existence of unlawful combinations of men organized for the resistance to the laws; for accumulating hidden deposits of arms, and encouraging contraband trade.

Although I am only ex-efficio member of the Board, and by reason of other engagements not able to be present at all their meetings, yet, from the free and full interchange of views among us, and the custom of the members to consult me on all important questions, and my knowledge of all their proceedings, I feel that I have a right to say, of my own personal knowledge, that the Board had no notice or information of any such combinations, if any such existed, which I have no reason to suspect.

Indeed, my experience of the fidelity of the Board, to its legal obligations during my whole official connection with it, and the common understanding between myself and my colleagues as to our course of duty since the present troubles began, justify me in saying that if any organization in this city for resistance to the laws could have been discovered by proper vigilance, they would have been found out and suppressed, to the extent of the powers conferred on the Board by law.

After the Board of Police had been superseded and its members arrested by the order of Gen. Banks, I proposed, in order to relieve the serious complication which had arisen, to proceed as the only member left free to act, to exercise the power of the Board as far as an individual member could do so. Marshal Kane, while he objected to the propriety of this course, was prepared to place his resignation in my hands whenever I should request it, and the majority of the Board interposed no objection to my pursuing such course as I might deem it right and proper to adopt in view of the existing circumstances, and upon my own responsibility, until the Board should be enabled to resume the exercise of its functions.

If this arrangement could have been effected, it would

have continued in the exercise of their duties the police force which is lawfully enrolled, and which has won the confidence and applause of all good citizens by its fidelity and impartiality at all times and under all circumstances. But the arrangement was not satisfactory to the Federal authorities.

As the men of the police force through no fault of theirs are now prevented from discharging their duty, their pay constitutes a legal claim on the city, from which, in my opinion, it cannot be relieved.

The new force which has been enrolled is in direct violation of the law of the State, and no money can be appropriated by the city for its support without incurring the heavy penalties provided by the Act of Assembly.

Officers in the Fire Alarm and Police Telegraph Department, who are appointed by the Mayor and City Council, and not by the Board of Police, have been discharged, and others have been substituted in their place.

I mention these facts with profound sorrow and with no purpose whatever of increasing the difficulties unfortunately existing in this city, but because it is your right to be acquainted with the true condition of affairs, and because I cannot help entertaining the hope that redress will yet be afforded by the authorities of the United States upon a proper representation made by you. I am entirely satisfied that the suspicion entertained of any meditated hostility on the part of the city authorities, against the General Government is wholly unfounded, and, with the best means of knowledge, express the confident belief and conviction that there is no organization of any kind among the people for such a purpose. I have no doubt that the officers of the United States have acted on information which they deemed reliable, obtained from our own citizens, some of whom may be deluded by their fears, while others are actuated by baser motives; but suspicions thus derived, can, in my judgment, form no sufficient justification for what I deem to be grave and alarming violations of the rights of individual citizens, of the city of Baltimore and of the State of Maryland.

Very respectfully,
GEO. WM. BROWN, Mayor

GEO. M. GILL'S STATEMENT TO THE MAYOR.

Baltimore, July 12, 1861,

To THE HON. GEO. WM. BROWN,

Mayor of the City of Baltimore:

In your communication to the City Council of yesterday, which I did not see until after it was communicated to the Council, you refer to the fact that I accompanied you on Friday, April 19th, to the Camden station. There were some additional circumstances which I deem it proper to state. You desired me to accompany you, hoping that I might aid in preventing any violence on that day, or interruption to the troops then about to pass through, in case any should be attempted. Your impression was that no such attempt would be made, but nevertheless you thought every precaution should be taken, in case of any such attempt to resist it. For the sole purpose of doing this I accompanied you.

After we reached the Camden Station there were manifestations of excitement among the crowd there assembled, and the Police Commissioners (excepting Mr. Hinks then absent from the City) gave directions to Marshal Kane, in my presence, to use his whole force in keeping order and protecting the troops from being interrupted. The reply of Marshal Kane then made was, that if he and his whole force lost their lives the troops should be protected.

After the first of the troops reached Camden Station a rush of people was made at the cars in which they then were, but the Police interfered and drove them off. A cry was then raised to tear up the track outside of the Camden Station, and a rush was made to accomplish this purpose, but the Police again interfered, and prevented this from being done.

I supposed for some time that all the troops would pass in safety, and such was my anxious wish, and to the extent of my ability I united in the effort to produce this result.

While I was at Camden Station the events on Pratt street took place, none of which did I see, and therefore cannot speak of them further than that I saw at a distance, and heard the firing of the troops as they passed up Pratt street.

My impression on that day was and still is, that the events arose from a sudden impulse which seized upon some of our people, and that after the firing commenced and blood was shed many persons took part, under an impression that the troops were killing our people, and without knowing the circumstances of provocation which induced the troops to fire.

Matters reached their height after Mr. Davis was killed, and the intense excitement resulting from this and other causes produced a state of feeling which for a time was beyond control on the part of the City authorities.

On Sunday, the 21st of April, whilst you were in Washington, where you had been summoned by the President, a regiment arrived from Pennsylvania, but were fortunately stopped at Cockeysville, about 14 miles off, by the disabled bridge at that point. Any rational man who witnesssed the condition of things in Baltimore on that day, can judge of the sad consequences which would have followed if the regiment had entered the City.

Yours very respectfully,

GEO. M. GILL.

Document [M.

BY THE HOUSE OF DELEGATES,

AUGUST 5th, 1861.

Read and 25,000 copies ordered to be printed.

By order M. Y. KIDD, *Chief Clerk.*

REPORT AND RESOLUTIONS

OF THE

JOINT COMMITTEE

OF THE

Senate and House of Delegates of Maryland,

UPON THE

REPORTS AND MEMORIALS OF THE POLICE COMMISSIONERS

AND THE

MAYOR AND CITY COUNCIL OF BALTIMORE.

———•———

ADOPTED IN THE HOUSE BY A VOTE OF 42 YEAS TO 7 NAYS,
AND IN THE SENATE BY A VOTE OF 12 YEAS TO 6 NAYS.

———•———

FREDERICK, MD.

E. S. RILEY PRINTER,

1861.

To the Honorable the President of the Senate
and the Speaker of the House of Delegates :

The Joint Committee on Federal Relations, to whom was referred the Report of the Police Board of Baltimore, enclosing a Memorial of Charles Howard, William H. Gatchell and John W. Davis, Esqs., members thereof, to the Congress of the United States, together with a communication from the Mayor of Baltimore, enclosing a Memorial of the Mayor and City Council of Baltimore to Congress, with accompanying documents ; respectfully ask leave to submit the following Report :

[Document A.]

BY THE SENATE,

APRIL 27, 1861.

Read and 5,000 copies ordered to be printed.

MESSAGE

OF THE

GOVERNOR OF MARYLAND

TO THE

GENERAL ASSEMBLY.

IN EXTRA SESSION, 1861.

· FREDERICK:

B. H. RICHARDSON, PRINTER.

1861.

MESSAGE OF THE GOVERNOR

TO THE

Legislature of Maryland.

State of Maryland, Executive Chamber, }
Annapolis, April 25th, 1861. }

Gentlemen of the Senate and House of Delegates:

The extraordinay condition of affairs in Maryland has induced me to exercise the constitutional prerogative vested in the Governor to summon the Legislature in special session, in the hope that your wisdom may enable you to devise prompt and effective means to restore peace and safety to our State.

I shall detail briefly the startling events which have induced me to summon you together, and which have so suddenly placed us in the state of anarchy, confusion and danger from which I sincerely trust you may be able to extricate us.

Believing it to be the design of the Administration to pass over our soil troops for the defence of the City of Washington, and fearing that the passage of such troops would excite our people and provoke collision, I labored earnestly to induce the President to forego his purpose. I waited upon him in person and urged the importance of my request. I subsequently communicated with him and his cabinet by special despatches, entreating an abandonment of their designs. To all my requests I could get but the reply: "that Washington was threatened with attack—that the government had resolved to defend it—that there was no other way of obtaining troops than by passing them over the soil of Maryland—and that the military necessity of the case rendered it impossible for the Government to abandon its plans, much as it desired to avoid the dangers of collision.'' My correspondence with the authorities at Washington is herewith submitted.

The consequences are known to you. On Friday last a detachment of troops from Massachusetts reached Baltimore, and was attacked by an irresponsible mob, and several persons on both sides were killed. The Mayor and Police Board gave to the Massachusetts soldiers all the protection they could afford; acting with the utmost promptness and bravery. But they were powerless to restrain the mob.

Being in Baltimore at the time, I co-operated with the Mayor, to the fullest extent of my power, in his efforts. The military of the city were ordered out to assist in the preservation of the peace. The railroad companies were requested by the Mayor and myself to transport no more troops to Baltimore city, and they promptly acceded to our request.

Hearing of the attack upon the soldiers, the War Department issued orders that no more troops should pass through Baltimore City, provided they were allowed to pass outside its limits. Subsequently, a detatchment of troops was ascertained to be encamped at or near Cockeysville, in Baltimore County. On being informed of this the War Department ordered them back.

Before leaving Baltimore, Col. Huger, who was in command of the U. S. Arsenal at Pikesville, informed me that he had resigned his commission. Being advised of the probability that the mob might attempt the destruction of this property, and thereby complicate our difficulties with the authorities at Washington, I ordered Col. Petherbridge to proceed, with sufficient force, and occupy the premises in the name of the United States Government; of which proceeding I immediately notified the War Department.

On Sunday morning last, I discovered that a detachment of troops, under command of Brig. Gen. B. F. Butler, had reached Annapolis in a steamer, and had taken possession of the practice ship Constitution, which, during that day, they succeeded in getting outside the harbor of Annapolis, where she now lies. After getting the ship off, the steamer laid outside our harbor, and was soon joined by another steamer, having on board the Seventh Regiment from New York City.

Brig. Gen. Butler addressed me, asking for permission to land his forces. It will be seen, from the correspondence herewith submitted, that I refused my consent. The Mayor of Annapolis also protested. But both steamers soon afterwards landed at the Naval Academy and put off the troops. Subsequently, other large bodies of troops reached here in transports and were landed. I was notified that the troops were to be marched to Washington. They desired to go without obstruction from our people ; but they had orders to go to Washington, and were determined to obey those orders. In furtherance of their designs, they took military possession of the Annapolis and Elk Ridge Railroad ; in regard to which act I forwarded to Brig. Gen. Butler the protest, and received the reply herewith submitted. On Wednesday morning the two detachments first landed took up the line of March for Washington. The people of Annapolis, though greatly exasperated, acting under counsel of the most prudent citizens, refrained from molesting or obstructing the passage of the troops through the city.

Seriously impressed with the condition of affairs, and anxious to avoid a repetition of events similar to those which had transpired in Baltimore, I deemed it my duty to make another appeal to the authorities at Washington. Accordingly, I sent a special messenger to Washington, with a despatch to the administration advising that no more troops be sent through Maryland ; that the troops at Annapolis be sent elsewhere ; and urging that a truce be offered with a view of a peaceful settlement of existing difficulties by mediation. I suggested that Lord Lyons, the British Minister, be requested to act as mediator between the contending parties. The result of the mission will be seen from the correspondence herewith submitted.

These events have satisfied me that the War Department has concluded to make Annapolis the point for landing troops, and has resolved to open and maintain communication between this place and Washington.

In the brief time allowed, it is impossible for me to go more into detail. The documents accompanying this message place before you all the information possessed by me. I shall promptly communicate such other information as may reach me.

Notwithstanding the fact that our most learned and intelligent citizens admit the right of the Government to transport its troops across our soil, it is evident that a portion of the people of Maryland are opposed to the exercise of the right. I have done all in my power to protect the citizens of Maryland and to preserve peace within our borders.

Lawless occurrences will be repeated, I fear, unless prompt action be taken by you.

It is my duty to advise you of my own convictions of the proper course to be pursued by Maryland in the emergency which is upon us. It is of no consequence now to discuss the causes which have induced our troubles. Let us look to our distressing present, and to our portentous future. The fate of Maryland, and perhaps of her sister Border Slave States, will undoubtedly be seriously affected by the action of your Honorable Body. Therefore should every good citizen bend all his energies to the task before us ; and therefore should the animosities and bickerings of the past be forgotten, and all strike hands in the holy cause of restoring peace to our beloved State and to our common country. I honestly and most earnestly entertain the conviction that the only safety of Maryland lies in preserving a neutral position between our brethren of the North and of the South. We have violated no rights of either section. We have been loyal to the Union. The unhappy contest between the two sections has not been fomented or encouraged by us, although we have suffered from it in the past. The impending war has not come by any act or any wish of ours. We have done all we could to avert it. We have hoped that Maryland, and the other Border Slave States, by their conservative position and love for the Union, might have acted as mediators between the extremes of both sections, and thus have prevented the terrible evils of a prolonged civil war. Entertaining these views, I cannot counsel Maryland to take sides against the General Government, until it shall commit outrages upon us which would justify us in resisting its authority. As a consequence, I can give no other counsel than that we shall array ourselves for Union and Peace, and thus preserve our soil from being polluted with the blood of brethren. Thus, if war must be between the North and the South, we may force the contending parties to transfer the field of battle from our soil, so that our lives and property may be secure. It seems to me that, independently of all other considerations, our geographical position forces us to this, unless we are willing to see our State the theatre of a long and bloody civil war, and the consequent utter destruction of every material interest of our people, to say nothing of the blood of brave men and innocent women and children which will cry out from our soil for vengeance upon us if we fail to do all that in us lies to avert the impending calamity.

The course I suggest has all the while been the sole groundwork of my policy. But for the excitement prevailing among our people during the past few days, I believe the object I have kept steadily in view during my administration would have been consummated. If it has failed, I have the full consciousness that, throughout the whole of my harass-ing and painful incumbency of the Gubernatorial Chair, I have labored honestly and faithfully for the peace, the safety, and the interests of Maryland, and of our common country. This consciousness has fully sustained me in all my troubles, and has enabled me to endure patiently all the cruel, unmer-ited, and heartless attacks that have been made upon my integrity.

I have also comfort in the conviction that my policy has been sustained by a large majority of the people, and noth-ing that has transpired since the recent lamentable occur-rences within our State has shaken that conviction. A momentary frantic excitement took the place of reason and good judgment, and men for the time threw aside all pru-dent thoughts of the future in the burning desire to avenge what they considered wrongs.

I submit my suggestions to your wisdom; and I appeal to you not only as devoted citizens of Maryland, but as hus-bands and fathers, to allow that prudence and christianlike temper, so honorable to all men, to guide your counsels; and I implore you not to be swayed by the passions which seem to be so fully aroused in our midst, to do what the gener-ations to come after us shall ever deplore.

In conclusion, gentlemen, I ask your indulgence if I have omitted to present to you any other matter of interest in connection with the important subject which you are sum-moned to consider. The short time I have had in which to prepare this communication, and the turmoil and excitement around me may have caused omissions; if so, they will be promptly supplied when indicated by you.

THOMAS H. HICKS.

[*Telegram to Mayor Brown.*]

ANNAPOLIS, April 21, 1861.

To the Mayor of Baltimore:

It is rumored here that men have been sent for from Baltimore to come here to prevent the landing of troops. Do not let them come. The troops will not land here.

TH. H. HICKS.

CORRESPONDENCE WITH BR. GEN. B. F. BUTLER.

STATE OF MARYLAND,
Executive Chamber, Annapolis, April 20, 1861.

To the Commander of the Volunteer Troops on Board the Steamer:

SIR:—I would most earnestly advise that you do not land your men at Annapolis. The excitement here is very great, and I think that you should take your men elsewhere. I have telegraphed to the Secretary of War, advising against your landing your men here.

Very respectfully,

Your obedient Servant,

TH. H. HICKS,
Governor of Maryland.

SEAL OF THE STATE OF MASSACHUSETTS.

OFF ANNAPOLIS, April 22d, 1861.

His Excellency Thos. H. Hicks, Governor of Maryland:

In reply to the communication from you on the 21st, I had the honor to inform you of the necessities of my command, which drew me into the harbor of Annapolis. My circumstances have not changed. To that communication I have received no reply. I cannot return, if I desire so to do, without being furnished with some necessary supplies, for all which the money will be paid. I desire of your Excellency an immediate reply, whether I have the permission of the State authorities of Maryland to land the men under my command, and of passing quickly through the State, on my way to Washington, respecting private property, and paying for what I receive, and outraging the rights of none—a duty which I am bound to do in obedience to the requisitions of the President of the United States?

I have received some copies of an informal correspondence between the Mayor of Baltimore and the President of the Baltimore and Ohio Railroad, and a copy of a note from your Excellency, enclosing the same to Capt. Blake, Commandant of the Naval School. These purport to show that instructions have been issued by the War Department as to the disposition of the United States militia, differing from what I had supposed to be my duty. If these instructions have been in fact issued, it would give me great pleasure to obey them.— Have I your Excellency's permission, in consideration of these exigencies of the case, to land my men—to supply their wants, and to relieve them from the extreme and unhealthy confinement of a transport vessel not fitted to receive them? To convince your Excellency of the good faith towards the authorities of the State of Maryland, with which I am acting, and I am armed only against the disturbers of her peace and of the United States, I enclose a copy of an order issued to my command before I had the honor of receiving the copy of your communication through Capt. Blake. I trust your Excellency will appreciate the necessities of my position, and give me an immediate reply, which I await with anxiety.

I would do myself the honor to have a personal interview with your Excellency, if you so desire. I beg leave to call your Excellency's attention to what I hope I may be pardoned for deeming an ill-advised designation of the men under my command. *They are not Northern troops—they are a part of the whole militia of the United States, obeying the call of the President.*

I have the honor of being your Excellency's obedient servant.

BENJ. F. BUTLER,
Brig. General in the Militia of the United States.

19

P. S.—It occurs to me that our landing on the grounds at
the Naval Academy would be entirely proper, and in accordance with your Excellency's wishes.   B. F. B.

SEAL OF THE STATE OF }
MASSACHUSETTS.   }

Special Brigade, Order No. 37.

HEADQUARTERS SECOND DIVISION MASS. VOL. MILITIA, }
On board steamer Maryland, off Annapolis, April 22d, 1861. }

Col. Munroe is charged with the execution of the following order:
At five o'clock A. M. the troops will be paraded by company and be
drilled in the manual of arms. Especially in loading at will, firing
by file, and in the use of the bayonet, and these specialties will be observed in all subsequent drills in the manual. Such drill to continue
until 7 o'clock, when all the arms will be stacked upon the upper
deck—great care being taken to instruct the men as to the mode of
stacking their arms, so that a firm stack, not easily overturned, shall
be made. Being obliged to drill at times with the weapons loaded,
great damage may be done by the overturning of the stack and the
discharge of the piece. This is important. Indeed, an accident has
already occurred in the regiment from this cause, and although slight
in its consequence, yet it warns us to increased diligence in this regard. The purpose which could only be hinted at in the orders of
yesterday has been accomplished. The frigate Constitution has lain
for a long time at this port substantially at the mercy of the armed
mob, which sometimes paralyzes the otherwise loyal State of Maryland. Deeds of daring, successful contests and glorious victories had
rendered "Old Ironsides" so conspicuous in the naval history of the
country, that she was fitly chosen as the school ship in which to train
the future officers of the navy to like heroic acts.

It was given to Massachusetts and Essex county first to man her;
it was reserved for Massachusetts to have the honor to retain her, for
the service of the Union and the laws.

This is a sufficient triumph of right, and a sufficient triumph for us.
By this the blood of our friends shed by the Baltimore mob is in so
far avenged. The Eighth Regiment may hereafter cheer lustily on all
proper occasions, but never without orders. The old Constitution, by

their efforts, aided untiringly by the United States officers having her in charge, is now safely "possessed, occupied and enjoyed" by the government of the United States, and is safe from all her foes.

We have been joined by the Seventh Regiment of New York, and together we propose peaceably, quickly and civilly, unless opposed by some mob, or other disorderly persons, to march to Washington, in obedience to the requisition of the President of the United States. If opposed we shall march steadily forward.

My next order I hardly know how to express. I cannot assume that any of the citizen soldiery of Massachusetts or New York could, under any circumstances whatever, commit any outrages upon private property in a loyal and friendly State. But fearing that some improper person may have by stealth introduced himself among us, I deem it proper to state, that any unauthorized interference with private property will be most signally punished, and full reparation therefore made to the injured party, to the full extent of my power and ability. In so doing I but carry out the orders of the War Department. I should have so done without those orders.

Col. Munroe will cause these orders to be read at the head of each company before we march.

Col. Leffert's command not having been originally included in this order, he will be furnished with a copy for his instruction.

By order of

B. F. BUTLER,
Brig. General.

{ Signed. }

WILLIAM H. CLEMENS,
Brig. Major.

STATE OF MARYLAND,
Executive Chamber, Annapolis, April 22, 1861. }

To Brig. Gen. B. F. Butler:

Sir—I am in receipt of your two communications of this date, informing me of your intention to land the men under your command at Annapolis, for the purpose of marching thence to the city of Washington. I content myself with protesting against this movement, which, in view of the excited condition of the people of this State, I cannot but consider an unwise step on the part of the Government. But I most earnestly urge upon you that there shall be no halt made by the troops in this city.

Very respectfully,

Your obedient servant,

TH. H. HICKS.

STATE OF MARYLAND,

Executive Chamber, Annapolis, April 23, 1861.

To Brig. Gen. B. F. Butler:

Sir: Having. in pursuance of the powers vested in me by the Constitution of Maryland, summoned the Legislature of the State to assemble on Friday, the 26th instant; and Annapolis being the place in which, according to law, it must assemble; and having been credibly informed that you have taken military possession of the Annapolis and Elk Ridge Railroad, I deem it my duty to protest against this step; because, without at present assigning any other reason, I am informed that such occupancy of said road will prevent the members of the Legi-lature from reaching this city.

Very respectfully, yours,

THOS. H. HICKS.

SEAL OF THE STATE OF
. MASSACHUSETTS.

HEADQUARTERS THIRD BRIGADE,
UNITED STATES MILITIA,
Annapolis, Md, April 23, 1861.

To His Excellency Thos. H. Hicks,

Governor of Maryland.

You are credibly informed that I have taken possession of the Annapolis and Elkridge Railroad. It might have escaped your notice, but at the official meeting between your Excellency and the Mayor of Annapolis, and the authorities of the government and myself, it was expressly stated as the reason why I should not land, that my troops could not pass the railroad, because the company had taken up the rails, and they were private property. It is difficult to see how it could be, that if my troops could not pass over the railroad one way, the members of the Legislature could pass the other way. I have taken possession for the purpose of preventing the carrying out of the threats of the mob, as officially represented to me by the Master of Transportation of this city, "that if my troops passed over the railroad, the railroad should be destroyed."

If the government of the State had taken possession of the railroad in any emergency, I should have long waited before I entered upon it. But, as I had the honor to inform your Excellency in regard to insurrection against the laws of Maryland, I am here armed to maintain those laws, if your Excellency desires, and the peace of the United States, against all disorderly persons whatever. I am endeavoring to save and not to destroy; to obtain means of transportation, so I can vacate the capital prior to the sitting of the Legislature, and not be under the painful necessity of occupying your beautiful city while the Legislature is in session.

I have the honor to be

Your Excellency's obedient servant,

BR. GEN. B. F. BUTLER.

HEADQUARTERS THIRD BRIGADE,
MASS. VOL. MILITIA,
Annapolis, Md., April 23, 1861.

To His Excellency Thos. H. Hicks,

Governor of the State of Maryland:

I did myself the honor, in my communication of yesterday, wherein I asked permission to land the portion of the militia of the United States under my command, to state that they were armed only against the disturbers of the peace of the State of Maryland and of the United States.

I have understood within the last hour that some apprehensions were entertained of an insurrection of the negro population of this neighborhood. I am anxious to convince all classes of persons that the forces under my command are not here in any way to interfere with or countenance any interference with the laws of the State. I am, therefore, ready to co-operate with your Excellency in suppressing most promptly and effectively any insurrection against the laws of Maryland.

I beg, therefore, that you announce publicly that any portion of the forces under my command is at your Excellency's disposal, to act immediately for the preservation and quietness of the peace of this community.

And I have the honor to be,

Your Excellency's obedient servant,

B. F. BUTLER,
General of Third Brigade.

STATE OF MARYLAND,
Executive Chamber, Annapolis, April 23, 1861.

To Brig. Gen. B. F. Butler:

Sir—I have the honor to acknowledge the receipt of your letter of this morning, tendering the force under your command to aid in suppressing a rumored insurrection of the slaves in this county.

I thank you most sincerely for the tender of your men; but I had, before the receipt of your letter, directed the Sheriff of the County to act in the matter; and am confident that the citizens of the county are fully able to suppress any insurrection of our slave population.

I have the honor to be,

Your obedient servant,

TH. H. HICKS.

COPY OF DISPATCHES FROM BRIG. GEN. BUTLER TO GOVERNOR CURTIN.

To His Excellency Andrew Curtin, Commander in Chief of the Forces of Pennsylvania:

Sir: Should this dispatch be forwarded to you, countersigned by His Excellency Thomas H. Hicks, Governor of Maryland, you will please to understand that the insurgents have surrendered Pikeville Arsenal, and that it, therefore, will not be necessary to advance your troops, as you were yesterday requested by me.

B. F. BUTLER,

Brigadier General.

Annapolis, April 24, 1861.

STATE OF MARYLAND,
Executive Chamber, Annapolis April 24th, 1861 }

To Brig. Gen. B. F. Butler:

Sir—A dispatch signed by you, addressed to Gov. A. Curtin, has been received by me, with a verbal request that I countersign it, and have it forwarded to its address.

In reference to the Arsenal at Pikeville, I have no official information. I do not know who is now in possession of it. I am cut off from all communication with other parts of the State; and have no means to forward your dispatch, if I were willing to countersign it.

I am compelled, therefore, to decline to accede to your request.

Very respectfully,

Your obedient servant,

TH. H. HICKS.

[Document B.]

BY THE SENATE,

Aprıl 27th, 1861.

Read and 3,000 copies ordered to be printed.

ADDRESS

TO THE

PEOPLE OF MARYLAND

BY THE

GENERAL ASSEMBLY,

IN EXTRA SESSION.

FREDERICK:

BEALE H. RICHARDSON, PRINTER.

1861.

TO THE PEOPLE OF MARYLAND.

Resolved, by the Senate and House of Delegates,

That the "extraordinary state of affairs" in Maryland and the Republic, justifies and demands that we should adopt and publish the following Address to the People of Maryland:

Under the Proclamation of your Governor, we have assembled to act, according to our best judgments, for the true interest of Maryland.

That Proclamation has declared the present to be "an extraordinary state of affairs;" and all must admit the correctness of that assertion. We have been convened to do all that we have the constitutional authority and the mental ability of accomplishing, to provide for your safety and welfare during the pendency of the present unfortunate and terrible crisis. At the commencement of our labors, we feel it to be our duty to you and to your General Assembly to solicit your confidence in the fidelity with which our responsibilities will be discharged. We are Marylanders, as you are. We have families, as you have. Our interests are identified with yours. Our duty, our wishes and our hopes will be to legislate for the true interests of all the people of our State.

We cannot but know that a large proportion of the citizens of Maryland have been induced to believe that there is a probability that our deliberations may result in the passage of some measure committing this State to secession. It is, therefore, our duty to declare that all such fears are without just foundation. We know that we have no constitutional authority to take such action. You need not fear that there is a possibility that we will do so.

If believed by us to be desired by you, we may, by legislation to that effect, give you the opportunity of deciding for yourselves, your own future destiny. We may go thus far, but certainly will not go farther.

We know that the present crisis has materially deranged the usual current of business operations in every department. We shall devote ourselves to the duty of making this change as little inconvenient as possible to our constituents. We invite their scrutiny to our every action. If results do not realise our hopes and anticipations, we ask that you will, at least, extend to us the charity of believing that the failure has occurred from lack of ability, but not of will.

JNO. B. BROOKE,	JAMES F. DASHIELL,
THOMAS J. McKAIG,	J. J. HECKART,
COLEMAN YELLOTT,	S. J. BRADLEY,
H. H. GOLDSBOROUGH,	TILGHMAN NUTTLE,
D. C. BLACKISTONE,	F. WHITAKER,
C. F. GOLDSBOROUGH,	OSCAR MILES,
JNO. E. SMITH,	WASHINGTON DUVALL,
ANTHONY KIMMEL,	TEAGLE TOWNSEND,
J. S. WATKINS,	ANDREW A. LYNCH.

[Document C.]

BY THE SENATE,

APRIL 27, 1861.

Read and ordered to be printed.

CORRESPONDENCE

BETWEEN THE

GOVERNOR OF MARYLAND

AND THE

SHERIFF OF FREDERICK COUNTY.

STATE OF MARYLAND,

EXECUTIVE CHAMBER,

FREDERICK CITY, April 27, 1861.

Gentlemen of the Senate :

I herewith transmit to your Honorable Body, a copy of a correspondence between this Department and the Sheriff of Frederick county.

The subject matter thereof, being an incident of the peculiar condition of affairs which you are assembled to consider, I respectfully submit it for your action.

THOMAS H. HICKS.

CORRESPONDENCE.

STATE OF MARYLAND,
EXECUTIVE CHAMBER,
FREDERICK CITY, April 26, 1861.

To the Sheriff of Frederick County:

SIR—I have received information to the effect that the Virginia troops, now stationed at or near Harper's Ferry, have seized upon and appropriated to their use some property belonging to a citizen of Maryland; said property being at the time of seizure within the limits of Maryland. I am also informed that you have official cognizance of the matter.

Will you do me the favor to furnish me, in writing, with such information as you possess in reference to said seizure.

Very respectfully, your obedient servant,

THOS. H. HICKS.

SHERIFF'S OFFICE,
FREDERICK, MD., April 27, 1861.

To His Excellency, the Governor of Maryland:

SIR—In reply to your inquiry of the 26th instant, I herewith give you a copy of the despatch, received by me, dated Point of Rocks, April 24th, 1861:

To the Sheriff of Frederick County:

My boat, loaded with grain, bound from Berlin to Georgetown, is detained at this point, by order of officers in command at Harper's Ferry. I demand your protection, and will hold the

State of Maryland responsible for said detention, and for all damages done said cargo. Answer.

C. F. WENNER.

To the Sheriff of Frederick County, and the State or Prosecuting Attorney.

I command you to protect my property, that is now being loaded in the cars to go to Harper's Ferry, against my wish or instructions, and I fall on my State for protection and damages. I demand your presence at this point. I will have my rights. The State is bound to give them to me.

Yours, in haste,

C. F. WENNER.

N. B.—There is about two hundred Virginia troops here; everything under their control, since they have taken my boat. It is truly warlike here, with clashing of swords.

They will have discharged by noon—feeding the troops with the oats. There are all troops here.

C. F. WENNER.

Mr. Wenner also called at my office in this city on the 25th instant, and stated the same as above detailed, and also stated that he gave some resistance, until the officers ordered the soldiers to fire, after a minute's notice; and that they refused to give him one of his mules to go home with. And while loading the grain on the cars, he insisted on the grain being weighed by the agent of the Baltimore and Ohio Railroad Company, that he might seek redress, which was denied him by the officers, who stated he might go to Harper's Ferry to see it weighed. He also stated that they took from him grain to feed near one hundred horses, without weighing or measuring; and that the bridge was then ready for destruction, having about six cords of wood and other combustible material thereto attached, to burn and blow up.

The above is all the information that has come to my knowledge respecting the matter.

Respectfully submitted,

MICHAEL H. HALLER.

[Document D.]

BY THE SENATE,
MAY 6th, 1861.
Read and 5,000 copies ordered to be printed.

REPORT

OF THE

COMMISSIONERS

APPOINTED TO WAIT ON THE

PRESIDENT OF THE UNITED STATES,

TO THE

GENERAL ASSEMBLY OF MARYLAND.

EXTRA SESSION, 1861.

FREDERICK:
BEALE H. RICHARDSON, PRINTER.
1861.

REPORT.

FREDERICK CITY, May 6th, 1861.

To the General Assembly of Maryland:

The undersigned, Commissioners, have the honor to report to the General Assembly of Maryland, that they waited in person on the President of the United States, on the 4th instant, and presented to him a copy of the joint resolutions adopted by your Honorable Bodies on the 2d instant.

They were received by the President with respectful courtesy, and they made such representations as were necessary to convey to him the sense of the General Assembly of Maryland in relation to the occupation of the Capital of the State by the Federal troops and the forcible seizure of the property of the State and of private citizens, in the Annapolis Railroad, and in the Washington Branch of the Baltimore and Ohio Railroad Company; and in this connection, his attention was called to the suspension of intercourse between Baltimore and Washington, and of all parts of the State with Annapolis, and to the indignity put upon a State still in the Federal Union by such an interference with the private rights of its citizens, and by such an occupation of its soil and ways of communication by the Federal Government.

Full explanations were exchanged between the undersigned and the Secretary of War and the Secretary of State, who were present, and participated in the discussion, as to the facts and circumstances that rendered necessary the extraordinary incidents accompanying the passage of Federal troops through Maryland, *en route* to the city of Washington, and especially in reference to those acts of the authorities of the city of Baltimore which arrested the progress of the troops by the railroads leading from Pennsylvania and Delaware into Maryland, and of the opposition to the landing of the troops subsequently at Annapolis by the Governor of the State; and in connection with this action of the authorities of the State, the hostile feeling manifested by the people to the passage of these troops through Maryland, was considered and treated with entire frankness by the undersigned, who, while acknowledging all the legal obligations of the State to the Federal Government, set forth fully the strength of sympathy felt by a large portion of our people for our Southren brethren in the present crisis.

Although many of the incidents and circumstances referred to were regarded in different lights by the undersigned and the Federal Government, even to the extent of a difference of opinion as to some of the facts involved, yet in regard to the general principles at issue, a concurrence of opinion was reached.

The President concurred with the undersigned in opinion, that so long as Maryland had not taken, and was not about taking a hostile attitude to the Federal Government, that the exclusive military occupation of her ways of communication, and the seizure of the property of her citizens, would be without justification, and what has been referred to in this connection so far as it occurred, was treated by the Government as an act of necessity or self-preservation.

The undersigned did not feel themselves authorized to enter into any engagements or arrangements with the Federal Government to induce it to change its relations to the State of Maryland, considering it proper under the circumstances to leave the entire discretion and responsibility of the existing state of things to that Government, making such representations as they deemed proper to vindicate the moral and legal aspects of the question; and especially insisting on its obligation to relieve the State promptly from restraint and indignity; and to abstain from all action in the transportation of troops that can be regarded as intended for chastisement or prompted by resentment.

The undersigned are not able to indicate to what extent or in what degree the Executive discretion will be exercised in modifying the relations which now exist between the State of Maryland and the Federal Government, and in the particular matter of the commercial communication between the city of Baltimore and other parts of the country, brought to the attention of the General Assembly by the Mayor and City Council of Baltimore; but they feel authorized to express the opinion that some modification may be expected. The undersigned feel painfully confident that a war is to be waged to reduce all the seceding States to allegiance to the United States Government, and that the whole military power of the Federal Government will be exerted to accomplish that purpose; and though the expression of this opinion is not called for by the resolutions of your Honorable Bodies, yet having had the opportunity to ascertain its entire accuracy, and because it will explain much of the military preparation and movement of troops through the State of Maryland, it is proper to bring it to your attention.

OTHO SCOTT,
ROBERT M. McLANE,
W. J. ROSS.

[Document E.]

BY THE SENATE,
MAY 14th, 1861.
Read and 5,000 copies ordered to be printed.

RESOLUTIONS

OF THE

COMMITTEE ON FEDERAL RELATIONS

OF THE

House of Delegates of Maryland,

WITH

SENATE AMENDMENTS.

EXTRA SESSION, 1861.

FREDERICK:
BEALE H. RICHARDSON, PRINTER,
1861.

HOUSE RESOLUTIONS.

WHEREAS, In the judgment of the General Assembly of Maryland, the war now waged by the Government of the United States upon the people of the Confederate States, is unconstitutional in its origin, purposes and conduct; repugnant to civilization and sound policy; subversive of the free principles upon which the Federal Union was founded, and certain to result in the hopeless and bloody overthrow of our existing institutions; and,

WHEREAS, The people of Maryland, while recognizing the obligation of their State, as a member of the Union, to submit in good faith to the exercise of all the legal and constitutional powers of the General Government, and to join as one man in fighting its authorized battles, do reverence, nevertheless, the great American principle of self-government, and sympathize deeply with their Southern brethren in their noble and manly determination to uphold and defend the same; and,

WHEREAS, Not merely on their own account and to turn away from their own soil the calamities of civil war, but for the blessed sake of humanity, and to avoid the wanton shedding of fraternal blood, in a miserable contest which can bring nothing with it but sorrow, shame and desolation, the people of Maryland are enlisted, with their whole hearts, on the side of reconciliation and peace: now, therefore, it is hereby

Resolved by the General Assembly of Maryland, That the State of Maryland owes it to her own self-respect and her respect for the Constitution, not less than to her deepest and most honorable sympathies, to register this, her solemn protest, against the war which the Federal Government has declared upon the Confederate States of the South, and our sister and neighbor Virginia, and to announce her resolute determination to have no part or lot, directly or indirectly, in its prosecution.

Resolved, That the State of Maryland earnestly and anxiously desires the restoration of peace between the belligerent sections of the country, and the President, authorities, and people of the Confederate States, having, over and over again, officially and unofficially, declared that they seek only peace and self-defence, and to be let alone, and that they are willing to throw down the sword, the instant that the sword now drawn against them shall be sheathed, the Senators and Delegates of Maryland do beseech and implore the President of the United States to accept the olive branch which is thus held out to him ; and in the name of God and humanity, to cease this unholy and most wretched and unprofitable strife, at least until the assembling of Congress in Washington shall have given time for the prevalence of cooler and better counsels.

Resolved, That the State of Maryland desires the peaceful and immediate recognition of the independence of the Confederate States, and hereby gives her cordial assent thereunto, as a member of the Union : entertaining the profound conviction that the willing return of the Southern people to their former Federal relations is a thing beyond hope, and that the attempt to coerce them will only add slaughter and hate to impossibility.

Resolved, That the present military occupation of Maryland, being for purposes, in the opinion of this Legislature, in flagrant violation of the Constitution, the General Assembly of the State, in the name of her people, does hereby protest against the same, and against the oppressive restrictions and illegalities with which it is attended; calling upon all good citizens, at the same time, in the most earnest and authoritative manner, to abstain from all violent and unlawful interference, of every sort, with the troops in transit through our territory, or quartered among us, and patiently and peacefully to leave to time and reason the ultimate and certain re-establishment and vindication of the right.

Resolved, That under existing circumstances, it is inexpedient to call a Sovereign Convention of the State at this time, or to take any measure for the immediate organization or arming of the militia.

SENATE AMENDMENTS.

And be it further Resolved, That a Committee be appointed to consist of four members of the Senate and four members of the House of Delegates, four of which Committee, (to be selected of themselves,) shall as early as possible, wait on the President of

the United States at Washington, and the other four of said
Committee shall wait on the President of the Southern Confederacy, for the purpose of laying the foregoing resolutions before
them ; and that said Committee be, and is hereby especially instructed to obtain, if possible, a general cessation of hostilities,
now impending, until the meeting of Congress in July next, in
order that said Body may, if possible, arrange for an adjustment
of existing troubles by means of negotiation, rather than the
sword.

Resolved, That said Committee consist of Messrs. Brooke,
Yellott, McKaig, and Lynch, of the Senate, and Messrs. ——,
——, —— and ——, of the House of Delegates.

Resolved, That said Committee be requested to report, if practicable, to the General Assembly, on the fifth day of June next.

[Document F.

BY THE SENATE,
JUNE 6th, 1861.
Read and 500 copies ordered to be printed.

REPORT

OF

THE COMMISSIONER

APPOINTED TO WAIT ON THE

GOVERNOR OF VIRGINIA,

TO THE

GENERAL ASSEMBLY OF MARYLAND.

EXTRA SESSION, 1861.

FREDERICK:
BEALE H. RICHARDSON, PRINTER.
1861.

REPORT OF COMMISSIONER HORSEY.

To the Honorable,

The General Assembly of Maryland:

The undersigned, appointed a Commissioner to the State of
Virginia, to enter into negotiations with the proper authorities
thereof, for the protection of the citizens of Maryland from injury
in person or property, by any unadvised acts of the military forces
of Virginia, and to obtain compensation for any injuries already
done, begs leave to report to your Honorable Body—

That, in the accomplishment of his mission, he proceeded at
once to Richmond, and received from Governor Letcher the most
distinct disavowal of the acts of the military, in molesting our
citizens, and seizing and holding their property, accompanied by
expressions of deep regret for any such acts of lawlessness, and
of earnest desire to maintain the most harmonious relations with
the citizens of our State. He expressed a readiness to make the
most liberal compensation for any injuries committed.

A gentleman was appointed to return with your Commissioner,
and institute inquiries into the nature and extent of any injuries
incurred by citizens of Maryland.

On their return to Maryland, they made a legal investigation
of the seizure of the boat and grain of C. F. Wenner, which, he
is happy to state, resulted in the satisfactory adjustment of the
claim of Mr. Wenner, whose receipt upon his petition to the
Executive, accompanies this report. The case of Mr. Wenner
was the only one of which the undersigned was apprised at the
time, and he believes it is the only instance of the interruption of
the Canal.

On his return to Maryland, your Commissioner received from
the Clerk of the Honorable House of Delegates the memorial of
certain citizens of Montgomery county, and the letter of Mr.
Biggs, of Washington county, with instructions to obtain accurate information in regard to the subjects thereof, and report the

same to that Honorable Body, with the result of any negotiations relating thereto with the authorities of Virginia.

Your Commissioner visited at once Montgomery county, and some of the petitioners, and ascertained that the apprehensions of molestation from the troops of Virginia were entirely groundless. He was informed by Mr. Darby, one of the petitioners, a respectable citizen, and owner of a large and important mill on Seneca Creek, near the Canal, that the petition had grown out of what they then considered well founded apprehensions of his neighbors, of injury to his mill property, in the continued security and operation of which they were all interested, arising from the fact of his supplying the Government with flour; but that he was now satisfied their apprehensions had been groundless, and his trade on the Canal, and his other branches of business, had not been threatened or molested by the troops of Virginia.

The undersigned made as thorough an examination of the condition of things on the Maryland mountain, opposite Harper's Ferry, as the pressure of circumstances, and the almost inaccessible nature of its approaches, would admit of.

Its top was occupied by four or five hundred Virginia troops, who had cut down four or five acres of the indifferent timber which clothes its summit, for the apparent purpose of constructing huts for their temporary shelter; and about the same space of land had been burnt over by the accidental contact of the dried leaves with their camp fires, as your Commissioner supposes.

That as soon as he had investigated all the complaints he returned to Richmond, and reached there on Wednesday, the 29th ultimo, when the authorities were engaged with the pressing duties arising from their reception of the President and Government of the Confederate States of America. That, on the evening of the 30th, he had a short interview with Governor Letcher, and brought to his notice the object of his mission, and the specific acts of aggression complained of, in the entrance upon our soil of the troops of Virginia.

The Governor was understood to say.that he would apply to the commanding officer at Harper's Ferry for information on the subject, and be prepared to reply more fully when the report of that officer was received; but he begged me to convey to your Honorable Body the distinct and earnest assurance, that if, at any time, the military forces of Virginia should trespass or temporarily occupy the soil of Maryland, it could only be justified by the pressing exigency of a military necessity, in defence and protection of her own soil from threatened or actual invasion, and certainly with no hostile intent towards the citizens of the State of Maryland, and that any and all damages to persons or property, consequent upon such occupation, should be fully and liberally compensated for.

Your Commissioner left with the Governor, at his request, a copy of the resolutions aforesaid, and the letter of Mr. Biggs, and regrets that the distracted state of the country, and the uncertainty of communication, compelled him to leave Richmond on Saturday morning, in order to be present at the assembling of your Honorable Body, and before he had received a definitive reply from the Governor of Virginia. That, as soon as he receives any further communication from him, he will make a further report to your Honorable Body.

Your Commissioner may be permitted to remark, that the people of the western counties of the State, and adjacent to the Canal, are much interested in preserving from molestation the trade along its line of navigation, and he has been particularly solicitous in removing all obstacles which threatened it. While the bed of the Canal is on the soil of Maryland, the dams which furnish it with water are dependant on the protection of the Virginia authorities; and while they have, as yet, manifested no disposition to withdraw their guardianship, and leave them liable to the depredations of malignant persons, your Commissioner has deemed it his duty to guard against, as far as possible, such a contingency, and he indulges in a well founded confidence that, the material interests of this great State work will not be seriously jeopardized.

O. HORSEY.

PETITION OF CHARLES F. WENNER.

To His Excellency, the Governor of Maryland:

The undersigned respectfully represents that he is a citizen of Frederick county, in the State of Maryland, resident at Berlin, on the line of the Chesapeake and Ohio Canal, and engaged in the business of forwarding grain and other produce over said canal to the terminus thereof at Georgetown, in the District of Columbia—that for the prosecution of said business, he owns two canal boats, to each of which are attached three hands for the management of the boats, and four mules, and has a warehouse for the storage of grain purchased by him or left with him on commission at Berlin; that on the 22d day of April, instant, he he had a boat loaded with grain on its way to Georgetown, and he left his home and went to Georgetown for the purpose of disposing of the cargo, and inquiring into prices of grain at that market, in order to determine on the time when he should ship the grain then in his warehouse; that being advised by his commission merchant at Georgetown that prices were high and rising, he on the same day of his arrival, (Tuesday, the 23rd inst.,) started for home, and riding all night on horseback, reached his home, at a distance of fifty-five miles from Georgetown, about sunrise on Wednesday morning, the 24th instant; that he immediately caused his boat, then at Berlin, to be loaded with the grain then in his warehouse, using great exertions to have it loaded as quickly as possible, in order to avoid probable detention on account of the water, which was being let out of certain portions of the canal for repairs; and that about 12 o'clock, M., on Wednesday, the 24th day of April, his said boat was loaded, and he was about to dispatch her to Georgetown, when a detachment of military rode up to him and demanded that said boat and cargo should be delivered up to them; that the officer in command of said squad, or detachment, announced that he acted under the order of the commander of the military force of the State of Virginia, then stationed at Harper's Ferry; that the undersigned immediately protested against the act, claimed that he was a citizen of

Maryland, and in no way amenable to the authorities of Virginia, and refused to surrender his property, then in Maryland, to any authority of Virginia, but stated that he was always ready to obey the authorities of his own State of Maryland; that the officer in command stated that the commander at Harper's Ferry was in correspondence with your Excellency, and he believed had authority from your Excellency for the seizure then being made; that the undersigned, refusing to surrender his property unless the orders of your Excellency were inspected by him, a soldier was dispatched to Harper's Ferry to procure said orders, and, in the meantime, the boat and cargo were taken possession of; and on the representation of the undersigned, that if said boat and cargo were detained until the arrival of said messenger, that the water would be so much lowered that he would not be able to proceed to Georgetown, in case the order of your Excellency, authorizing said seizure, should not be produced, the officer in command determined that the undersigned should conduct said boat to the Point of Rocks, a distance of six miles, guarded by his detachment of men, and should there await the return of said messenger. During the evening the messenger returned without any orders of your Excellency, but accompanied and followed during the night by three several additional detachments, numbering in all, over eighty men, and the whole force, under the command of Colonel Baylor, of the Virginia forces, took forcible possession of the mules, boat and grain, in defiance of the protest of the undersigned, and with the repeated threats to shoot him, unloaded the grain, sent part of it over the bridge at Point of Rocks into Virginia, and other portions of it had been transferred to cars on the Baltimore and Ohio Railroad, and taken to Harper's Ferry. All the grain in the boat was appropriated by the military, and the boat, mules and hands were left in their hands, when the undersigned came to Frederick to seek redress; and on his return, found that the hands with said boat had been permitted by the military to return with the boat and mules to Berlin.

The cargo of said boat, seized by said military and appropriated to its own use, consisted of two thousand bushels of oats, of which the selling price at Georgetown, on the 26th day of April, the day on which said boat would have arrived, and said cargo been ready for sale, was seventy-five cents per bushel; two hundred bushels of white corn, of which the selling price on said day was $1.20 per bushel; six hundred bushels of yellow corn, of which the price as aforesaid was $1.05 per bushel; and twenty-five bushels of wheat, of which the price as aforesaid, was $1.75 per bushel. From that time to the present, said boat, with team and hands, has been unused, wholly because the undersigned has feared similar seizures. The average earnings of said boat and team has been about $10 per day, which has been lost entirely to the undersigned.

Your Excellency will understand that all the occurrences aforesaid, were on the soil of Maryland. The undersigned respectfully appeals to the constituted authorities of the State, of which he is a citizen, for indemnity and vindication, on account of the outrage which has been perpetrated upon him, and has the honor to be,

Your Excellency's humble servant,

CHARLES F. WENNER.

State of Maryland,

    Frederick County, to wit:

I hereby certify, that on this 30th day of April, 1861, before the subscriber, a Justice of the Peace of the State of Maryland, in and for Frederick county, personally appeared Chas. F. Wenner, and made oath on the Holy Evangely of Almighty God, that the matters, facts and things in the aforegoing memorial contained, are true as stated.

W. MAHONY.

Received, June 4th, 1861, of O. Horsey, Esq., Commissioner of the State of Maryland to the State of Virginia, one thousand six hundred and ninety-three dollars and seventy-five cents, ($1,693.75,) the amount allowed by the State of Virginia, in satisfaction of the within claim, and which I hereby receive in full satisfaction and discharge of said within stated claim.

CHARLES F. WENNER.

[Document G.

BY THE SENATE,
JUNE 6th, 1861.

Read and 500 copies ordered to be printed.

MESSAGE

OF THE

GOVERNOR

IN RELATION TO HIS

Disarming the State Military,

IN RESPONSE TO AN ORDER OF THE

SENATE OF MARYLAND.

EXTRA SESSION, 1861.

FREDERICK:

BEALE H. RICHARDSON, PRINTER.

1861.

MESSAGE OF THE
GOVERNOR OF MARYLAND,

IN RESPONSE TO THE ORDER OF THE SENATE OF JUNE 5, 1861, IN RELA-
TION TO HIS DISARMING OF THE STATE MILITARY.

STATE OF MARYLAND,
EXECUTIVE CHAMBER,
FREDERICK CITY, June 5, 1861,

Gentlemen of the Senate:

In response to your order of this date, asking me "to furnish the Senate, at my earliest convenience, with a statement of the facts which induced me to reclaim the arms formerly confided to certain military companies of Baltimore city; also, with the reasons why said arms were sent, by my order, to Fort McHenry; and, also, what security I have for the restoration of said arms, when demanded by the proper authorities of Maryland," I have to say—

That, although I cannot acknowledge any right on the part of the Senate to make such inquiries, yet it gives me pleasure to respond to them, inasmuch as I desire the people of the State to be acquainted with the motives of all my official actions, and had, therefore, determined to give the public the reasons for my action in the premises.

I issued orders for reclaiming the arms referred to, because I had become satisfied that many of them had been carried beyond the limits of the State of Maryland, for disloyal purposes, whereby our citizens, the loyal as well as the disloyal, have become obnoxious to the charge of aiding and abetting those persons who are now in rebellion against the United States Government; and whereby, also, the State, in addition to a pecuniary loss, has been deprived of the protection designed to her citizens by the purchase of said arms. Having good reason to believe that more of said arms would be carried off for a like purpose, unless they were promptly secured, I ordered them to be reclaimed, thinking it to be my duty to do so, for the protection of the interests of the State.

I have ordered the arms to be deposited at Fort McHenry, as a place of security, because other arms belonging to the State had previously been stolen from the depository selected in Baltimore city; and I did not deem it prudent to again incur a similar risk.

The security I have "for the restoration of said arms, when demanded by the proper authorities of Maryland," lies in the honor of the United States Government, and of its loyal officers. I should have deemed it absurd and insulting to have required any other security.

THOS. H. HICKS.

[Document H.]

BY THE SENATE,
. JUNE 11, 1861.
Read, and 1,000 copies ordered to be printed.
By order,   WILLIAM KILGOUR, *Secretary.*

REPORT

OF THE

Committee on Federal Relations,

WITH THE REPORT OF THE

𝕻𝖊𝖆𝖈𝖊 𝕮𝖔𝖒𝖒𝖎𝖘𝖘𝖎𝖔𝖓𝖊𝖗𝖘

APPOINTED TO WAIT ON

PRESIDENTS LINCOLN AND DAVIS

BY THE

GENERAL ASSEMBLY.

FREDERICK:
BEALE H. RICHARDSON, PRINTER.
1861.

REPORT

OF THE

COMMITTEE ON FEDERAL RELATIONS.

To the Honorable,

The Speaker of the House of Delegates:

The Committee on Federal Relations, to whom were referred the Message and Correspondence of the Governor, the Bill calling a Sovereign Convention, &c., &c., ask leave respectfully to report as follows:

The Message of His Excellency, the Governor, demands the consideration of the Legislature, from two points of view—first, in regard to the state of public affairs which it discloses; and, secondly, as to the remedy which it suggests to the people of the State for the perilous contingencies which surround them.

So far as we can ascertain the views of the Governor, from the brief presentation of them, which the haste of our meeting had, as he states, permitted him to make, it appears that he regards the circumstances which have transpired since the attack upon the Massachusetts regiment, in Baltimore, on the 19th of April, as constituting all the facts to which it is necessary your attention should be drawn. Your Committee, of course, recognize the propriety of avoiding at this moment all unnecessary recurrence to discussions which have already been far overstepped by the rapid progress of events; but they find it, at the same time, quite impossible to do justice to the questions before them, without a frank and explicit reference to at least a portion of the public events which had preceded and were so closely connected with the occurrences alluded to.

The President of the United States, by his Proclamation of the 15th of April, had called upon a portion of the States to place at his disposal a body of militia, to the number of seventy-five thousand men. The Proclamation was directed against the people of the newly-formed Southern Confederacy, and its purposes and policy were obvious, although its terms were technically shaped in conformity with the Act of Congress of 1795. It recited, with formal precision, in the language of the Act, "that the laws of the United States were opposed, and the execution thereof was obstructed," in the seven seceded States, "by combinations too powerful to be suppressed by the ordinary course of judicial proceedings, or by the powers vested in the Marshals," and it called forth the militia of the other States, in the further language of the statute, "to suppress such combinations, and to cause the laws to be duly executed." In pursuance of another section of the law, it then commanded "the insurgents to disperse and retire peaceably to their respective abodes" within twenty days. If there is any proposition clear beyond dispute, it must be, that if the occasion which authorises the President to call out the militia, under the Act of 1795, existed at all, it was declared, by the explicit terms of the Proclamation, to exist only in the States of the Southern Confederacy, which were therein enumerated. It is equally indisputable, as matter of law, that the militia, if called out lawfully at all, were lawfully empowered to execute the laws and suppress unlawful combinations in the seven States named, and in none other. Such a conclusion of law is not only obvious and unavoidable, as matter of construction, but equally to be insisted upon as matter of principle and self-protection on the part of the people; for the exercise of the military power, in a free government, is never to be permitted, except within the limits and under the severest restrictions and checks of the law. If a President of the United States, under the fraudulent pretence of suppressing unlawful combinations in Louisiana and Florida, could be permitted to call out troops, to be used for any purpose in Maryland or Virginia, no soil of any State would be free from invasion, and no right of the citizen anywhere would be secure against overthrow.

It was not, however, because of any apprehension that the militia which were called out by the President would be used in other than the designated quarters, that the Proclamation created an intense and immediate excitement in the Southern and Border Slave States. On the contrary, it was the very purpose announced by Mr. Lincoln which kindled so intense a flame of resentment and resistance. His Proclamation was regarded as a declaration of war against the Southern Confederacy—as a deliberate summons to the people of the two sections, into which his party and its principles had so hopelessly divided the land, to shed each other's blood, in wantonness and hate. A scheme so full of wickedness—so utterly subversive of every principle upon which our government was founded, and so sure to involve the destruction of that government, let the fortune of war be what it might—could not but excite almost to frenzy every feeling of those who sympathized with the people against whom it was fulminated. Independently, too, of its wantonness and inhumanity, it was felt and known to be a gross violation of the Constitution, and without color of lawful authority. The people of the seceded States, whether constitutionally or unconstitutionally, had separated themselves from this government, and established a federal government of their own, with all the forms of a constitution, and all the substantial attributes of actual independence. Through their constituted authorities and in their collective capacity, as communities, they had withdrawn themselves from the Union—repudiated its laws and excluded its officers, of all sorts, from the exercise of all functions and jurisdiction. The United States Government no longer had among them either courts to issue, or marshals to execute process. They had substituted their own courts and their own processes, to which they yielded cheerful obedience. The authority of the Federal Government was in fact dead within their limits. They were in an attitude towards it, not only of independence, but of forcible resistance, for they had repelled the assertion of its authority over any portion of their soil, and had subdued for their own protection, one of its fortifications within their borders. The Confederate Government and that of the United States were, in fine, belligerents, engaged in actual, though undeclared war, and with all the rights and responsibilities which it gives and entails. This last is none the less true, because of their being engaged in civil war, for that is like any other war, when waged among civilized people. Vattel defines the relations which exist in such cases in terms too clear to be misunderstood, and too well recognized to be disputed.

"A civil war," he says, "breaks the bands of society and government, or at least suspends their force and effect. It produces in the nation two independent parties, who consider each other as enemies, and acknowledge no common judge. These two parties, therefore, must necessarily be considered as thenceforward constituting, at least for a time, two separate bodies, two distinct societies. Though one of the parties may have been to blame in breaking the unity of the State and resisting the lawful authority, they are not the less divided in fact. Besides, who shall judge them? Who shall pronounce on which side the right or the wrong lies? On earth they have no common superior. They stand, therefore, in precisely the same predicament as two nations, who engage in a contest, and being unable to come to an agreement, have recourse to arms." (Vattel, Book 3, ch. 18, sec. 293.) To attempt to apply, under such circumstances, to a belligerent people, an Act of Congress, which was meant as a domestic remedy, in aid of civil process and to secure obedience to the laws under judicial proceeding—in States still recognizing the authority of the Union and the jurisdiction of its tribunals—was to trifle with the understandings of educated men. To issue a proclamation to three millions of free Americans, composing seven powerful States, and asserting the sacred and indfeasible right of self-government, with arms in their hands, and "command" them as "insurgents" to "retire peaceably to their respective abodes," like a mob at a street corner, was an absurdity too gross to be here respectfully discussed. No government would venture to palm such an imposition upon a people, except in the well-assured confidence of absolute power. Nay, in the passionate excitement of the moment, the President forgot even the suggestions of political decorum, and did not hesitate to transgress all possible constitutional limits, and confess a purpose of animosity and revenge, by distinctly calling on the people, whom he summoned to the field, "to redress wrongs already long enough endured." The Proclamation, therefore, meant war, and nothing but war. It could signify nothing else, and to attempt to cloak its meaning and purpose under the flimsy pretext of "executing the laws," and "suppressing unlawful combinations," was but to cover up a flagrant usurpation with words.

Neither the Constitution nor the laws of the United States can be tortured into conferring the war-making power upon the President in any contingency. Where foreign nations are concerned, the plain language of the fundamental law entrusts it to Congress only. As against the States of the Union, the possibility of such a thing is not even contemplated, much less provided for. Like parricide at Athens, it was held too heinous and impossible to be named, even for the purpose of punishment. As early as the fifth day after the meeting of the Convention for the formation of the Federal Constitution, "the use of force against a State," by the rest of the Union, as contemplated in the plan of Mr. Randolph, was denounced by Mr. Madison, and on his motion the resolution providing for it was indefinitely postponed by unanimous assent. Mr. Madison announced it as his deliberate opinion that "a union of the States, containing such an ingredient, seemed to provide for its own destruction." From that day forward such an idea ceased to be a part of the theory of those by whom the Constitution was framed. When Gen. Hamilton was called to express his opinion upon it, he asked, "How can this force be exerted on the States collectively? It is impossible; it amounts to a war upon the parties. Foreign powers, also, will not be idle spectators. They will interpose; the confusion will increase, and a dissolution of the Union will ensue." The reasoning was unanswerable, and the Constitution happily was not stained with the perilous folly, against which these two great statesmen so earnestly protested. There was not a discussion in the debates on the Federal Constitution, whether in the Convention which framed it or the State Conventions which adopted it, that does not confirm this view of its spirit and purpose. The essays of the Federalist are pregnant with demonstrations to the same effect, and there is no constitutional lawyer who does not know, that the whole theory of the Government is to act, through the courts, upon individuals, and not through the Army and Navy upon the States. The brave and wise men who framed and upheld it, would have died in the breach before they would have submitted themselves to it upon any other basis. It could never have been adopted, it would never have been ratified, upon any other understanding. The States would have endured anarchy, distracted counsels, and all the evils of the old Confederation, aggravated tenfold, before they would have surrendered themselves to any system in which the Federal Government, and least of all, the Federal Executive, was clothed with the constitutional power of coercing them by force of arms. They entered into a constitutional Union, depending for its permanence upon the good faith and good feeling of its members, and deriving its strength from their consent only. They did not abandon themselves to the bayonets of a military despotism enthroned upon popular majorities.

But, illegal and unconstitutional as was the war which the Proclamation summoned one section of the country to wage against the other, the causes and purposes of that war made it chiefly obnoxious to the people of Maryland and of the Slave States of the Border. It was a war of propagandism and of sectional aggression and domination. It was a war of the North upon the South. It was a war in which the dominant section had seized upon the name and flag, and resources and powers, of the General Government, and was abusing them for its own ends, and for the permanent establishment of its dominion over the other section. It was a war, to the unholy purposes of which the sacred associations and memories of the Union were prostituted, and in which its honored name was taken in vain. It was a war waged against a people of our own name and blood, who sought peace and kindly relations with us, and who asked only to be let alone and to be permitted to govern themselves. It could bring no good, for it could end only in the defeat of the invaders or the subjugation of the invaded, and in either case the Union, which our fathers left to us, must be at an end. Subjugated provinces could not be sister States, and a Federal Government, professedly Republican, maintaining its authority by armies, could not be other than the worst and most unprincipled and uncontrollable of despotisms. The South had entrenched itself upon the principle of self-government. It had offered to negotiate, peaceably and honorably, upon all matters of common property and divided interest, claiming only that three millions of people had a right to throw off a Government, by which they no longer desired to be ruled, and to live under another Government of their own choosing. Unless the American Revolution was a crime, the Declaration of American Independence a falsehood,

and every patriot and hero of 1776 a traitor, the South was right and
the North was wrong, upon that issue. The people of Maryland,
therefore, could have but one choice in such a contest, and while
as devoted to the Union and as loyal to the Constitution as the
people of any of the thirteen States, who had formed the one
and pledged themselves to the other, they could not but throw
the whole weight of their sympathies upon that side to which
common interests and institutions inclined them, and with which
they felt that the right and the truth were. Nor was it a matter
of sympathy merely. The breach of the Constitution involved in
the coercive policy of the Administration, was a breach of their
rights, and not less than unlawful aggression upon the rights of
the Southern people. It was an overthrow of the principles of
free government, and could end in nothing but an ignominious
annihilation of the noble institutions of the Republic. The people of Maryland were summoned to take part, as soldiers, in the
strife, and as citizens they were asked to contribute their means
to its prosecution, and were to bear their share of its unconstitutional burdens; their stake in the struggle, therefore, was one of
political and individual self-preservation. They were bound by
every principle and pressed forward by every impulse of right and
self-respect, to make every protest against the wrong to their
brethren, and the oppression to themselves, which their situation
and circumstances would permit. To the requisition upon them
for troops, to take part upon the side of the Government in such
strife, their answer, if they could have given it with their own
voice, would have been an instant and indignant refusal.

It is deeply to be regretted that the respone of his Excellency,
the Governor, should have fallen so far short, in this regard, of the
manly and patriotic spirit with which the Governors of Virginia
and North Carolina, Tennessee, Kentucky and Missouri, threw
back the insulting proposition of the Administration. Indeed,
the Committee are unable to determine, from the correspondence
with which the Governor has furnished the Legislature, whether
His Excellency does not still contemplate complying with the
requisition as made. His letter of April 20th, to the Secretary of
War, is the only one which gives a key to his intentions, and in
that he merely announces that he thinks it "prudent to decline
(for the present")—not because of the illegality and wickedness
of the demand, and the disgrace which the State would incur
from acceding to it—but on account of the then alleged disorderly
condition of the militia themselves. Your Committee are not
prepared to admit the accuracy of the statement made by the Gov-
nor in the letter referred to, to the effect that "the principal part
of the organized military forces" of Baltimore took part with the
"disorderly element" in the affair of the 19th of April. On the
contrary, they have every assurance and every reason to believe
that the organized military of Baltimore, under the direction of
the constituted authorities, and in implicit obedience to their

orders, did all that could have been expected from brave men and good citizens to preserve the public tranquility. But whether the hasty statement of the Executive be well or ill-founded in that particular, the determination of the State of Maryland, upon the question of furnishing her quota of militia to make war upon the Southern States, ought not, in the opinion of your Committee, to rest a moment longer upon any such collateral and accidental issue. It becomes the self respect of the State that she should speak out openly and decidedly upon the point, and the question should no longer be left dependent upon what may be hereafter regarded as "prudent" by the Executive. For this purpose, your Committee have prepared and reported a resolution, which is appended to this report, and the adoption of which they respectfully recommend.

It is but justice to the Executive of the State to observe, in this connection, that His Excellency appears to have been misled, in his action upon the requisition of the United States Government, by the two letters of the Secretary of War, dated April 17, in which that gentleman informs him that "the troops to be raised in Maryland will be needed for the defence of the Capital and of the public property in that State and neighborhood." "There is no intention," the Secretary adds, "of removing them beyond these points." In conformity with this information, the Proclamation of the Governor—of which he has not furnished a copy to the General Assembly, but which is matter of public notoriety—informs his fellow-citizens to the same effect, and holds out the idea that troops from this State may be furnished for the purposes indicated. Your Committee would be happy to persuade themselves that in suggesting the possibility of its being "prudent," at any time, for the Maryland quota to be furnished to the Government, His Excellency could only have contemplated their employment, in any contingency, for the limited purposes in question. But it does not become the House of Delegates to allow themselves to be deceived by any such intimations from the Government, as those which imposed upon the Governor. The Proclamation of Mr. Lincoln, under which the troops of Maryland have been called into the field, is directed (as has already been observed) against the seceded States, and none other. The militia were summoned to execute the laws and suppress unlawful combinations in South Carolina, Georgia, Florida, Alabama, Mississippi, Louisiana and Texas, and not in Maryland or the District of Columbia. The very requisition of the Secretary of War upon the Governor is in direct and absolute contradiction to the assurance contained in his letter. The one asks for troops to be used in the South, and not at the Federal Capital; the other declares that their employment, at the Federal Capital and not in the South, is the only purpose contemplated.

One of two things, therefore, is perfectly clear. Either the Government had called out troops under the pretence of needing

10

them for one purpose, while intending to use them for another, or it contemplated employing a portion of them at Washington, as a guard and a reserve, but in aid, at the same time, of its offensive movements to the south of the Potomac. In the one case, it can have no claim upon our confidence; in the other, we should be false to ourselves and to free institutions, if we were to hesitate about refusing it our co-operation. Whatever destiny the people of Maryland may be able or willing to shape for themselves, now or hereafter, the Committee would be pained to believe it possible, that a single citizen of the State could be forced or persuaded to take part, directly or indirectly, in the slaughter and subjugation of our Southern brethren and the overthrow of Constitutional Government by usurpation and brute force. If the Government desires to put an end to all doubts as to the safety of the Capital, it can do so at a word, by putting an end to its own purposes of coercing the South.

What the Committee have already suggested in regard to the character and purposes of the conflict, which Mr. Lincoln has inaugurated, under the pretence of enforcing the laws, is so manifestly and indisputably corroborated by his course since the Legislature was convoked, that the Committee cannot discharge their duty without alluding to that course in this connection. Reference is especially had to the Proclamation of the 3rd of May, calling out over forty-two thousand additional volunteers, to serve in the militia for a period of three years, and increasing the regular force of the United States by an addition of nearly twenty-three thousand men to the army, and eighteen thousand seamen to the navy. The most unscrupulous advocate of the Administration and its policy would be compelled to shrink from the task of pointing out any legal or Constitutional authority of any sort for this unprecedented measure. The right of increasing the army and navy is one which belongs exclusively to Congress, and over which the President has no more Constitutional control than the humblest citizen. His right to call out the militia is expressly limited by the restriction that their use shall only continue "if necessary, until after the expiration of thirty days after the commencement of the then next session of Congress." (Act of 1795, sec. 2.) The Proclamation is therefore without any color whatever of right, and is as plain and bald a subversion of the letter and spirit of the Constitution and the laws, as was ever attempted by the military power, in any Government ostensibly free. The pretence of "existing exigencies" is but the shape in which military revolutions have always begun, since the prestige of free institutions has rendered it necessary, even for usurpers, to make a show of apology for overthrowing them.

If ever a triumphant illustration could be given of the wisdom of our fathers, in providing by the constitution, that the government should operate upon its individual citizens through the laws, and not upon the States by military coercion, it is to be found in the fact, that the first administration daring to depart from this fundamental and consecrated principle, has rushed, in the short space of sixty days, into the assertion of absolute control over the whole military resources of the country, in open and reckless defiance of every legal and constitutional restraint. The Committee hazard nothing in saying, that there is not a citizen of Maryland, whatever be his political opinions, who must not shudder at the palpable and ominous presence of this usurpation, and who does not recognize, for the first time, in his own experience or the history of Maryland, that he is living and moving and holding his civil and political rights at the pleasure of an unrestricted military power, and subject to the arbitrary and anti-republican caprices of what is entitled "military necessity." For any man to be able to persuade himself, under such circumstances, that the policy of the administration ever meant peace and not war—the "enforcement of the laws,"—the "defence of the capital"—and not subjugation—requires a peculiarity of mental construction with which reason is at a loss how to deal. To suppose that a blockade of the whole sea coast, from the capes of the Chesapeake to the extreme borders of Texas, with a land army extraordinary of one hundred and fifty thousand men, and a naval increase of eighteen thousand, can be intended only in aid of "the ordinary course of judicial proceedings, or the powers vested in the Marshals," and is therefore within the scope of the President's civil functions, and not of the war-making power, which only Congress can exercise, implies a facility of conviction, to which nothing can be regarded as impossible.

The Committee are of course not unacquainted with the familiar doctrine laid down by the Supreme Court of the United States in the case of Martin vs. Mott, (12 Wheaton, 19,) and so often cited by those who maintained the absolute authority of the President over the whole question of calling out the militia. The Committee might readily dispose of it if they were willing to stand upon the same grounds with the Administration, by applying to it the doctrine of the inaugural of Mr. Lincoln, and might insist upon confining the ruling of the Court to the particular case and the individual parties concerned, repudiating its controlling authority, upon the one side or the other, on a question of administrative government. Believing, however, that the true and only "loyalty" of a free people consists in their reverence for the laws and constitution, and their obedience to the tribunals by which these are expounded, the Committee assume that the people of Maryland will cheerfully bow to whatever the Supreme Court has determined, upon the question under discussion, or any other. The case of Martin vs. Mott was a controversy between a private of militia and one of the United States Marshals, who had seized his goods, in enforcement of a fine imposed by court-martial, for failure to enter the service upon requisition, according to law, during the war of 1812. The jurisdiction of the court-martial, and the authority of the President to issue the Proclamation under which the militia were called out to repel invasion, were both considered in the case; the question in chief, however, of course being the right of the individual citizen to judge, for himself, whether the legal occasion existed, upon which the President might rightfully summon the citizens to arms. This latter was the real and only point in controversy, and the Court decided, that under the Act of 1795, it was for the President, exclusively, to determine whether the exigency contemplated by the law had arisen, and that no soldier or officer had any choice but to obey.

The principle of military subordination upon which this adjudication is distinctly placed by the Court, is too obvious to be .confounded with the recognition of arbitrary and irresponsible power, to which the decision is sought to be perverted, by the supporters of the existing order of things. To determine that the President is the exclusive judge of whether an exigency has arisen, in a case to which his discretion is lawfully applicable, is one thing. To give to him the exclusive and irreversible authority to determine, not only the existence of the exigency, but the existence of the case in which it may lawfully arise, is quite another thing. The first is what the Supreme Court has done, the second is what no respectable Court, it is confidently assumed, can be persuaded or forced to do, except under the pressure of "military necessity." The one gives to the President the exercise of a discretion, in certain named and ascertained cases. The other gives him absolute power in all cases. The one endows him with a necessary executive function. The other makes him supreme over all law, by granting him the exclusive control of its application. If the President cannot only invoke the military power at his discretion, in cases of invasion, insurrection and resistance to the laws, but can create invasion, insurrection and resistance, by merely proclaiming that they exist, whether, in fact, they do so, or not; there is not a moment of his term, at which he cannot constitutionally compass the absolute subjugation of the people, through the mere official assertion of a falsehood. Assume for a moment, for the sake of the argument, that the attitude of the United States, is not, in fact or law, a case authorizing the President to call out the militia, under the act of 1795, is it to be pretended that he makes it such a case simply by calllng it such, in a proclamation? Is it to be gravely argued, under a constitutional government, that the nation is bound to acquiesce in it as a fact, against the public knowledge to the contrary, and must accept the war, indorse the bloodshed, pour out the treasure, and submit to the usurpation, with no other remedy than articles of impeachment, or the chances of the next Presidential election?

The commonest intelligence—the most superficial acquaintance with the scheme and spirit of republican institutions—revolts at

conclusions so monstrous. And yet precisely such must be the
conclusions to which any man must yield who supposes the Supreme Court to have decided, as has been pretended. That
high tribunal never meant to decide, and never did decide, a
principle so wholly irrational and despotic. It is a disrespect to
its character to put such a question even in dispute. The way
in which the States and the people may and ought to deal with
such a usurpation is a matter apart, but that it does not cease to
be a usurpation, because of the insertion of a form of words in a
Proclamation, is a matter which the Committee will not disparage the manliness and sense of the House by discussing further.
Indeed, in his letter of May 4th, 1861, to the United States Minister at Paris, which has appeared during the preparation of this
report, the Secretary of State does not hesitate to throw aside all
the masks and pretenses of the Proclamation, and to admit that
it is no longer a simulated question of "enforcing the laws" and
"defending the Capital," but a downright case of "civil war"—
of "open, flagrant, deadly war," which the United States have
"accepted." Such a confession—nay, such a bold and defiant
annunciation—that the President has assumed upon himself the
power of peace and war, in glaring and indisputable subversion
of even the Constitution, leaves to the people of Maryland nothing further to consider, in this connection, but the fact, that they
are face to face with a military despotism, whose only law is its
will.

If the Committee are justified, by what has been said, in their
view of the constitutional position of the Federal Government,
and especially if the missions now made by it, without disguise,
show but the consummation of an original and persistent illegal
scheme on the part of the Administration, it follows, as a matter
of necessity, that the troops called out by the President were and
are an unauthorized body of men, passing across our territory for
illegal and unconstitutional purposes, and carrying with them
none of the constitutional safeguards, which would undoubtedly
accompany any force of the United States exercising the right of
transit for lawful and justifiable ends. They were, in fact, not
United States soldiers, but "Northern troops," as they were properly designated by the Governor in his correspondence, and
"Northern troops," too, whose presence in Maryland, without
the consent of her constituted authorities, was indubitably an
aggression upon her dignity, her safety and tranquility. Your
Committee, of course, admit, without question, that only the
authorities of the State were competent to deal with such a case,
and that it would only have been dealt with properly, even by
them, in distinct recognition of the fact, that Maryland is still a
State of the Union, with all the obligations which that relation
imposes upon her.

But they cannot shut their eyes to the other part, equally indisputable, that it was primarily the fault of those who marched the

Massachusetts soldiery through Baltimore, upon an unconstitutional and illegal errand, if the popular passions were unfortunately stimulated by their presence, into a lawless outbreak, too sudden and too violent to be restrained, for the moment, by the ordinary appliances of a free government. The Committee, therefore, cannot but commend the repeated efforts of the Governor to induce the President to forego his purpose of passing troops across our soil, both before and after the fatal occurrence of the 19th of April. They can only regret that the indignant feeling manifested by his Excellency in regard to the misdeeds of the "rebellious element" at home, was not testified, with equal vigor of remonstrance against the illegality and wrong, involved in the proceedings of the Government.

The events which have occurred since the period referred to, the Committee do not feel themselves called upon to discuss in any detail. They have taken occasion to allude, in a previous report, to the humiliating facts which are disclosed by the present position of Maryland. A State of the Union, held to the obligations of that relation, and having never through her constituted authorities pretended to repudiate or abjure them, she is treated as a conqured enemy. Her soil is occupied; her property and that of her citizens are sequestered; her public highways are seized and obstructed; her laws are suspended; her capital is converted into a military post; her Legislature is compelled, in the language of her Executive, to consult its "safety" by holding its sessions at a distance from her offices and archives; troops are quartered around the peaceful homesteads of her people; her citizens are subjected to the illegal and arbitrary violence of military arrest and confinement; her very freedom, in fine, all that distinguished her from a Neapolitan province, before Naples was liberated, is under the armed heel of the Government. That such a fate is imposed upon her, without constitutional authority; that indeed no respect to the Constitution is even pretended in her regard; the frank admission of the Federal authorities to the Commissioners recently accredited to them by this Legislature, renders a mortifying and almost intolerable certainty.

The State of Maryland is under military rule. Partly for military convenience, and partly for chastisement, her free institutions have been temporarily suspended by the War Department, and her name blotted out, for the time, from the list of free governments. It is not the desire of the Committee to aggravate by comment the humiliation which is inseparable from these facts in in their simplest statement. It is not their disposition to provoke a review of the unhappy policy, in her own councils, which has contributed to plunge the State into so hopeless and helpless a condition. They wish to deal only with the practical questions it suggests for present determination; and this brings them to consider the recommendations of the message transmitted by the Governor.

The Committee understand His Excellency as recommending, in general terms, a policy of peace. So far as that naked proposition goes, they give to it their warmest and heartiest concurrence, but they are not sure that they exactly apprehend the mode in which the Governor proposes that the policy he so favors should be carried out. His language is as follows: "I honestly and most earnestly entertain the conviction that the only safety of Maryland lies in preserving a neutral position between our brethren of the North and South." He then enters into a consideration of the part which Maryland has taken in the sectional contest that has been waged, and adds: "Entertaining these views, I cannot counsel Maryland to take sides against the Federal Government, until it shall commit outrages upon us which would justify us in resisting its authority." What class of outrages would furnish such justification for resistance he does not announce, but proceeds to say: "As a consequence, I can give no other counsel than that we shall array ourselves' for union and peace, and thus preserve our soil from being polluted with the blood of brethren. Thus, if war must be between the North and the South, we may force the contending parties to transfer the field of battle from our soil, so that our lives and property may be secure."

The Committee confess their difficulty in perceiving how, consistently with a policy purely pacific, these counsels can possibly be made available. No matter how decidedly and enthusiastically we "array ourselves for union and peace," it is altogether impossible for us to preserve our soil from the pollution of fraternal blood, unless we possess the means and assert the power to force back the tide of war, if it comes surging across our borders. And that we should consolidate and employ such power, to the extent which the exigency may demand, is obviously the counsel of the Governor, for he proceeds to tell us, that by the action he advises, we may be able, "if war must be," to *force the contending parties to transfer the field of battle from our soil,* so that our lives and property may be secure." Surely we cannot "force" belligerent armies from our midst, without employing force of our own. It is out of the question that we can prevent them from making our homes their battle-field, unless we have the strength to repel them, and are willing and prepared to use it.

No peaceful "array" whatever—no legislative protest—no Executive remonstrance—from Maryland, can stay the strife of contending squadrons. A deputation from the Peace Society would have been as effectual in arresting a charge at Solferino. If, then, the "neutrality" of the Governor means anything, (speaking with all respect,) it must mean a neutrality armed and resolute—prepared to assert its policy, and able to vindicate it on the field. Otherwise it would be nothing, and would come to nothing. It would only irritate both parties, and stay the arm of neither.

And yet although this is the result and the only practical result of the recommendation of the Message, it is difficult to reconcile such a conclusion with the other views which the Governor announces. Upon the authority of "our most learned and intelligent citizens," he admits the right of the Government to transport its troops across our soil. He recognizes the unbroken relations and the continuing loyalty of Maryland to the Union. He does not impeach the constitutionaltty of the action of the Federal authorities. His protests against the landing of the troops, and the seizure of the railroad at Annapolis, are based upon no denial of the right. They amount to remonstrance and advice, but to nothing more.

His theory is, and he has always steadfastly maintained it, that nothing has occurred to alter the reciprocal rights and obligations of this State and the General Government. The Constitution he believes is still over both, and the old bonds still unite them together. If all this be true, then the State of Maryland can hold no neutrality when the Union is at war. She is part of the Union; at war when it wars; at peace when it is peaceful. She "takes sides" against it the instant that she fails to take sides with it. Neutrality, in such a case, is nullificatien pure and simple, and an armed neutrality is merely rebellion, and not union or peace. The position of His Excellency in the premises is, therefore, in the judgment of the Committee, wholly untenable, and it is not surprising that it should have placed him at so obvious a disadvantage, in the correspondence which he has furnished the House between himself and the astute officers of the Government. Differing from the Governor in opinion as to the course and rights of the Federal authorities, to the wide extent herein before indicated, the Committee have no hesitation in asserting and maintaining the right of the State, and its duty, to protest against the unconstitutional action of the Administration, and refuse obedience to its unconstitntional demands. Recognizing, however, to the same extent as the Governor, that Maryland is still a State of the Union, the Committee cannot counsel this Honorable Body, or the people whom it represents, to assume, under the guise of "neutrality," a hostile relation to the Government, or attempt, by any policy whatever, to "force" it from the position in which it is entrenched. If no better argument existed against such a project, a sufficient one would be found in its hopeless futility.

The present—and the only possible present attitude of the State towards the Federal Government is, in the judgment of the Committee, an attitude of submission—voluntary and cheerful submission on the part of those who can persuade themselves that the Constitution remains inviolate and the Union unbroken, or that the Union can survive the Constitution—unwilling and galling submission on the part of those who think and feel differently; but still, peaceful submission upon both sides. It is not for the

Committee to ignore this state of things, because of the humiliation which comes with it. They feel it their duty to confess the
inexorable logic of facts, and leave the future to be shaped by the
people of Maryland, to whom, exclusively, that prerogative belongs, and who, doubtless, will exercise it in their own way and
at their own good time.

This expression of the views of your Committee, at so much
necessary length, leaves very obvious the recommendations which
they ask leave to report, upon the two leading subjects submitted
to their deliberation: the calling of a Sovereign Convention of the
people, and the re-organization and arming of the militia of the
State.

At the time when the Legislature was called together, there
was certainly but little difference of opinion among its members,
of all parties, as to the propriety of speedily adopting measures
to secure both the objects referred to. Since that time, the rapid
and extraordinary development of events, and of the warlike purposes of the Administration; the concentration of large bodies of
troops in our midst and upon our borders, and the actual and
threatened military occupation of the State, have naturally enough
produced great changes of opinion and feeling among our citizens.
The members of the Committee, judging from their own correspondence and that of their fellow members, of all shades of opinion,
as well as from the memorials and other expressions of the public will, which have reached the House, have no hesitation in
expressing their belief, that there is an almost unanimous feeling
in the State against calling a Convention at the present time.
The reasons for this conclusion are doubtless various, in different
portions of the State, and the opinions of individuals as to the
probable result of the deliberations of a Convention, at this moment, are of course very wide apart. To the Committee, the
single fact of the military occupation of our soil by the Northern
troops in the service of the Government, against the wishes of
our people, and the solemn protest of the State Executive, is a
sufficient and conclusive reason for postponing the subject, to a
period when the Federal ban shall be no longer upon us. It does
not become the dignity of the State of Maryland to attempt the
performance of an act of sovereignty, absolute or qualified, at a
moment when not only her sovereignty but her Federal equality
is subordinated to the law of the drum-head. No election, held
at such a time, and with such surroundings, could by possibility
be fair or free. No result which could be reached by it would
command the confidence or secure the willing obedience of the
people. The Committee therefore feel it their duty to recommend
the postponement of the subject for the present.

For reasons almost identical, the Committee take leave to
report against the arming of the State, and the organization of
our military defences at this time. If the holding of a Sovereign
Convention were not regarded as a hostile movement by the Fed-

3

eral Government, the re-establishment of the military force of the State, in a condition of present efficiency, certainly would be, however unjustly. It avails nothing to say that the arming and organization of a suitable militia, are declared by the Constitution of the United States to be "necessary to the security of a free State," and therefore especially guaranteed to us as peaceful and fundamental rights. The Constitution is silenced by the bayonets which surround us, and it is not worth while for us to fancy ourselves beneath its ægis. It would be criminal as well as foolish for us to shut our eyes to the fact that we will not be permitted to organize and arm our citizens, let our rights and the Constitution be what they may. The interview of our Commissioners with the President sets that point at rest. It is not easy for free men to realize such a state of things; but it is not our fault that we are helpless, nor our shame that our helplessness is abused.

The Committee respectfully recommend that no action be taken towards the re-organization of the militia at this time, or the doing of any act which might be construed into hostility to the Government, and that, if any purchase of arms be indispensable, it be confined, at the farthest, to such reasonable quantity as may be manufactured in our own State, for local purposes; and may aid in the equipment of the militia, when a plan for their proper enrollment and distribution shall be matured at some future day. The purchase of such a quantity can give no just ground for complaint in any quarter, as the slightest inquiry will show that the total disuse of the militia system, for many years past has left us almost wholly defenceless in many parts of the State, and renders some such arrangement indispensable as a measure of domestic police.

The Committee regard it as within their province further to suggest to this Honorable Body the propriety of adjourning over to some named day, as soon as its present and pressing duties are discharged. In their opinion, the exigencies of the present crisis do not permit a final adjournment, with any proper regard to the responsibilities and dangers which may, at any moment, be precipitated on the State.

Finally, the Committee respectfully submit to the House the following resolutions, and pray to be discharged from the further consideration of the matters before them.

S. T. WALLIS,
J. H. GORDON,
G. W. GOLDSBOROUGH,
JAMES T. BRISCOE,
BARNES COMPTON.

WHEREAS, In the judgment of the General Assembly of Maryland, the war now waged by the Government of the United States upon the people of the Confederate States, is unconstitutional in its origin, purposes and conduct; repugnant to civilization and sound policy; subversive of the free principles upon which the Federal Union was founded, and certain to result in the hopeless and bloody overthrow of our existing institutions; and,

WHEREAS, The people of Maryland, while recognizing the obligation of their State, as a member of the Union, to submit in good faith to the exercise of all the legal and constitutional powers of the General Government, and to join as one man in fighting its authorized battles, do reverence, nevertheless, the great American principle of self-government, and sympathize deeply with their Southern brethren in their noble and manly determination to uphold and defend the same; and,

WHEREAS, Not merely on their own account and to turn away from their own soil the calamities of civil war, but for the blessed sake of humanity, and to avoid the wanton shedding of fraternal blood, in a miserable contest which can bring nothing with it but sorrow, shame and desolation, the people of Maryland are enlisted, with their whole hearts, on the side of reconciliation and peace: now, therefore, it is hereby

Resolved by the General Assembly of Maryland, That the State of Maryland owes it to her own self-respect and her respect for the Constitution, not less than to her deepest and most honorable sympathies, to register this, her solemn protest, against the war which the Federal Government has declared upon the Confederate States of the South, and our sister and neighbor Virginia, and to announce her resolute determination to have no part or lot, directly or indirectly, in its prosecution.

Resolved, That the State of Maryland earnestly and anxiously desires the restoration of peace between the belligerent sections of the country, and the President, authorities, and people of the Confederate States, having, over and over again, officially and unofficially, declared that they seek only peace and self-defence, and to be let alone, and that they are willing to throw down the sword, the instant that the sword now drawn against them shall be sheathed, the Senators and Delegates of Maryland do beseech and implore the President of the United States to accept the olive branch which is thus held out to him; and in the name of God and humanity, to cease this unholy and most wretched and unprofitable strife, at least until the assembling of Congress in Washington shall have given time for the prevalence of color and better counsels.

Resolved, That the State of Maryland desires the peaceful and immediate recognition of the independence of the Confederate States, and hereby gives her cordial assent thereunto, as a member of the Union: entertaining the profound conviction that the willing return of the Southern people to their former Federal relations is a thing beyond hope, and that the attempt to coerce them will only add slaughter and hate to impossibility.

Resolved, That the present military occupation of Maryland, being for the purposes, in the opinion of this Legislature, in flagrant violation of the Constitution, the General Assembly of the State, in the name of her people, does hereby protest against the same, and against the oppresive restrictions and illegalities with which it is attended ; calling upon all good citizens, at the same time, in the most earnest and authoritative manner, to abstain from all violent and unlawful interference, of every sort, with the troops in transit through our territory, or quartered among us, and patiently and peacefully to leave to time and reason the ultimate and certain re-establishment and vindication of the right.

Resolved, That under existing circumstances, it is inexpedient to call a Sovereign Convention of the State at this time, or to take any measure for the immediate organization or arming of the militia.

SENATE AMENDMENTS.

And be it further Resolved, That a Committee be appointed to consist of four member of the Senate and four members of the House of Delegates, four of which Committee, (to be selected of themselves,) shall as early as possible, wait on the President of the United States at Washington, and the other four of said Committee shall wait on the President [of the Southern Confederacy, for the purpose of laying the foregoing resolutions before them ; and that said Committee be, and is hereby especially instructed to obtain, if possible, a general cessation of hostilities, now impending, until the meeting of Congress in July next, in order that said Body may, if possible, arrange for an adjustment of existing troubles by means of negotiation, rather than the sword.

Resolved, That said Committee consist of Messrs. Brooke, Yellott, McKaig, and Lynch, of the Senate, and Messrs. ——, ——, —— and ——, of the House of Delegates.

Resolved, That said Committee be requested to report, if practicable, to the General Assembly, on the 5th day of June next.

REPORT

OF THE

COMMITTEE OF THE GENERAL ASSEMBLY,

APPOINTED TO WAIT ON THE

PRESIDENT OF THE UNITED STATES.

The undersigned, a portion of the Committee appointed by the Legislature to present and enforce its Resolutions to Presidents Lincoln and Davis, beg leave to report—

That the manifest purpose of those resolutions was, in the opinion of your Committee, to secure, if possible, through the instrumentality of Maryland, peace to our distracted country; and, if failing in that, then a cessation of hostilities on the part of the armies of the Federal and Confederated troops, until Congress should express its opinion on the subjects which now agitate the people. These purposes being defeated by the movement of the Federal troops on Virginia, and an active commencement of hostilities, we have considered our mission as ended, and, therefore, have not felt authorized, on the part of the Sovereign State of Maryland, to present a request which has in advance been repudiated.

The dignity of the State, as well as self-respect, seemed to demand this of us.

All of which is respectfully submitted.

JNO. B. BROOKE,
G. W. GOLDSBOROUGH,
GEO. H. MORGAN,
BARNES COMPTON.

REPORT

OF THE

COMMITTEE OF THE GENERAL ASSEMBLY,

APPOINTED TO WAIT ON THE

PRESIDENT OF THE SOUTHERN CONFEDERACY.

To the *Honorable*,

The Senate and House of Delegates of Maryland:

The undersigned, being that portion of the Joint Committee selected to proceed to Montgomery, Alabama, and to submit for the consideration of the President and Cabinet of the Confederate States of America the resolutions as passed by the Legislature of the State of Maryland, beg leave most respectfully to report—

That your Committee, in performance of their mission, proceeded to Montgomery, Alabama, and were there received by the President of the Confederate Government, a majority of his Cabinet being present, with a frank cordiality and that consideration due to the representatives of the sovereign State of Maryland. In answer to the resolutions thus presented, the President of the Confederate States caused to be delivered to your Committee the paper accompanying and made part of this report.

Believing that any expression of opinion relative to the object your Honorable Bodies wished to accomplish, or to the probable final result of the fratricidal and sectional war which is now being inflicted upon the country, would be transcending the limits of the power entrusted to your Committee, your Committee therefore content themselves with simply asking the attention of your Honorable Bodies to the answer of President Davis to the resolutions thus laid before the Confederate Government.

THOMAS J. McKAIG,

COLEMAN YELLOTT,

CHARLES A. HARDING.

LETTER OF PRESIDENT DAVIS.

Montgomery, 25th May, 1861.

Gentlemen:

I receive with sincere pleasure the assurance that the State of Maryland sympathises with the people of these States in their determined vindication of the right of self-government, and that the people of Maryland "are enlisted with their whole hearts on the side of reconciliation and peace." The people of these Confederate States, notwithstanding their separation from their late sister, have not ceased to feel a deep solicitude in her welfare, and to hope that, at no distant day, a State whose people, habits and institutions are so closely related and assimilated with theirs, will seek to unite her fate and fortunes with those of this Confederacy.

The Government of the Confederate States receive with respect the suggestion of the State of Maryland, that there should be "a general cessation of hostilities now impending, until the meeting of Congress in July next, in order that said body may, if possible, arrange for an adjustment of existing troubles, by means of negotiation, rather than the sword," but is at a loss how to reply, without a repetition of the language it has used on every possible occasion that has presented itself, since the establishment of its independence. In deference to the State of Maryland, however, it again asserts, in the most emphatic terms, that its sincere and earnest desire is for peace; that whilst the Government would readily entertain any proposition from the Government of the United States tending to a peaceful solution of the pending difficulties, the recent attempts of this Government to enter into negotiations with that of the United States, were attended with results which forbid any renewal of proposals from it to that Government.

If any further assurance of the desire of this Government for peace were necessary, it would be sufficient to observe that, being formed of a confederation of sovereign States, each acting and deciding for itself, the right of every other sovereign State to the same self-action and self-government is necessarily acknowledged. Hence, conquests of other States are wholly inconsistent with the fundamental principles, and subversive of the very organization of this Government. Its policy cannot but be peace—peace with all nations and people.

Very respectfully,

JEFFERSON DAVIS.

Messrs. McKaig, Yellott and Harding, Committee of Maryland Legislature.

[Document I.]

BY THE SENATE,
JUNE 21, 1861.

Read, and 2,000 copies ordered to be printed.

By order,   WILLIAM KILGOUR, *Secretary.*

REPORT

OF THE

COMMITTEE ON JUDICIAL PROCEEDINGS

˙UPON THE MESSAGE OF THE

Governor of Maryland,

GIVING HIS REASONS FOR

DISARMING THE STATE MILITIA.

FREDERICK:

BEALE H. RICHARDSON, PRINTER.

1861.

REPORT

OF

MESSRS. McKAIG AND MILES

OF THE

COMMITTEE ON JUDICIAL PROCEEDINGS

UPON THE

MESSAGE OF THE GOVERNOR

OF THE 5TH OF JUNE, 1861.

IN THE SENATE OF MARYLAND,

FRIDAY, *June* 21, 1861.

Messrs. McKaig, and Miles, from the Committee on Judicial Proceedings, submitted the following

REPORT AND RESOLUTION:

The Committee on Judicial Proceedings, to whom was referred the Message of the Governor, of the 5th of June inst., in answer to an order of the Senate, asking him "to furnish the Senate with a statement of the facts which induced him to reclaim the arms formerly confided to certain military companies of Baltimore city, also with the reasons why said arms were sent by his order to Fort McHenry," beg leave to report :

That after having given the questions involved in the message and orders of the Governor a full and careful consideration, they are satisfied that the Governor had no authority of law to issue such orders, or to dispose of the arms of the State in the manner he has done.

By the eighth Article of the Code, two armories are established in the State, one at Easton, and the other at Frederick. It is

made the duty of the Governor, by and with the advice and con·
sent of the Senate, to appoint, bi-ennially, an Armorer at Frederick, and an Armorer at Easton, to take charge of and keep in
repair and fit for use, all public arms and accoutrements in those
armories. The Armorers are each required to give bond, with
security, for the faithful discharge of their duty.

There is no charge, on the part of the Governor, that the
armories had been robbed, or that the Armorers had not done
their duty; but he does say that the State, in addition to a pecuniary loss, has been deprived of the protection designed to her
citizens by the purchase of said arms.

It is manifest, however, to your Committee, that the loss referred by the Governor, was sustained to the State by the neglect
of the Governor and Adjutant General to comply with the positive requirement of the act of the 27th February, 1860, chapter
188, which made it their duty that, when the arms were so purchased, they should "be deposited in the armories of the State,
and distributed by the Adjutant General according to the mode
prescribed, *to the several volunteer companies of the State.* Not
distributed by the Govenor nor by his order, but by the Adjutant
General; not to individual citizens—for neither the Adjutant
General nor Governor has any power to distribute the arms of
the State amongst individual citizens, though the Governor has
illegally issued such orders, but "to the several volunteer companies of the State."

By the fifth section of the eighth Article of the Code, it is
made the duty of the Quarter Master, General, and the Brigade
and Regimental Quarter Masters, whenever they have reason to
believe that any of the public arms are not properly preserved,
or have fallen into the possession of those who have no right to
retain them, such as ununiformed associations of individuals or
disbanded companies—to cause such arms to be seized and transported to the nearest State Armory. The State has, therefore,
made ample provision for the safe keeping of all the public arms
of the State. The laws have designated the places where they
shall be kept, who shall keep them—and has provided for their
safety and their proper preservation, by requiring bond, with
ample security, from the Armorers.

By the act of the 27th February, 1860, it was made the duty
of the Governor and Adjutant General, to purchase for the use of
the State such number of rifles, carbines, pistols, sabers and
horse equipments, for calvary, of the most approved paterns, as in
their judgment may be necessary; and when so purchased, it
was their duty to have them deposited in the armories of the
State; and when so deposited, the Adjutant General was required "to distribute them" in accordance with the provisions of
the one hundred and tenth section of the sixty-third Article of the

Code of Public General Laws, to the several duly organized and uniformed volunteer companies of the State.

Your Committee report that the Governor and the Adjutant General failed to comply with the requirement of this act by not having the arms purchased by them deposited in the armories of the State, and by reason of that failure, part of the arms was lost to the State.

By the provisions of the one hundred and tenth and one hundred and eleventh sections of the sixty-third Article of the Code, "the Adjutant General (not the Governor), is required to furnish the captain of any uniform volunteer company with such arms or accoutrements, for the use of his company, as he may apply for, if the same be on hand or in any of the armories of the State, *and not appropriated;* provided, the company numbers at least thirty-two men, and is duly organized and uniformed, and the captain executes, to the State of Maryland, a bond, with satisfactory security, in such penalty as the Adjutant General shall approve, conditioned for the safe keeping, preservation and return or delivery of said arms or accoutrements, to one of the Armorers of the State, within the space of twenty days after the company, for whose use they were furnished, shall have been dissolved or disbanded."

When a uniformed volunteer company has thus been supplied with arms and given bond for the same, according to law, the Governor has no authority, by law, to interfere with or take away their arms, as long as they preserve their organization. Any order issued by the Governor to strip the company of their arms, as long as they are a legally organized company, is a gross violation of law. If they do not preserve the arms and keep them fit for duty, their bond is responsible. But the Governor has no power to seize the arms. If, however, under any circumstances, he could be justified in seizing the arms, he violated the provisions of the law by ordering the arms to be deposited at Fort McHenry—a Fort not belonging to the State of Maryland.

The disarming, therefore, of the regular organized uniformed companies of Baltimore, and the removal of the public arms from the armory at Easton, and placing them in Fort McHenry, and the distribution of the public arms that were in the armory at Frederick, to ununiformed citizens or association of citizens, by order of the Governor, were all, and each of them, a palpable usurpation of authority, which ought not to be tolerated. The law has invested the Governor with no such power.

The forty-third section of the sixty-third article authorizes the Governor to adopt measures to collect, preserve, distribute, deliver and re-deliver the arms, accoutrements and ammunition belonging to the State; but this section cannot be construed without a manifest perversion of the provisions of the militia system into an authority, to the Governor, to strip the organized and uniformed volunteer companies of the State of their arms, for which they had bonded according to law. The provisions of this section were intended to give the Governor the power to collect and re-deliver or place in the armories the arms of the State, in the hands of disbanded companies, and companies whose members do not amount to thirty-two men in uniform.

The Governor says, in his message, that he "issued the orders for reclaiming the arms referred to, because he had become satisfied that many of them had been carried beyond the limits of the State of Maryland, for disloyal purposes." He does not point to any source from which proof could be obtained to establish the charge against the disarmed companies; nor does he say from what source he obtained his information, whether it was "from a reliable source not accessible to the people," or from anonymous letters. Your Committee, however, have not been able to discover that any of the arms of the State were so carried beyond the limits of the State.

If the Governor is to be justified in the orders he says he has given, then the right of our people to "a well regulated militia, as the proper and natural defence of a free government," and the statute laws of the State, are all to give way and be disregarded whenever the Governor "becomes satisfied," and so orders.— Yield in this matter to the Governor, and he becomes a military despot, and the citizens of Maryland an enslaved people.

The Governor says, also, in his message, that he "cannot acknowledge any right on the part of the Senate to make such inquiries." If the Governor be right in assuming this position, which your Committee utterly deny, it follows as a necessary consequence, that the Governor of the State of Maryland can violate all the statute laws of the State, and there is no power in the State to question his authority or stay his hand.

Your Committee are of opinion that this is the first time in the history of Maryland, that such powers have been claimed by any Executive officer of the State, and that it is the imperative duty of the Legislature to make a direct issue with the Governor on the powers thus claimed, and to confine him to the exercise of the powers and duties confided to him by the Constitution and the laws.

The undersigned recommend the passage of the following Joint Resolution:

Resolved by the Senate and House of Delegates of Maryland, That the Governor be requested to return to the armories of the State, the arms which have been removed by his order from said armories, and deposited in Fort McHenry, or placed in the hands of ununiformed companies, or associations of individuals; and that he return to all regularly organized and uniformed volunteer companies, of the State, the arms reclaimed from them, or either of them, by his order.

THOS. J. McKAIG, *Chairman;*

O. MILES.

Which was read.

REPORT

OF

MESSRS. GOLDSBOROUGH AND SMITH

OF THE

COMMITTEE ON JUDICIAL PROCEEDINGS.

Messrs. Goldsborough, of Talbot, and Smith, of Carroll, sub-mitted, as a substitute, the following

REPORT:

The undersigned, a portion of the Committee on Judicial Pro-ceedings, to whom was referred the message of the Executive respecting the return of the arms of the State furnished certain military companies in Baltimore city and elsewhere, and the rea-sons why the same have been sent to Fort McHenry, beg leave to report—

That after having carefully considered the same, they are of opinion that the Governor has in this matter acted within the limits prescribed by the Code of General Laws, and the Consti-tution of the State.

Without any elaborate explanation of their views, they think that the forty-third section of the sixty-third Article of the Code of General Laws, amply provides for what has been done by the Governor, as it empowers him, "from time to time, to adopt such measures and give such orders as he shall deem necessary for the collection, distribution, delivery and re-delivery of the arms, accoutrements and ammunition belonging to the State, and to provide and issue such ammunition as, *in his opinion,* may at any time be necessary.

[Document J.]

BY THE SENATE,
June 22, 1861.

Read, and 2,000 copies ordered to be printed.

By order, William Kilgour, *Secretary.*

RESOLUTIONS

OF THE

GENERAL ASSEMBLY

IN REGARD TO THE RELATIONS OF THE

State of Maryland

TO THE

FEDERAL GOVERNMENT.

EXTRA SESSION, 1861.

FREDERICK:

BEALE H. RICHARDSON, PRINTER,

1861.

RESOLUTIONS

OF THE

GENERAL ASSEMBLY IN REGARD TO THE RELATIONS OF THE STATE OF MARYLAND TO THE FEDERAL GOVERNMENT.

"WHEREAS, We hold these truths to be self-evident, that all men are created equal; that they are endowed by their Creator with certain unalienable rights; that amongst these are life, liberty and the pursuit of happiness; that to secure these rights, governments are instituted among men, deriving their just powers from the consent of the governed; that whenever any form of government becomes destructive of these ends, it is the right of the people to alter or abolish it, and to institute a new government, laying its foundations on such principles, and organizing its powers in such form as to them shall seem most likely to effect their safety and happiness;" and,

WHEREAS, The doctrine of non-resistance against arbitrary power and oppression is absurd, slavish and destructive of the good and happiness of mankind; and,

WHEREAS, Standing armies are dangerous to liberty, and ought not to be raised or kept up without the consent of the Legislature; and,

WHEREAS, In all cases and at all times the military ought to be under strict subordination to, and control of, the civil power, and that the people of this State ought to have the sole and exclusive right of regulating the internal government and police thereof; and that in all criminal prosecutions, every man hath a right to be informed of the accusation against him, to have a copy of the indictment or charge in due time (if required) to prepare for his defense, to be allowed counsel, to be confronted with the witnesses against him, to have process for his witnesses, to examine the witnesses for and against him on oath, and to a speedy trial by an impartial jury, without whose unanimous consent he ought not to be found guilty; and,

WHEREAS, The Constitution of the United States declares that *Congress* shall have power to declare war, to raise and support armies; that "the privilege of the writ of *habeas corpus* shall not be suspended, unless when in cases of rebellion or invasion, the public safety may require it," nor then unless by Congress. "That a well regulated militia being necessary to the security of a free State, the right of the people to keep and bear arms shall not be infringed;" that "the right of the people to be secure in their

houses, persons, papers and effects against unreasonable searches
and seizures, shall not be violated, and no warrant shall issue but
upon probable cause, supported by oath or affirmation, and particularly describing the place to be searched, and the persons or
things to be seized;" and,

WHEREAS, Maryland is yet a State in the Union, submitting
peaceably to the Federal Government, yet, nevertheless, the President has raised and quartered large standing armies upon her
territory, has occupied the houses of her citizens without their
consent, has made the military superior to and above the civil
power, has assumed to regulate the internal police and government of the State, has seized upon and appropriated our railroads
and telegraphs, has seized and searched our vessels, has forcibly
opened our houses, has deprived our people of their arms, has
seized and transported our citizens to other States for trial upon
charges or pretended charges, has taken the private property of
our citizens, has caused peaceable travellers to be stopped and
their persons, trunks and papers to be searched, has arrested and
caused to be imprisoned, without any civil process whatever, the
persons of our citizens, and by the military power kept and still
keeps them in confinement against and in contempt of all civil
process. Now, therefore, be it

Resolved by the General Assembly of Maryland, That recognizing our relations to the Federal Government, we feel that whilst
we cannot do more, we can do no less, than enter this, our solemn protest, against the said acts of the President of the United
States, and declare the same to be gross usurpation, unjust, oppressive, tyrannical and in utter violation of common right and
of the plain provisions of the Constitution.

Resolved, 2.—That the right of separation from the Federal
Union is a right neither arising under nor prohibited by the Constitution, but a sovereign right, independent of the Constitution,
to be exercised by the several States upon their own responsibility.

Resolved, 3.—That prudence and policy demand, that the war
now being waged, shall cease, that if persisted in, it will result
in the ruin and destruction of both sections, and a longer continuance of it will utterly annihilate the last hope of a reconstruction
of this Union; therefore we want peace, and are in favor of a
recognition of the Southern Confederacy and an acknowledgment
of its government.

Resolved, 4.—That we deem the writ of Habeas Corpus, the
great safe-guard of personal liberty, and we view with the utmost
alarm and indignation, the exercise of the despotic power that
has dared to suspend it in the case of John Merryman, now confined in Fort McHenry.

[Document K.]

BY THE SENATE,
JUNE 22, 1861.
Read, and 1,000 copies ordered to be printed.
By order,   WILLIAM KILGOUR, *Secretary*.

PROTEST

OF THE

GENERAL ASSEMBLY

AGAINST THE

ILLEGAL ARREST AND IMPRISONMENT

BY THE

FEDERAL GOVERNMENT

OF

CITIZENS OF MARYLAND.

FREDERICK:
BEALE H. RICHARDSON, PRINTER.
1861.

RESOLUTIONS

IN REGARD TO THE ILLEGAL ARREST AND IMPRISON-
MENT OF CITIZENS OF MARYLAND.

———————

WHEREAS, Ross Winans, a member of the House of Delegates of Maryland, from the city of Baltimore, on his way to his home from the discharge of his official duties, on the 14th of May last, was arbitrarily and illegally arrested, on a public highway, in the presence of the Governor of this State, by an armed force under the orders of the Federal Government, and was forcibly imprisoned and held in custody, thereafter, at Annapolis and Fort McHenry, without color of lawful process or right, by the command and at the arbitrary will and pleasure of the President of the United States; and

WHEREAS, Sundry other citizens of Maryland have been un-lawfully dealt with, in the same despotic and oppresive manner, by the same usurped authority, and some of them have in fact been removed by force beyond the limits of the State of Mary-land and the jurisdiction of her tribunals, in utter violation of their rights as citizens, and of the rights of the State, as a mem-ber of the Federal Union; and

WHEREAS, The unconstitutional and arbitrary proceedings of the Federal Executive, have not been confined to the violation of the personal rights and liberties of the citizens of Maryland, but have been extended into every department of oppresive ille-gality, so that the property of no man is safe, the sanctity of no dwelling is respected, and the sacredness of private correspon-dence no longer exists; and

WHEREAS, The Senate and House of Delegates of Maryland, recognizing the obligation of the State, as far as in her lies, to protect and defend her people against usurped and arbitrary power—however difficult the fulfillment of that high obligation may be rendered by disastrous circumstances—feel it due to her dignity and independence, that history should not record the overthrow of public freedom, for an instant, within her borders, without recording, likewise, the indignant expression of her resentment and remonstrance: now, therefore, be it

Resolved, That the Senate and House of Delegates of Maryland, in the name and on behalf of the good people of the State, do accordingly register this, their earnest and unqualified protest against the oppresive and tyrannical assertion and exercise of military jurisdiction, within the limits of Maryland, over the persons and property of her citizens, by the Government of the United States, and do solemnly declare the same to be subversive of the most sacred guarantees of the Constitution, and in flagrant violation of the fundamental and most cherished principles of American free government.

Resolved, further, That the resolutions be communicated by the President of the Senate and the Speaker of the House, to the Hon. James Alfred Pearce and the Hon. Anthony Kennedy, Senators of Maryland in the Senate of the United States, with the request that they present the same to the Senate, to be recorded among its proceedings, in vindication of the right and in perpetual memory of the solemn remonstrance of this State against the manifold usurpations and oppressions of the Federal Government.

Document [L.]

BY THE SENATE,

August 1, 1861.

1,000 copies ordered to be printed.

REPORT

AND

ACCOMPANYING DOCUMENTS

OF THE

HOUSE COMMITTEE,

APPOINTED TO EXAMINE INTO THE AFFAIRS OF THE

MARYLAND PENITENTIARY.

FREDERICK, MD.

B. H. RICHARDSON, PRINTER.

1861.

REPORT.

The special Committee appointed under the resolution of June 11th, 1861, to examine generally into the affairs of the Maryland Penitentiary, beg leave respectfully to report that they organized in the city of Frederick on the 25th of June, and selected Mr. Thomas H. Moore as clerk, and adjourned to meet on the 1st of July, in the city of Baltimore, at the Maryland Penitentiary.

Their duties, as pointed out in the resolution and order above referred to, consisted of an investigation of the following matters:

1st. The memorial of John H. Duvall and William Howard, asking relief from losses growing out of the destruction of their property by fire.

2d. The memorial of Charles Murdock, asking relief by a modification of his contracts with the Directors of the Penitentiary and the equitable settlement of claims in dispute between them.

3d. An investigation of the manufacturing department of the Institution generally.

4th. An examination of the financial affairs and condition, and

5th. An enquiry into its general management and discipline.

Taking the points to be examined in the order they appear, the Committee commenced with the memorial of Messrs. Duvall and Howard.

The memorial states that on the 3d of October, 1859, they entered into a written contract with the Directors of the Maryland Penitentiary for the rent of certain shops and yard room, and the employment of convict labor in the manufacture of barrels, and in the prosecution of that business had invested a large amount of money in the purchase of patent rights, machinery, and the necessary stock to carry it on successfully; that while in the prosecution of a successful business, on the 23d of December, 1860, their work shops were fired by some of the convicts, and their property almost destroyed, entailing, as they allege, a loss over and above the amount of insurance of $23,150, and avers that said fire was caused partly by the refusal of the Directors to permit them to have their own watchman on the premises on Sunday, (the fire having oc-

curred on that day,) whereby their property was left in an
unprotected state on Sundays, and partly by a want of proper discipline on the part of the officers of the Institution,
by which the convicts were enabled to obtain access to the
shops and commit the incendiary act; and the memorialists plead that as the loss was by no act of their own, but
was indirectly caused by the officers of the State, as above
stated, that the Legislature should grant them relief by
reimbursing in whole, or in part, the loss sustained.

The magnitude of the claim, and the importance of it to
the memorialists, who were entirely ruined by the fire, as
well as to the State, whose finances are not in a condition
to bear any burdens that are justly avoidable, demanded
of the Committee the most careful and thorough examination of the case, it was conducted and argued by eminent
counsel on both sides. Numerous witnesses were examined, whose evidence will be found in the proceedings of
the Committee, pages 1 to 53, herewith submitted; and
while deeply sympathising with the memorialists in the
heavy loss they have sustained, the Committee have been
unable to arrive at the conclusion that the case presents
any just grounds for a claim on the State, the allegation
that the Directors refused to permit the presence of a private watchman on Sundays, was not sustained by the
evidence, and although it was proved that the shops were
fired on Sunday by some of the convicts, yet it did not
appear to have arisen from any lack of ordinary discipline
on the part of the officers, it being utterly impossible with
few officers and many prisoners, strictly to carry out the
prison rules which requires a prisoner to be always under
the eye of an officer, neither have the Committee been able
to arrive at the conclusion that a loss by fire, even if
proved to have been caused by negligence on the part of
the officers, would afford just cause for a claim on the State.

The second portion of the investigation was the memorial of Charles Murdock, asking a modification of his contracts with the Directors and the arbitration of a disputed
account between them.

It appears that Mr. Murdock for some ten years past has
rented work shops and employed the convict labor of the
Institution, principally in the manufacture of cedar ware,
and at the time of his memorial, had in his employment
one hundred convicts whose time would expire July 1,
1861, and fifty, whose time, under his contract, would
expire January 1, 1865. Mr. Murdock deemed himself
justified in asking relief from his contracts on the ground
that the existing war and blockade of the Southern States
had seriously embarrassed him in the prosecution of his

business, the raw material that he uses being derived entirely from the South, and his manufactured goods finding an exclusive market there, thus completely shutting him out on both sides, and rendering it impossible to carry on his busines until peace should be restored.

Before the Committee proceeded to take evidence in this case, an arrangement and settlement was happily made between the Directors and Mr. Murdock, by which the latter pays in full to the Directors the amount in dispute, and retains the labor of 50 men at 50 cents per day until January 1, 1865. This, with the rent of the shops, will give the Institution a revenue from that source of about $8,300.

The 100 men whose time with Mr. Murdock expired on the 1st of July, the Directors propose to employ in the weaving department.

The Manufacturing Department.

This department is devoted to the manufacture of plaid cottons, with a few linseys and coarse carpets, and the Committee regret to report it in a very depressed condition. At no time has it been a source of much revenue to the Instition, arising from the inability of hand loom labor to compete successfully with power looms; still, the superior quality of its manufactured goods and its wide-spread reputation has heretofore insured their immediate sale, but the embarrassment growing out of the blockade of the Southern States has produced the same results as in the case of Mr. Murdock; nearly all the yarns used are the product of Southern mills, while the manufactured goods find a market exclusively in the Slave States. The consequence is, that no sales have been made by the Directors for the past three months, and none of any consequence can be made until the Southern markets shall be re-opened. No revenue, therefore, can be expected from this department as long as the present unfortunate state of affairs continues to exist. The stock of manufactured goods now on hand amounts to $10,500, and of materials to $2,300, which, when manufactured, will increase the stock of goods to $15,000, all of which, in ordinary times, could be made available to pay the debts and expenses of the Institution.

The Committee, after a patient and thorough investigation of this branch of the subject, are satisfied that the entire system of labor at the Institution is wrong, and demands a radical change, as at present conducted, it must always be, as it has been, a heavy burden on the State. It has not been furnished by the State with the cash capital necessary to carry on successfully a manufacturing business; its operations are, necessarily, on a credit basis, and the disadvantages of this system may be illustrated by the single fact that it has paid during the last five years the sum of $13,015 for interest alone, to say nothing of the increased cost of supplies when purchased on credit, and the saving of the discount which always accompany cash payments.

A careful analysis of the operations of this department for the past five years exhibits the fact that the nett earnings of all the convicts employed by the Institution average but eleven cents per day, and this, without making any allowance for cost and depreciation of machinery, while about the same number of convicts employed by the contractors at 50 cents per day, gave a revenue of $28,800 for labor, and $700 for rent of work shops. It is true that the labor employed by the latter was of better quality, but that would account for but a small portion of the difference.

The Committee would recommend the total abolition of all manufacturing on account of the Institution, and the substitution of a system farming the convict labor to contractors. Under this system, the Institution can be made to support itself and the State relieved from a heavy burden, while the prisoners will be taught some useful trade, the knowledge of which, by giving them the means of procuring an honest livelihood, would in many instances prevent them from relapsing into crime.

It is very true that the difficulties of the present time will prevent this plan from being carried out at once, but with peace will come the ordinary demand for labor, when it can be successfully accomplished.

It will not be out of place here to illustrate the proposition by an estimate of its results.

The expenses of all kinds of maintaining the Institution, simply as a prison, may be estimated at about $37,000. This, by a judicious economy, might be probably reduced to $35,000. The prisoners average about 420 in number, of which 400 are males. Suppose the sick, the infirm, and those necessary to perform the ordinary house work of the Institution to amount to 100, there remains 300 whose labor may be made available. These would not be equally valuable, and may be thus classified :

200 worth 50 cents per day,	-	-	-	-	$31,300
50 " 25 " " "	-	-	-	-	3,912
50 " 12½ " " "	-	-	-	-	1,956

Producing - - - - - - $37,168

A sum fully equal to all the expenses of the Institution. This change would not entail any expense on the State, inasmuch as the work shops now used for spinning and weaving would be sufficient and answer for any other occupation.

The Financial Condition of the Institution.

In the investigation of this branch of the inquiry every facility was afforded by the Board of Directors, and Mr. J. J. C. Dougherty, the financial clerk and book-keeper.

The Institution has been singularly fortunate in securing the services of the latter officer, whose books and accounts are kept in a manner highly creditable to himself and those who appointed him.

This examination produced the following results:

Liabilities of the Institution, over and above cash on hand July 1st, 1861, } $45,298 41.

ASSETS.

Appropriation at April session not yet collected,	$25,000	
Active debt due (good) by contractors,	6,764.65	
Suspended debt,	5,414.47	
Manufactured goods and materials on hand,	12.669.29	49,848.41.
Nominal surplus,		$4,550.00

The stock of manufactured goods on hand is not available for reasons before stated, and the suspended debt is in the same condition, from the same causes; it consists of the notes of merchants, hitherto of undoubted solvency, doing business in the South, whose business is now prostrate, and whose only chance of paying their debts is in the probability of being able at some future day to collect the debts due them in the Southern States.

From this exhibit it will be seen that until peace is restored, and trade resumes its accustomed channels, the Institution must become a heavy burden on the State, and that to carry it through the next twelve months an additional appropriation of not less than $25,000 will be absolutely necessary.

The General Management and Discipline.

On this subject it affords the Committee much pleasure to speak of the faithful and efficient manner in which the Directors and officers have discharged their duties, under the immediate management of Mr. Alfred D. Evans, the Warden, and his deputy, Mr. Isaac G. Roberts. The entire prison presents an air of neatness and cleanliness rarely met with in public buildings of the kind, and would indeed be creditable to any private house ; the prisoners were well clad and cleanly in their persons, and the food sufficient in quantity and quality. The discipline, if not at all times carried out to the strict letter of the law, is as perfect as the limited number of officers and guards would admit of.

But there are some matters in this connection which humanity demands at the hands of the Legislature as early action as the finances of the State will justify. The law requires that each prisoner shall be confined in a separate cell ; this from the want of necessary accommodations cannot be carried out ; five, six, and sometimes as many as eight are confined in one room, subject to all the evils that arise from free intercourse between criminals ; in addition to this the basement cells of the eastern dormitory (some fifty in number) are under ground and unfit for the confinement of human beings—it is true the present Warden, by flooring the brick pavement, has improved their condition somewhat, still they are not fit to be used.

A new dormitory, with not less than 150 cells, should be erected as soon as the means of the State will permit.

There is another evil that requires Legislative action— it is too much the practice of the courts throughout the State to send persons to the Penitentiary for small offenses whose proper destination would be the County Almshouse or the Insane Hospital. There are now in the Institution many of both classes, some who commit a petty theft for the sole purpose of being provided with a home, and others idiotic or insane at the time of commitment.

One case may be instanced by way of illustration ; the commitment is from Calvert County and reads thus :—

"George Norfolk, presented for feloniously entering the dwelling of Wm. Ogden and taking therefrom a bottle of whiskey, a pan of milk, and some bread and meat. Verdict of the jury, *Guilty, and insane at the time of the committal of the act and insane now*, and sentenced by the Court to be confined in the Penitentiary house of the State of Maryland *until he shall recover his reason*, and be discharged by due course of law."

This is virtually an imprisonment for life for the offense of stealing something to eat, the party being idiotic and insane at the time, and the effect is to transfer his support from the county to which he belongs to the State at large.

All of which is respectfully submitted.

LAWRENCE SANGSTON,
CHARLES H. PITTS,   } Committee.
JOHN THOS. FORD,

FREDERICK CITY, June 25, 1861.

The Committee appointed by the House of Delegates of Maryland to examine into the questions in dispute between Messrs. Duvall and Howard, and Mr. Charles Murdock and the Board of Directors of the Maryland Penitentiary, as also to inquire into the financial condition of the same, assembled this day in Frederick, at 12 o'clock, M.

Present—Messrs. Sangston, Pitts and Ford, of the Committee.

Mr. Thos. H. Moore was unanimously selected as clerk to the Committee.

After consultation, the Committee adjourned to meet in Baltimore city, on Monday, July 1st, 1861, at the office of Charles H. Pitts, Esq., at 11 o'clock, A. M.

By order,

THOMAS H. MOORE.

BALTIMORE, July 1st, 1861.

The Committe appointed to examine the questions in dispute between Messrs. Duvall and Howard, and Charles Murdock and the Board of Directors of the Maryland Penitentiary, as well as to inquire into the financial condition of said Institution, assembled this morning at the office of Charles H. Pitts, Esq., St. Paul street, pursuant to adjournment.

Present—Messrs. Sangston, Pitts and Ford, of the Committee. Thomas H. Moore, Clerk.

The Clerk was directed to notify the Board of Directors that the Committee would visit the Penitentiary on to-morrow, July 2d, for the purpose of examining into the facts connected with the contract of Messrs. Duvall and Howard.

· The Committee then adjourned.

By order,

THOS. H. MOORE, Clerk.

The Committee of the Legislature of Maryland assembled this morning at the room of the Directors of the Maryland Penitentiary, at 10 o'clock, pursuant to adjournment.

Present—Messrs. Sangston and Ford, of the Committee.

Mr. John H. Duvall, George M. Gill, Esq., his counsel, and Messrs. John Hurst, John Hilbert, Wm. Chestnut, R. Middleton and Lefevre Jarrett, of the Board of Directors.

The Clerk proceeded to read the memorial of John H. Duvall and William Howard to the Legislature of Maryland.

Isaac G. Roberts, Deputy Warden, was sworn on the Holy Evangely of Almighty God.

Examined by Mr. Sangston.—Question. Were you the bearer of an order from the monthly Committee of the Board of Directors to Mr. Duvall, directing him to dispense with the services of a watchman on Sunday?

Answer. No; not that I recollect. The order was given me by the Warden to tell Messrs. Duvall and Murdock that there should be no more Sunday work, and to stop all work of that kind.

Question. Did that order extend to the services of Mr. Duvall's watchman?

Answer. They did not tell me that; they only said no more fires should be made on Sunday.

Question. Who was the watchman?

Answer. I believe his name was Gambrill.

By Mr. Gill.—Question. You gave the same directions to Mr. Murdock?

Answer. I do not recollect whether I gave him or Mr. Kimball the directions. I know that Mr. Duvall's man was at work on Sundays.

By Mr. Duvall.—Question. Did you not deliver the order to me in this way, "Your men must not be about here on Sundays?"

Answer. No, sir; the order was, that Sunday work should be stopped throughout. The order I received from the Warden was general.

By Mr. Gill.—Question. Did you tell Mr. Murdock, or his man either, that they should not have a watchman on Sunday?

Answer. The prisoners attended to Mr. Murdock's work; he did not have a watchman on Sunday in daytime.

Question. Do you recollect any conversation had with Mr. Murdock, or did you tell Mr. Murdock that you had told Mr. Duvall the watchman should not be there on Sunday?

Answer. I do not recollect such conversation. The directions given to Mr. Duvall was some time before the 23d December, 1860. The man employed by Mr. Duvall was attending to the dry-houses, who was also night watchman. The fire took place after dinner on Sunday, between 2 and 3 o'clock; before 3 o'clock, 23d December, 1860.

Question. Did you investigate into the causes of the fire?

Answer. I did, and was under the impression that Samuel Green, Edward Perry, John Butler and Joe Wheatley, all colored, committed the act. The men could very easily get from the church to the shop—about sixty yards.

Question. Were they permitted to go about without an officer under the proper discipline of the establishment?

Answer. It is customary to go about without an officer. The officers on the wall are constantly on the look out, with arms in their hands. If they had attended to their duty, the prisoners could not enter the shop of Mr. Duvall except at one point in the rear ; Mr. Murdock's dry-house obscured the view from the officer's box, leaving a space of three or four feet a prisoner could enter. The dormitories are cleaned between 10 and 12 o'clock. The fire took place about fifteen minutes of 3 o'clock. I ascertained from investigation, that three of the parties were guilty, and one was present. Wheatley said that Green had a box with yellow cotton in it ; Green set the cotton on fire in the dormitory. Green and Perry went to Duvall's shop together, when they built the fire. Wheatley said the whole four were connected ; that he, Wheatley, set the fire, but the others assisted. Yellow cotton is an article used in the manufacturing department, and makes a very good slow-match. A piece three feet long would burn two hours.

Question. How far is the dormitory where the cotton was set on fire from Duvall's shop?

Answer. About seventy-five yards.

Cross-examined by Mr. Hurst.—Question. Did the Court rule your testimony out?

Answer. It did upon the second trial, because the information I derived was through stratagem.

By Mr. Jarrett.—Question. How long have you been connected with the Penitentiary?

Answer. Three years under William Johnson Waden, one year under I. M. Denson, and upwards of three years under A. D. Evans.

Question.—Are the present officers as great in number as those of former administrations?

Answer. There are four more than under the late Warden, Mr. Merryman.

Question. How does the discipline of this Institution as at present, compare with that of former wardens?

Answer. I think it might be more strict ; my own orders are to carry out the strictest discipline, and I have endeavored to do so.

Question. Has not Mr. Duvall been notified that the condition of his shops prevented the officers from having a strict supervision over the same?

Answer. I have notified him several times that the quantity of barrels prevented the officers from having a full view of the entire shop during work hours.

By Mr. Sangston.—Question. Who was the watchman on duty nearest the shop of Mr. Duvall?

Answer. Mr. Suter was the guard.

Question. Was any action taken by the Board in relation to the negligence of the guard?

Answer. Yes. Mr. Suter was discharged.

James Gambrell, sworn.

By Mr. Gill.—Question. You recollect the fire at Mr. Duvall's shop, 23d December, 1860?

Answer. Yes. I do.

Question. How long prior to that fire had you been employed by Mr. Duvall?

Answer. Seven months and nineteen nights and days. I commenced about the 4th May, 1860.

Question. What was your duty?

Answer. Watch out for fires; put out all fires used in shop after prisoners had left; not to permit any fires after Saturday night, 12 o'clock.

Question. When you first attended, what did you do on Sundays?

Answer. The first two Sundays I was not admitted to the yard of the Institution until my hour for duty arrived.

Question. What did you do for the subsequent time on Sundays?

Answer. On and after the third Sunday, I cleaned out the boilers of the engine, and watched for anything that might be wrong until Mr. Duvall's foreman or sons arrived, which continued until three or five Sundays before the fire, when I stopped coming to the Institution until my hour arrived for night duty, about sun-down. I stopped then by Mr. Duvall's directions. I understood from him that the Directors were not satisfied with his men coming upon the premises on Sunday; after which notice I did not watch on Sundays.

Question. Was any work done on Sundays after you entered Mr. Duvall's employment?

Answer. Nothing was done except cleaning the boilers, which was done by me until stopped, as before mentioned, by Mr. Duvall.

Cross-examined by Mr. Jarrett.—Question. When Mr. Duvall told you that your services on Sunday were dispensed with, no work was then required of you?

Answer. I had the same watching to do.

By Mr. Ford.—Question. Did you understand from any person connected with the Institution that objection was raised against your being there as watchman simply?

Answer. I had no information on the subject.

Cross-examined by Mr. Jarrett.—Question. Did the officer in charge of Mr. Duvall's shop complain in your hearing of the condition of the shop?

Answer. I did hear him complain, and have seen him take Mr. Duvall's men and remove the cause of complaint.

Question. Have you seen Mr. Evans, the Warden, pass through at late hours of the night and examine Mr. Duvall's shop?

Answer. I have.

Question. Did the Warden sometimes previous to the fire express to you his apprehensions that because of the non-employment of the convicts, and the unsafe condition of Mr. Duvall's shop, a fire would result therefrom?

Answer. I do not think the convicts were referred to, but he did complain of the condition of the shop, and requested me to keep a bright look out.

Direct examination resumed by Mr. Gill.—Question. If you had continued up to the time of the fire, would you not have been able to prevent the fire?

Answer. I think I would.

Question. Could the regular watch of the Institution prevent the convicts from going into Mr. Duvall's shop?

Answer. I think they could.

Mr. Charles Murdock, sworn for Complainant.

Examined by Mr. Gill.—Question. Prior to the fire, was a watchman on duty on Sunday in Mr. Duvall's shop?

Answer. I have seen one on duty, presuming he was from what I have seen him do, the impression on my mind being that both Mr. Lamb and Mr. Gambrell have attended to the fires on Sunday, although I am not sure of the same.

Question. Had you any conversation with Mr. Roberts prior to or subsequent to the fire in relation to the direction he had given Mr. Duvall as to the watchman being there on Sunday?

Answer. After the fire Mr. Roberts admitted to me that he had given the order to Mr. Duvall forbidding his watchman on Sundays. The order to stop the watchmen was given one or two months prior to the fire.

By A. D. Evans. I understood Mr. Roberts to say that the watchman was stopped from doing whatever he had been previously doing?

By Mr. Jarrett.—Question.—Have you heard any objections from any Director to a watchman being employed by a contractor?

Answer. No, sir; because I have had to employ no watchman.

By Mr. Ford.—Question. Did you understand the order as forbidding all persons employed by contractors coming upon the premises?

Answer. I did so understand the order.

By Mr. Hurst.—Question. After the order was given, did you not see persons at work on Sunday in the shop of Mr. Duvall?

Answer. I cannot say.

By Mr. Jarrett.—Question. Have you ever expressed any apprehensions from fire because of the condition of Mr. Duvall's shop.

Answer. I believe I have.

Mr. Gambrill, recalled by Complainant.

By Mr. Gill.—Question. Did you know of any work being done on Sunday while you were acting as watchman?

Answer. I do not know of any.

Michael Conner, sworn by Complainant.

Examined by Mr. Gill.—Question. You were the foreman of Mr. Duvall in the manufacturing department?

Answer. Yes, sir, from the 28th February, 1860. I had no knowledge of any order being given, except that no prisoners should be worked on Sundays, and no fires be permitted in the dry houses on that day.

The Committee then adjourned until to-morrow, Wednesday morning, at 10 o'clock.

————

WEDNESDAY, July 3d, 1861.

The Committee met pursuant to adjournment. Present, Messrs. Sangston and Ford.

Mr. Murdock, recalled by Complainant.

Examined by Mr. Gill.—Question. If the rules and regulations of the Penitentiary, as laid down in the Code and printed orders, had been followed on the day when the shop of Mr. Duvall was fired, would not such fire have been prevented in your opinion?

Answer. I understand that under such rules an officer should have had the supervision of the prisoners, and if this had been so, it would be impossible, in my judgment, for the fire to have occurred. It would be difficult among so large a number of convicts to have *at all times* an officer with each convict. When the rules and regulations were made, the number of shops were less, and the prisoners were not so scattered, although no difference existed on Sundays.

Question. Is there, or not, more danger on Sundays from fire by the convicts than on other days? If so, state the reasons?

Answer. On Sundays there is less danger from accidents; but more danger from incendiaries, because on Sunday if the prisoners are allowed in the shops the fire would not be so readily discovered, there being so few persons about.

Question. How long have you been employed in the Penitentiary?

Answer. The best part of ten years, with very few intervals.

Cross-examined by Mr. Hurst.—Question. Were the prisoners allowed to go into the shops of Mr. Duvall, or any of them, on Sundays?

Answer. I do not know that they were, except by special permission, although I have seen them in the shops on Sunday, and I understood from Mr. Roberts that it would not be permitted for the future. I never supposed that they were permitted to enter unless they had business.

By Mr. Jarrett.—Question. So far as you know, have not the rules and regulations, as far as practicable, been carried out?

Answer. I have no knowledge of what the rules and regulations are, unless as printed; in many respects they have not been carried out as printed, in others they have.

Question. What is your opinion of the general discipline of the Institution for the past three years?

Answer. In some respects I have considered the discipline has been very good, the difference between the present and former administrations exists in the fact, that I have been enabled to compel my men to work under the present administration, when they were disposed to object; I have had more control over the men; a great portion of the discipline of the Institution I have no means of knowing anything about, as it does not come under my supervision or observation. The discipline in the shops under my control has been somewhat better than under former administrations; I have thought that the rules were defective in not placing the watchman on Sundays on duty at noon instead of at night.

Question. Is it not an utter impossibility for the officers to have their eyes on every prisoner during work hours?

Answer. I believe it is.

Question. Was your shop ever burnt out by fire?

Answer. Several times; in 1857 by a very heavy fire; I lost all my machinery.

Question. Did you ever make a claim against the State for damages resulting from fire?

Answer. No. I did not. At the fire of 1857 the Directors gave me the labor of a considerable number of men, free of charge, until my shops were re-built.

Question. Was the same routine in regard to the enforcement of the rules and regulations on Sundays carried out then as now?

Answer. I do not know, not being present on Sundays.

Question. Has not a disposition been manifested always by the Board of Directors and officers to give your property every protection and security against loss by fire?

Answer. As far as I know, it has.

Cross-examined by A. D. Evans, Warden.—Question. Do you remember of there ever being a watchman in the yard on Sundays previous to the fire of Mr. Duvall's shop?

Answer. I had supposed so until I ascertained much to my surprise about three years ago, that the watchman did not go on duty until Sunday night. I refer to the watchman of the Institution. I do not know whether I ascertained this fact prior to, or since the present administration.

Cross-examined by Mr. Jarrett.—Question. Have you not considered that Mr. Duvall kept his fires at too great a degree of heat in the dry houses, and thereby endangered the premises?

Answer. I considered that at times he did keep the fires hotter than I deemed prudent to keep mine, but I had no knowledge of the degree of heat, except from what I heard from others.

By Mr. Evans.—Question. What degree of heat do you deem proper and safe?

Answer. I think it dangerous to go above 125 degrees; the material used by me, however, being lighter than that used by Mr. Duvall.

The testimony for complainant here closed for the present.

Mr. A. D. Evans, Warden of Penitentiary, sworn for Directors.

Examined by Mr. Jarrett.—Question. Has the same protection been given to Mr. Duvall's property as has been given to Mr. Murdock's and the property of the State?

Answer. Yes, sir, fully as much, no complaint of want of protection has ever been made to me by either Mr. Duvall or Mr. Murdock.

Question. Has any extra advantages or favors been extended to Mr. Duvall in the prosecution of his business?

Answer. In the selection of good workmen, in the increase of the hours of labor, when other contractors did not desire it; an extra officer placed in the wagon yard to facilitate the delivery of the barrels; and giving the convicts their breakfasts earlier, so that the time of labor was increased, for the space of three days, which was changed at Mr. Duvall's request.

Question. Did not Mr. Duvall keep his shop in an unsafe condition, and did you not notify him of the same?

Answer. The shop was in a very unsafe condition for a long period of time, so much so, that it was constantly complained of by the officer, Mr. Lefevre, that he could not perform his duties as he would like. I told Mr. Duvall the Directors thought his shop was in an unsafe condition, and I thought so too, and that the shop must be cleared; Mr. Duvall said he could not do it, because he had no other place for his stuff, and that the Directors had no authority or control over his shop, as the contract did not mention anything of that character.

Question. Was not the State deprived of the services of convicts from accidents occurring in Mr. Duvall's shop?

Answer. Yes, of a large number.

Question. Did you make it your duty or practice to go through Mr. Duvall's shop during the week and on Sundays more than through other shops?

Answer. Some six or eight weeks prior to the fire, I did visit his shop more than any other, because the shop was lumbered more than formerly, and in a dangerous condition, and I feared it might be fired either by accident or design.

Question. While Mr. Duvall's shop was in such a condition, was he not absent a great part of the time?

Answer. Yes, a week at a time.

William A. Wisong, sworn.

Examined by Mr. Hurst—Question. Have you not had frequent opportunities to witness the operation of the Institution, and what is your opinion of the general discipline of the same?

Answer. I have, and I believe the discipline to be as good as that of any other of the kind, and a good deal better than some. I have been connected with the Penitentiary, as agent of the Prison Association, for two years past, and believe that the rules are fully enforced.

Cross-examined by Mr. Gill.—Question. Did you ever go into the shops on Sunday?

Answer. I never did. I visited only the chapel and hospital on Sundays.

The Committee adjourned to meet on Friday morning, at 10 o'clock.   By order,

THOS. H. MOORE, Clerk.

2

BALTIMORE, July 5, 1861.
The Committee met. Present Messrs. Ford and Sangston.

Mr. John H. Duvall, sworn and examined.

By Mr. Gill.—Question. What was the first direction and order received by you in relation to the employment on Sundays of any persons acting for you, and when and by whom? What was the second order, and from whom and when? And what was done after each of these orders?

Answer. Some time prior to the accident by which I was shot, on the 21st of April, 1861, I received an order from Mr. Evans, the Warden of the Penitentiary, that no more work should be done in my shops on Sunday, at the Penitentiary, such as firing the dry houses, &c. Some time prior to the fire, I do not know how long, the Deputy, Mr. Roberts, told me he was instructed by the Committee to say to me that any watchman or any of my men must not be about there on Sundays. I directed the firing of dry houses to be discontinued on Sundays. It was discontinued. After the second order from Mr. Roberts, I directed the watchman, Mr. Gambrill, not to be there on Sundays until the hour of going on duty at evening, which was obeyed to the best of my knowledge.

Question. Did you employ a watchman to take care of the property in the shops carried on by you in the Penitentiary, and especially on Sundays, and when did he cease to do that duty, and why?

Answer. I did employ a watchman; the first one, Mr. Lamb, who continued until about the first of May, 1860, when the fire of Mr. Murdock's shops occurred; that one of the Directors, Mr. Bryson, I think, sent by Mr. Howard when I was confined to bed, that Mr. Lamb ought to be discharged; he was accordingly discharged, and Mr. Gambrill appointed in his stead, at the solicitation of Mr. Bryson. Gambrill continued in my employment until the 23d of December, 1860, when the fire took place, it may have been a little later. Gambrill's duty was to watch the place at night and on Sundays, and attend to the dry houses. The duty was performed until the order was given herein before stated, as given by Mr. Roberts· After which order Gambrill ceased to be there on Sunday in the day time.

Question. At what time on Sunday, the 23d of December, did the fire at your shop occur, and to what cause do you attribute the same, and if your watchman had been on duty as before the order was given by Mr. Roberts, would or would not the fire have been prevented in your judgment?

Answer. The fire occurred on Sunday, 23d December, about half-past two to three o'clock, the cause I attribute to the act of incendiary convicts. If my watchman had been on duty as previously to the order of Mr. Roberts, the fire could not have occurred in my judgment.

Question. Are you acquainted with the rules and regulations of the Maryland Penitentiary, and especially in relation to convicts, and the course pursued to them on Sundays, and state what they were? Also state if such rules and regulations had been pursued on Sunday, the 23d December, 1860. Would or would not, in your judgment, the fire at your shop on that day have been prevented?

Answer. I know of no rules and regulations except the published ones, a copy of which was handed me soon after my contract. I have no information in regard to the management of prisons on Sundays, except from what I have derived from observation. It is usual for a portion of the negro convicts, some fifteen or twenty in number, to be employed in cleansing the dormitories and carrying off the filth to the pen; in doing which they have to pass through a large portion of the yard and around most of the shops. If properly supervised by an officer, they could not enter the shops without the knowledge of the officer. I think the fire would have been prevented if the rules and regulations had been enforced.

The Committee here adjourned until to-morrow morning at 10 o'clock.

———

BALTIMORE, JULY 6, 1861.

The Committee met pursuant to adjournment. Present, Messrs. Sangston and Ford.

The examination of Mr. Duvall resumed.

By Mr. Gill.—The particular rule to which I refer, which, if observed, would have prevented the fire, is to be found in the Code of General Laws, Art. 73, Sec. 82: "The Warden must not permit any prisoners to be together at any time without the proper supervision of an officer."

Question. Were there or not any fires in and about your shop at the Maryland Penitentiary immediately prior to the fire of the 23d December, 1860, or on the premises connected therewith? How did the fire which destroyed your property occur as you have been advised, and what were the circumstances thereof? State all of them? What precautions might have been and ought to have been taken to prevent the convicts from getting into your shop on that day, and if taken, what would probably have been the effect thereof?

Answer. We were running our engine the day before (Saturday) with the usual fire, and on the same day some fire may have been in other stoves, as it is usual to have them at that season; all of which were extinguished, to my knowledge, about 5 o'clock, P. M., of that day, (Saturday.) In the usual course of business there would be no fires during the whole day of Sunday, and as far as I know there was no fire on that Sunday; but I was not there until after the fire.

From what I have learned from the Deputy Warden, the fire was the act of incendiary convicts, as he had ascertained by their confessions, accomplished by the use of slow-matches and powdered sulphur and rosin. That they had applied the matches in the early part of the day, probably about 11 o'clock.

After Mr. Roberts had ascertained these facts, in company with some of the officers in the Warden's Lodge, an experiment was tried with the yellow cotton yarn, which the convicts confessed to have used as matches. The experiment proved that the yarn made a good slow-match, and that it would have been easy to have communicated the fire by such matches.

The convicts who cleaned the dormitories are engaged on Sundays at this work about 10½ A. M., or later, while religious services are performed.

The distance from the door of the dormitory to the pen is, say 150 to 200 yards, this route would pass my shop, and would also pass two of Mr. Murdock's shops and dry-houses, the State dry-house and smoke-house, and also Mr. Murdock's broom corn shed. Convicts passing those shops, if properly supervised by an officer or officers, could not have obtained access to them.

Question. Who were interested in the business carried on by you at the Maryland Penitentiary?

Answer. My son-in-law, William Howard, and myself were interested in the business referred to.

Question. What was the amount of loss sustained from the fire of the 23d December, 1860, by you and your partner; state the details, and show how such loss is made up.

Answer. According to an estimate made by Mr. Conner and myself:

Materials prepared in the shop, &c., destroyed, would have made up 82,500 barrels. The barrels were sold for 35 cents a piece. Hoops and labor 9 cents—26 cents—
amounting to $21,450.00
Besides on hand 1200 barrels, at 36 cents,   432.00
Loss in machinery, dry houses, cost $9,500 worth, 7,100.00

                                                  $28,982.00

Less insurance money received,   5,600.00

My claim being $23,382.00

 Question. What amount did you pay the Directors of the Maryland Penitentiary for the hire of convicts prior to the fire, and what did you pay after the fire, and under what circumstances did you make such payment after the fire?

Answer. During the contract, and before the fire, I paid $7,031.07 to the Directors for labor, &c.

After the fire I paid $1,075.59 to the Directors, according to an account which I produce with my answer and file as part of it, (marked A.) The fire ruined my business, soon after which the Directors desired to know of me what was my intention about going on with the contract. I informed them that our misfortunes at the fire had destroyed our business, and I was unable to do it. I was asked the question by one of the Directors, if I was aware that I could be required to build the shop, and pay for the prisoners, while it was going on. This induced me to consult my counsel, Mr. Gill, who informed me that under the contract I could be so held. My counsel, therefore, advised me to make the best settlement I could with the Directors, and I accordingly did so, as the paper alluded to, marked A, shows.

(A)

BALTIMORE, December 31, 1860.

Messrs. John H. Duvall & Sons,
         In account with Maryland Penitentiary.

Work done in smithing, October, 1860, - - - $ 3.22
Water rent from July 1 to Nov. 1, 1860, $240, - 80.00
Work done in smithing, November, 1860, - - - 4.57
Rent from August 31 to Nov. 30, 1860, $200, - - 50.00
Hire, November, 1860, - - - - - - - - 180.05
"   from Dec. 1, 1860, to 22d, inclusive, - - ⎫
"   1,157¾ days, at 60 cents, - - - - ⎬ 694.65
"   19 · "   at 25 " - - - - - - ⎭ 4.75
Work done, December, 1860, - - - - - - - 1.68
Rent from Nov. 30 to Dec. 31, 1860, - - - - - 16.67
"   Water " 1 "   "   " - - - - - 40.00

                                  $1,075.59

                CR.
By 101 lbs. tobacco, at 20 cents, - - - - - - 20.20

                                  $1,055.39

Cr.

1861. January 30, By cash, - - - - - - -   140.00
_____
$915.39·

Cr.

By R. Norris, Jr's., note, dated January 31, 1861,
  at 3 mos., for $800, less interest 3 mos., $12,   788.00
_____
$127.39
Received balance by check, January 31, 1861.

JNO. J. C. DOUGHERTY, Clerk.

After we had agreed on the terms of settlement, I
informed the Directors that my only means of payment
was the property then on hand, and not destroyed. I
asked permission to remove some of it, and dispose of it
for that purpose. This permission was refused, and they
would not allow me to do so until the settlement was
made.

To make the settlement I had to encounter great inconvenience and difficulty, in consequence of the misfortune
of the fire.

Mr. Gill, in his opinion, also advised that no suit could
be maintained against the State or the Directors as such.
If they could have been sued, he would have advised me to
bring suit.

Cross-examined by Mr. Brune.—Question. What work was
done on Sundays, before the order which you say was given
by Mr. Evans?

Answer. There was no general work done on Sundays,
except making fires in dry houses. There was occasionally
other work done. It was not the practice to do work on
Sundays, except from necessity. The orders given by Mr.
Evans were followed, and the fires discontinued, so far as I
know, after such order had been given.

Question. Who was your watchman at the time of this
order from Mr. Evans, and when precisely was this order
given?

Answer. Mr. Lamb was the watchman when the order
was given by Mr. Evans. I cannot state more specifically
than I have done in my direct answer, the time when Mr.
Evans gave the order referred to.

Question. Why was Mr. Lamb discharged, and was there
or not a fire or fires at the Penitentiary while he was your
watchman?

Answer. I do not know why Mr. Lamb was discharged, except as already stated. There was only one fire of importance while Mr. Lamb was my watchman. That was at one of the dry houses, and in January, 1860. There was nothing that destroyed anything. On one occasion, while at work at shop, some boards took fire, and they were immediately put out. Mr. Lamb was not then present; beside these there was the fire on Mr. Murdock's premises in May, 1860, and which led to Lamb's discharge.

Question. Who were the Monthly Committee at the time the order of Roberts, spoken of by you in answer to the first direct question, was given, and was such order *in writing*, through Mr. Roberts?

Answer. I do not know who constituted the Monthly Committee of the Penitentiary when the order given to me by Roberts was received. The order from Roberts was verbal.

Question. Did you, after this order was given to you by Roberts, make any application to the Monthly Committee or to any of the Directors in relation thereto, and if you did state to whom you so applied?

Answer. I did not. I obeyed the order without making any complaint about it or seeing any of the parties.

Question. Did you, or your sons, or your foreman of machinery, Mr. Murdock, ever go into the shops on Sunday after this order?

Answer. I do not know that any one but myself did go over to the Penitentiary on Sunday after the order from Roberts; I did sometimes go over on Sunday in the morning, and sometimes in the afternoon.

Question. Have you any recollection of Mr. Murdock's covering a pully with wood on a Sunday?

Answer. I recollect that a pully was covered with wood on Sunday by Mr. Murdock, but I think it was done prior to the order from Mr. Roberts.

Question. Before the order which you state came from Mr. Roberts, was it the habit of Mr. Gambrill to make a fire on Saturday night and keep it up during Sunday? If not, when was the fire made on Sunday before and after said order, and what time was the watchman expected to come on duty every day and go off, and who watched while he was off duty?

Answer. Before the order from Roberts it was not the habit of Mr. Gambrill, the watchman, to make up the fires on Saturday night and keep them up on Sunday. After the order from Mr. Evans they stopped firing at 12 o'clock on Saturday, and began again at 12 o'clock on Sunday night. Some time after this I got permission from Mr. Hilbert to make the fires at dark on Sunday night, and to stop them at *daylight*. The watchman usually came on about supper time during the week, he would be there on Saturday night, and was relieved on Sunday morning at about 10 o'clock, when witness would sometimes relieve him, and would return at about 12 or 1 o'clock, and sometimes later, to resume his duties; this was before the order given by Mr. Roberts, afterwards he quit when the state watchman would go away in the morning, and not return again. When not relieved by witness, the watchman would go for his meals during Sunday from the premises—before the order from Roberts.

Question. Why did you extinguish the fires on Saturday, the 22d of December, at 5 P. M., if you had under Mr. Hilbert's permission right to continue them until Sunday at daylight?

Answer. We had no fires on Saturday, the 22d, or for some days prior to that time in the dry houses. They had been unable for some weeks, say six weeks, to procure a supply of hoops, and during that time had not finished barrels. There was an intermission of that particular kind of work. There was a good deal of other work done, such as cutting and drying timber. They had kept on at that until every place was full where they could put it in the shop or dry houses.

Question. Did Mr. Gambrill remain all night of Saturday, the 22d of December? Do you know when he left in the morning of Sunday?

Answer. Mr. Gambrill did remain all night, so far as I know on Saturday night, the 22d of December, 1860. I do not know when he left on Sunday morning, the 23d of December, 1860.

Question. Can you say from your own knowledge or observation that the negro convicts in cleaning the dormitories on Sunday, the 23d of December, were not properly supervised?

Answer. On that day I was not present at the Penitentiary until after the fire broke out. I cannot say.

Question. With what Committee or Directors was the agreement (A) made?

Answer. The agreement was made at a Board meeting. Mr. Hurst was present, and Mr. Jarrett, and three or four others.

Question. At the time this agreement for settlement with the Board was made, did you complain of the orders of Messrs. Evans and Roberts, or either of them, or set up any claim on your part against the Directors or the State of Maryland?

Answer. I do not recollect that anything was said about the orders of Mr. Evans or Mr. Roberts at the time of the agreement for settlement, nor did I then complain of such orders or either of them, and at that meeting I did not set up any claim against the State or the Directors. I did not mean to speak of that and did not.

Question. Did you not express to the Board or to some members of it, at that meeting or subsequently, that you thought they were dealing liberally with you, or words to that effect?

Answer. When the settlement was made, I thanked the Board for the settlement because I was glad to make it to enable me to get some of my property out of the place to live upon.

(Copy of Bond filed.)

Question. Did you not, subsequently to the agreement for a settlement, obtain premission from the Directors that your goods might remain on the premises for some time, and did you not verbally or in writing propose to the Board to renew your contract on certain terms?

Answer. At the time of the settlement I did get permission to permit goods to remain until they wished to re-build. Subsequently I received notice that the rent would be $25 per week for the premises burnt. I asked the Board if they would make a contract with me on certain terms, which they declined.

Question. Where was your property insured, and was the insurance money paid, and why was it not insured for a larger amount?

Answer. The property was insured at the Lynchburg Office and the Valley Insurance Company at Virginia, and it was not insured for a large amount, for the reason that it was difficult to procure good insurance. Application was made and declined by several offices, because the risk was too great.

The Committee adjourned to Monday morning next, at 10 o'clock.

By order,

THOMAS H. MOORE, Clerk.

———

MONDAY, July 8th, 1861.

The Committee met pursuant to adjournment. Present, Messrs. Sangston and Ford.

The cross-examination of J. H. Duvall continued by Mr. Brune.

A letter marked (B,) now exhibited and filed.

(B)

BALTIMORE, March 21, 1861.

To the Directors of the Maryland Penitentiary:

GENTLEMEN :—

" With the view of arranging so as to enable me to make another contract with you, I propose to ask you the following questions, viz:

1st. Would you rebuild the shop so as to afford the largest possible amount of yard room, and enable me thereby to dispense with a portion of the dry houses; building say 25 or 26 feet wide, two stories, one end of it for the accommodation of machinery, &c., say 40 or 50 feet square, with celler under such portion of it as might be wanted, and shed for boiler and engine?

2d. Would you buy my boiler and engine at fair price, say $2,000, to be put and kept in order by me, and to be paid for as may be agreed by the labor of the prisoners for which I may contract?

3d. Would you contract for, say thirty-five first class prisoners, as far as you may have them, the same as worked for me before—that I may select, at fifty cents per day, and ten to fifteen second class at twenty-five cents—this latter class to be healthy and strong, but say short term, and such as you always have, that cannot be employed to better advantage, either by the State or a contractor, the fifty cent men at all times to be first class; and if upon trial of, say one month, any such shall be found not to answer the purposes for which they were taken, to be exchanged. All to work for three months, as they are taken to learn at twenty-five cents per day—I to take such portion of them from time to time as I may require them—and take all by a day to be agreed upon; and have the privilege of increasing from time to time, as I may want them—the fifty cent men, say to the number of sixty, and the twenty-five cent men to the number of twenty-five; and to have such labor as may . be wanted in fitting up the shop for commencement without charge?

4th. What will you charge for the rent of the shop, and boiler and engine, including water rent?

Which I respectfully sumbit.

Very truly,

Your obedient servant,

JOHN H. DUVALL.

Question. Look at paper B, now presented to you, and say whether it is in your hand-writing.

Answer. It is.

Question. Were you here on Sundays, so as yourself to see the way in which the dormitories were cleaned by the negroes, as spoken of in your examination in chief?

Answer. I have been present on Sundays and witnessed the manner in which the negroes carried off the filth from the dormitories to the filth pens.

Question. Did you ever complain to the Warden or Directors, or any of them, and if so, when and how¿ that the negroes thus engaged were without the proper supervision of officers?

Answer. I have no recollection that I ever did.

J. G. Roberts, recalled by Directors.

By Mr. Brune.—Question. In your previous examination you stated, in answer to a question in regard to the present discipline of the Institution—"I think it might be more strict; my own orders are, to carry out the strictest discipline, and I have endeavored to do so." Will you explain the apparent discrepancy in portions of your said answer?

Answer. I meant to say that the discipline was as good as it could be under existing circumstances; by existing circumstances I mean the contract system as it now prevails; the contract system has prevailed for the last three years to my knowledge. I was assistant Warden nine years before the present term; when I was first here no contract system prevailed.

Cross-examined by Mr. Gill.—Question. You were not present when the fire took place?

Answer. No, sir.

Question. You were then Deputy Warden?

Answer. Yes, sir.

Question. How long had you been absent before the fire?

Answer. About two weeks.

Question. Why were you absent so long?

Answer. I had been confined for a long time and obtained leave of absence from the Board for two weeks.

Question. Who was appointed in your absence?

Answer. I believe Mr. Sparks discharged my duty.

Question. Do you know who filled your position on the day of the fire?

Answer. I do not know.

Question. Have you ever said to Mr. Charles Murdock, that if you had been present on the day of the fire, the same would not have occurred?

Answer. I might have said so, I do not recollect it; I have had frequent conversations with him on the subject of the fire.

Question. Have you not said to Mr. Murdock that during your absence from the Penitentiary, there was a want of discipline therein, and that you attributed the fire to such want of discipline, and state what you did say to Mr. Murdock in reference to the discipline of the Penitentiary, and the effect thereof in producing the fire at Mr. Duvall's shop?

Answer. If I did say so, it was in assent to a remark from him.

Mr. Charles Murdock, recalled.

By Mr. Gill.—Question. Had you any conversation with Mr. Roberts after the fire, relating to his absence at the time of the fire at Mr. Duvall's shop, and the effect thereof in his judgment, if so, state it?

Answer. I have had conversation with Mr. Roberts.

Question. Did Mr. Roberts say to you, that if he had been present, in his opinion, the fire would not have occurred?

Answer. I have heard Mr. Roberts express his opinion, that if he had been here, the fire would not have occurred. I understood him to mean if he had been on duty. I never heard him say specifically why the fire would not have occurred, if he had been present.

Mr. Gill here exhibits and filed a printed copy of the rules and regulations for the government of the Maryland Penitentiary, 1853.

(C)

The officers are required to preserve harmony and kind feelings among themselves, to the end that a desirable official intercourse may obtain. They must, therefore, be respectful in their intercourse and communications with each other, and indulge in no undue liberties.

The Deputy Keepers must yield that ready obedience to their superior officers, so necessary to secure the beneficial results of effective co-operation and good government.

Whenever a Deputy Keeper may be absent from sickness, or other *necessary cause*, the Warden shall designate one of the approved supernumeraries to take his place, at such Deputy Keeper's expense.

Mr. Conner recalled and cross-examined by Mr. Brune.—Question. What were Mr. Gambrill's duties as watchman after he came and down to the time of the fire; was he a day or night watchman, and what were his hours for going on and coming off duty?

Answer. I understood the duties of Mr. Gambrill, during the time that staves were in the dry houses, to keep up fires and to get steam on the steam boxes in the morning, so that the men could get to work. On Saturday evening or Sunday morning, after the boiler was "blown off," he cleaned the boiler out, no change took place in the duty that I am aware of down to the time of the fire. I never considered him a day watchman, he would generally go on duty about the time the men would leave off work, about supper time. I was never present when he came off duty in the morning.

Question. At what time did you come on duty in the morning?

Answer. I generally came on at 6½ to 7 o'clock in the morning.

Question. Was Gambrill generally gone when you came on duty?

Answer. He was, every day excepting when Mr. Murdock was away; this does not apply to Sundays. It was very rarely I came on Sundays.

Question. Did you make any examination of the property manufactured and the machinery remaining after the fire. If so, state for what purpose, and was it carefully done and in connection with Mr. Duvall?

Answer. I made an examination of the loss in stock at Mr. Duvall's request, for the Insurance Company; it was carefully done.

Question. Will you be so good as to state to the Committee, as well as you now can, the result of such inquiry and the statement of loss to the stock?

Answer. The statement prepared for Insurance Company made the amount of stock in the main shop to be one million of pieces, from what I could understand from Mr. Duvall and his sons, we estimated these pieces to be $7 per thousand pieces, were dried and ready, the greater portion to put in barrels. We estimated either 90 or 95 thousand pieces were not damaged, there were four dry houses, two were destroyed entirely and two damaged, one damaged to the extent of one-half. In two of the houses I considered a total loss had occurred; I considered the loss to be 200,000 pieces, at $7 per thousand, $14,000. For the other two houses I considered the loss to be one half, making $700 of loss. 1,200 barrels fully completed were ready for delivery, with the exception of a few hoops, the value of each barrel I believed to be 35 to 36 cents per barrel. I did not make an examination of the loss to the machinery, that was done by Messrs. Denmead and Pool.

Question. Was the property remaining or any part of it sold, and if so, to whom, and for about what amount?

Answer. Yes, sir, the barrels on hand, those not burnt entirely through were sold to Mr. Everitt at 12½ cents per barrel; I think between 500 or 600 were sold him; they were sold for about $60. I understood from Mr. Duvall that he sold all the leavings or remnants for $100 ; the cost of the labor of cleaning up the remains of the fire would have been much more than he received from the sale.

Examination resumed by Mr. Gill.

Question. How many barrels would the stuff destroyed by the fire have made?

Answer. According to the estimate made for the Insurance Company, about 46,154 barrels.

Question. Did that estimate include the whole quantity destroyed?

Answer. It did not, because Mr. Duvall said that the amount of loss was so far above the insurance, it was unnecessary for me to go fully into the examination.

Question. Was or not, in your judgment, a much larger amount of stuff destroyed than covered by estimate of insurance, and how much more?

Answer. I believe there was more, but how much more I am unable to say.

Question. Do you recollect having any conversation with Mr. Duvall shortly prior to his application to the Legislature, in relation to the amount of stuff lost by the fire, as compared with estimate made to Insurance Company, and what amount of barrels you stated to him the stuff would have made up.

Answer. I remember having a conversation with Mr. Duvall upon the subject, and in that interview he exhibited some papers, among which was the estimate that had been made to the Insurance Company, another was an estimate to prove to the Legislature Committee, and by whom the amount of stuff he had on hand, and the number of barrels he could have made. I do not remember to have expressed any opinion as to the number of barrels that could have been made. Before and subsequent to the fire it was commonly observed among us, that we had stuff enough to make 100,000 barrels, but it was not my opinion ; I do not believe it would have made one-half of that number, if that. Mr. Duvall had contracted to sell the barrels to two parties at 36 cents, and to one other party at 35 cents per barrel. I estimate the cost of finishing each barrel about 9 to 10 cents. I have no knowledge of the agreement by which Mr. Duvall employed Mr. Gambrill. I am now a substitute officer in the employment of the Penitentiary.

John R. Hynson, sworn.

Question. Are you now an officer of the Maryland Penitentiary, what office do you hold, and how long have you held it?

Answer. I am an officer of the Maryland Penitentiary, and have been watchman of the yard since May, 1860.

Question. Did you know Mr. Gambrill, who was formerly in the employ of Mr. Duvall? If so, will you state when he was in the habit of going on and coming off duty; state particularly when he went on on Saturday evening, and when he went off on Sunday mornings?

Answer. Yes, sir; he would go on duty usually about the time of locking up in the evening, and he came off when Mr. Duvall's hands went to work. On Saturday evening he would go on about the usual time; on Sunday morning he would go off duty some time before I did. I went off on Sunday morning at 7 o'clock; I was a night watchman.

Question. Was Mr. Gambrill in the habit at any time, while he was in the employ of Mr. Duvall, of coming to the Institution on Sundays after he left in the morning, before the evenings when you came?

Answer. I never saw him at the Penitentiary on Sunday mornings, as I was not here myself; although I have heard him say he had attended and cleaned the boilers, we would frequently come together when about to go on duty for the night.

Question. Where did he get his meals on Sundays; and is it not necessary for a night watchman to get rest during each day?

Answer. As far as I know he did not get them in the Institution on Sunday. It is necessary for a night watchman to get rest during the day.

By Mr. Sangston.—I do not think that I ever came to the Institution on Sundays.

Mr. A. D. Evans, Warden, recalled.

Question. What time did Mr. Gambrill leave the Institution usually on Sunday mornings? Where did he get his meals, and when did he usually return, and state your means of knowledge?

Answer. Mr. Gambrill would leave the Institution in the morning about 7 o'clock, and would leave about the same time on Sundays as on week days. He did not get his meals at the Institution. He usually returned a little before dusk, although I have seen him here somewhat earlier. My means of knowledge are derived from personal observation.

Question. Had you ever any knowledge that Messrs. Lamb and Gambrill were day watchmen for Mr. Duvall?

Answer. I never knew it; I did know that they were night watchmen.

Wm. J. Bryson, a Director, sworn.

Question. Had you ever notice in any way from Mr. Duvall, or did you know in any way that Mr. Gambrill or Mr. Lamb had been appointed day watchmen by him, or that it was part of their duty to watch the premises occupied by Mr. Duvall during the day time on Sundays?

Answer. I never did; I was here a great deal on Sundays, and I never saw Mr. Gambrill on Sundays, with one or two exceptions. I solicited the appointment of Mr. Gambrill as a watchman, and I always supposed his position to be a night watchman.

John Hilbert, a Director, sworn.

Question. Had you ever notice in any way from Mr. Duvall, or did you know in any way that Mr. Gambrill or Mr. Lamb had been appointed day watchmen by him, or that it was part of their duty to watch the premises occupied by Mr. Duvall during the day time on Sundays?

Answer. I never had notice of such fact; I am seldom absent on Sundays, and never yet saw Mr. Gambrill on duty on Sundays. I visit the Institution generally between 9 and 10 o'clock in the morning, and leave between 12 and 1 o'clock. I have frequently visited Mr. Duvall's shop on Sundays, and complained of the hands doing work on that day; it was on account of this work a resolution passed the Board instructing the Monthly Committee to notify the Warden to stop all work of convicts on Sunday. I cannot fix the time of the resolution.

Cross-examined by Mr. Gill.—The directions given by the Board was, that no convicts could be worked on Sundays, and that no fire should be allowed in the dry houses; the resolution referred to was passed 29th of March, 1860, upon reference to the proceedings of the Board of that day, and reads as follows:

"*Resolved*, That on and after this date there be no fire allowed either in the State's or any other dry houses on the Sabbath day; nor shall the prisoners be allowed to work on the Sabbath."

Question. Was any other resolution passed restricting the said work except the one of 29th of March, 1860?

Answer. None that I am aware of.

Lefevre Jarrett, a Director, sworn.

Examined by Wm. Brune.—Had you ever notice in any way from Mr. Duvall, or did you know in any way that Mr. Gambrill or Mr. Lamb had been appointed day watchmen by him, or that it was part of their duty to watch the the premises occupied by Mr. Duvall during the day time on Sundays?

Answer. I had no notice of such fact. I always regarded the appointment of Mr. Gambrill as a night watchman.

Question. Was any other resolution passed by the Board restricting the work on Sundays except the one of 29th of March, 1860?

Answer. None that I am aware of.

Mr. Richard Middleton, a Director, sworn.

Question. Had you ever notice in any way from Mr. Duvall, or did you know in any way that Mr. Gambrill or Mr. Lamb had been appointed day watchmen by him, or that it was part of their duty to watch the premises occupied by Mr. Duvall during the day time on Sundays?

Answer. I had no notice of such fact. I always supposed they were night watchmen.

Question. Was any other resolution passed by the Board restricting the work on Sundays, except the one of 29th of March, 1860?

Answer. None that I am aware of.

Mr. Hilbert recalled by Mr. Brune.

Question. Please state as to the regulation on Sundays in regard to watching the wall and yard, and particularly during the religious services at the Institution? State when the prisoners are locked up on Sundays?

Answer. The watch goes on the wall the same on Sundays as during the week; some of the prisoners attending Sunday School are let out of the dormitories sooner than those who do not; the religious services commence at quarter past 10 o'clock, A. M., where all are required to be, with the exception of those engaged in cleaning the dormitory and old buildings. All at Sunday School and at church are under the supervision of officers. The prisoners go direct from church to the refectory for dinner, and after dinner to their cells, where they are locked up.

Cross-examined by Mr. Gill.—*Question.* Were you present on the day of the fire?

Answer. Yes, sir. I was there until nearly 1 o'clock. I do not know what officer was present or had charge of the convicts who were employed on that day in cleaning

3

the dormitories. I do not recollect seeing any officers. Mr. Sparks acted as Deputy Warden during Mr. Roberts' absence.

Question. Is it not the rule that all persons cleaning the dormitories are placed in the charge of an officer? Have you any doubt that an officer was so employed on the day of the fire?

Answer. It is the rule, and I have no doubt that an officer was so employed on the day of the fire.

Question. If the officer in charge had accompanied the convicts engaged in cleaning the same from the dormitory to the filth pen, could those convicts thus employed have entered Mr. Duvall's shop and set it on fire without his knowledge?

Answer. I cannot answer, because I do not know whether the convicts set the shop on fire or how it originated.

Mr. Hurst, a Director, sworn.

By Mr. Brune.—Question. Had you ever notice in any way from Mr. Duvall, or did you know in any way that Mr. Gambrill or Mr. Lamb had been appointed day watchmen by him, or that it was part of their duty to watch the premises occupied by Mr. Duvall during the day time on Sunday?

Answer. I never had such notice or knowledge.

Question. Were you not one of the Committee, and personally engaged in making the agreement of settlement between Mr. Duvall and the Board, and had you not frequent interviews with Mr. Duvall in relation to said agreement, and did he to you or to the Board up to the time of such settlement complain of the action of the Board in connection with his loss by the fire? State all that you think important in relation to such agreement of settlement?

Answer. I was appointed by the Board of Directors to effect a settlement or compromise with Mr. Duvall, subject to the ratification of the Board; I had frequent interviews with him, he never complained to me of the action of the Board, but thanked me and the Board, through me, for our liberality in settling with him, and I never knew that he set up any claim against the Board or the State until I saw the application in the newspapers.

Question. Were you on the Committee to investigate the cause of the fire on Mr. Duvall's premises, of which a report was made to the Board on the 17th of January, 1861? If so, state whether any and what specific charges of neglect of duty were proved to the Committee in reference to officers Mills and Suter?

Answer. I was on the Committee; it is the duty of the wall guard to be on duty when ever the prisoners are not in their cells, and it is not expected that the officer who has charge of the men cleaning the dormitory to follow every man as he goes to the filth pen, but that they are under the supervision of the wall guards. That although there was no proof against the guard named Wills, I thought proper to suspend him for three days. Mr. Suter was a substitute, acting as a wall guard, at the time of the fire. I dismissed him, believing it would increase the efficiency of the officers.

Mr. Gill here files an extract from the proceedings of the Board of January 17, 1861, marked (D.)

(D)

Copy from Proceedings of the Board,

January 17th, 1861.

Your Committee ordered a thorough examination into the cause of the fire, and placed the examination in the hands of the Warden and Deputy-Warden, which was conducted in a manner so skilful as to meet our warm approbation, and resulted in the fact, that the place was set on fire by four prisoners, all colored, viz: Joseph Wheatly, John Madison, —— Butler, Samuel Green and E. Perry, who have all acknowledged their guilt. We are indebted to prisoners Burkhiser and Offutt for valuable information.

In this connection, we have suspended officers Wills and dismissed substitute Suter for inattention and neglect of duty while on the wall the morning of the fire.

In connection with Col. Chesnut, appointed by the Board, and with the assistance of Messrs. Middleton and Hilbert, we have settled all differences existing between the State and Messrs. Murdock and Duvalls by first calling to our aid the professional advice and assistance of F. W. Brune, Esq., of the firm of Brown & Brune, Attorneys-at-Law. With Mr. Murdock we have agreed to terminate his old contract of one hundred men, and to make a new one for the same number of hands from the 1st January, 1861, for four years, giving Mr. Murdock power to terminate the same on the 1st of July, 1861, or the 1st of January, 1862, by his giving us the three months' notice of the same.

We have made two propositions to Mr. J. H. Duvall, to which he promptly accorded, but he has not yet informed us which one he would select; we to terminate the

contract of Mr. Duvall upon his paying the rent of his
shop, the hire of his men and water rent to January 1st,
1861, or to surrender to the State the bricks in his dry
house, and to pay his hire of prisoners up to the date of
the fire, to wit: the 23d December, 1860, and water rent
of shop to 1st January, 1861.

The sixty hands that has been returned to the State
upon the termination of the above contract we are placing
on the looms as fast as circumstances will permit.

Question. Will you state to the Committee the value to
the State of Maryland, in a financial point of view, of the
contract system in the management of the Maryland Penitentiary, and how long such system has continued here,
and state also how the sums realized by the Institution
under the contracts made by the present administration,
until the commercial and political troubles of the country
arose, will compare with the amounts received under previous administrations?

Answer. I consider the contract system has been a benefit, in a financial point of view. It went into operation a
short time before the present Board came into power. The
Institution under the contract system, which we increased
more than double after we came here, came nearer paying
the expenses of the same than formerly. I did not consider the contract with Mr. Duvall as profitable, for many
reasons. From the nature of the employment, extra clothing was required by the convicts, and they were subject to
casualties.

Cross-examined by Mr. Gill.—Question. In the conversation you had with Mr. Duvall prior to or at the time of the
settlement testified to by you, was anything said in relation to the cause of the fire at Mr. Duvall's shop?

Answer. I think not.

Question. Were you not aware that, owing to the loss
Mr. Duvall sustained by fire, that he had no other means
to rebuild and carry out the first contract?

Answer. I had no knowledge of Mr. Duvall's means, any
further than that I heard him say that his all was invested
in the business.

To the General Assembly of the State of Maryland:

The Memorial of Charles Murdock, of the City of Baltimore, respectfully represents that he has been for some years engaged in the business of manufacturing brooms and wood-ware, and to enable him to conduct this business, he has heretofore made various contracts with the Directors of the Maryland Penitentiary for the rent of shops of the Penitentiary and ground belonging to the Penitentiary, on which your memorialist built shops, and for the hire of convicts in the said Penitentiary, to be employed in the said manufacture ; that your memorialist commenced the said business in the year 1850 on the said Penitentiary grounds, and has continued ever since, under various written contracts, which he is prepared to present at the proper time and place, and is still so engaged ; that various questions have arisen between your memorialist and the Directors of the Maryland Penitentiary, about which your memorialist, although believing himself to be in the right, has yet been compelled to submit to the decision of that body, having no tribunal or third party to whom he could appeal.

Your memorialist further states, that he has invested a large sum of money in the Penitentiary grounds, in buildings, machinery, &c., and has paid annually large sums of money to the Directors of the said Penitentiary, and for the last year nearly the entire income thereof has been derived from the payments made by your memorialist, arising from the rent of buildings and employment of convicts by him ; the amount paid by your memorialist from April, 1860, to April, 1861, being $21,811.43.

Your memorialist further states, that at the present time a difference exists between your memorialist and the said Directors in relation to the present indebtedness by your memorialist to them ; that your memorialist has offered to pay all he now owes, but this has been refused, and a large amount claimed, which is denied to be due by your memorialist ; and the Directors of the said Penitentiary have refused to permit your memorialist to remove any of his manufactured articles from the said Penitentiary until he pays an amount which he believes not to be due, and which the Directors have, in his view, no right to exact or claim ; and that thereby his business has been seriously injured.

Your memorialist further states, that owing to the change of times which, as is well known, has effected all kinds of business and the value of all property, your memorialist has found himself unable to conduct the business at the

Penitentiary, and to employ, according to the terms of his contract, the number of convicts agreed upon and as regularly as agreed upon; that your memorialist has been unable to obtain the necessary supply of materials for manufacturing purposes, owing to the fact that, by the existence of war and the blockade of ports, this supply has been cut off, and that even if this difficulty were removed, it would be found to be impossible, or nearly so, to dispose of the articles when manufactured, because the usual and customary markets are closed against their reception.

Your memorialist, finding himsef thus deprived of the power to continue the manufacture of goods at the Maryland Penitentiary according to his contracts, has applied to the Directors thereof for a modification of his contracts, but in vain; they insist upon a literal compliance therewith, even if by so doing your memorialist will be ruined; that finding no relief can be had from the Directors, your memorialist has appealed, as he now does, to your Honorable Body for relief in the premises; and he now prays that such a settlement shall be made as to you may seem just, and that such modifications and alterations in his contracts may be made as will do justice to both parties, and at the same time secure to the State such income and revenue as can be obtained from the Maryland Penitentiary in the existing circumstances and condition of the country.

Your memorialist would further state, that owing to causes already set forth, he will be compelled, unless some material change be made in his arrangements with the Directors of the Maryland Penitentiary, or some unexpected change should take place in the affairs of the country, to discontinue his manufacturing business at the Penitentiary, in which event there will necessarily be a large loss in the revenues heretofore derived from that Institution.

CHARLES MURDOCK.

To the General Assembly of the State of Maryland:

The Memorial of John H. Duvall and William Howard respectfully states, that on the fourth day of October, in the year of our Lord, one thousand eight hundred and fifty-nine, one of your memorialists—viz., John H. Duvall—entered into an agreement with the Directors of the Maryland Penitentiary to rent the blacksmith's shop at the Penitentiary grounds, in the city of Baltimore, and certain yard room for the storage of wood, and for hiring of thirty male convict prisoners, to be employed in the manufacturing of barrels, with the privilege of increasing the number of convicts, the particulars of which agreement will appear by the written agreement entered into, a copy of which is hereto annexed, and the original of which will be produced whenever called for.

Your memorialists further state that, after making the said agreement, the said John H. Duvall became connected in the business of manufactoring barrels with the said William Howard, who furnished capital to carry on the same—that your memorialists invested at the said Penitentiary, in machinery, buildings and fixtures necessary for their business, more than eight thousand dollars in addition to the value of patent rights and materials for manufacturing—that they continued to perform the agreement entered into by John H. Duvall until the 23d December, 1860, and paid from the time of making the said agreement and the said 23d December, 1860, for the labor of the prisoners employed by them the sum of $7,031.07—that on Sunday, the 23d December, 1860, their shops were fired by incendiary convicts and their contents nearly destroyed, and that the loss sustained by your memorialists amounts to $23,150.

Your memoralists further state, that after making the said agreement by the said John H. Duvall, your memorialists, believing it to be proper to do so, employed a watchman to guard their property at the Penitentiary during the night, and on Sundays during the day time, that while this watchman remained in charge and on duty no damage was done, but that prior to the fire, which occurred, as aforesaid, notice was given to your memorialists through the Deputy Warden, Isaac G. Roberts, by the monthly Committee of the Penitentiary, that their watchman would not be permitted to be at their shop in the Penitentiary on Sundays, and your memorialists were thereby required to withdraw their watchman on Sundays, which they accordingly did, being compelled to obey such order—that their property was fired and burned on Sunday, 23d December, 1860, by a portion of the convicts at the said Penitentiary, which would have doubtless been prevented if their watchman had been at his post and on duty as he had been prior to the time of giving the aforesaid order, not to be on duty on Sundays.

Your memorialists further represent, that after they had been prevented by the order of the Monthly Committee of the Penitentiary from having their private watchman on the premises on Sundays, they had a right to expect, and did expect and believe that the vigilance and activity of the officers of the Penitentiary in guarding and taking care of their property at the Penitentiary on Sundays would be increased, but on the contrary, when on Sunday, the 23d December, 1860, the fire took place, there was no proper or sufficient care taken ; and it was owing to the gross remissness and negligence of these officers that these convicts at the Penitentiary obtained access to the work shops, and thus were able to set fire to them and reduce them to ashes.

Your memorialists further state, that the rules and regulations prescribed for the government of the Penitentiary would, if faithfully carried out on the Sunday when the fire took place, have prevented the loss which then took place, but it can be made to appear beyond all doubt that these rules and regulations were disregarded and not maintained. Your memorialists, who were not permitted to maintain a proper guard over their property, which they had done until ordered to discontinue it, have been subjected to heavy loss by the conduct, omission and negligence of the officers of this State.

Your memorialists further state, that after the heavy loss they had sustained by the fire, and under the circumstances hereinbefore mentioned, they were required to settle for the rest of the property and hire of convicts up to the 31st December, 1860, and to pay to the Directors of the Maryland Penitentiary the sum of $1,075.59 from the payment of which they ought, as they insisted, when making said payment, and still insist, to have been excused and relieved.

Your memorialists further state, that they have been advised that if they had made an agreement with individuals, or a body corporate, liable to be sued, that they might have maintained an action at law, and recovered, under the circumstances, the amount of their loss ; but that, inasmuch as no suit can be maintained against the Directors of the Maryland Penitentiary, and none against the State of Maryland, they have no redress except by application to your Honorable Body.

Your memorialists, finding that their only redress, under the circumstances in which they have been placed, must come from your Honorable Body, which has the power to grant full and adequate relief, have made this application in the hope and belief that you will cause a full and complete examination into all the circumstances of this transaction to be made, and do what is just, proper and equitable ; and they therefore pray that you will make good their loss and grant full relief to them, &c.

JOHN H. DUVALL,
June 10, 1861.   WILLIAM HOWARD.

These articles of agreement made and concluded between the Directors of the Maryland Penitentiary on the one part, and John H. Duvall, of the city of Baltimore, on the other part, witnesseth, that the said Directors on their part do covenant and agree with the said John H. Duvall.

1st. To rent unto him the blacksmith shop now vacant at the Penitentiary, with all the rooms and conveniences thereunto attached, except the carpenter shop, the engine and boiler, one of the blacksmith furnaces, to be placed in the south-west corner of the shop for the use of the Institution, to be worked at no time by more than two hands, for the remaining portion of the year eighteen hundred and fifty-nine, and for five years thereafter, for the annual rent of two hundred dollars, with the privilege of removing the present engine and boiler, and of erecting others of more power, and also of erecting steam boxes and dry houses, and removing a portion of the fire places and chimneys, and of making such other changes and additions, without injury to the premises, as may be necessary for the convenience of manufacturing barrels by machinery, and also for the use of yard room for the storage of one hundred cords of wood; all said changes and additions to be at the cost of John H. Duvall, and to be made under the supervision and directions of the Directors and Warden.

2nd. That the said Directors agree to hire unto the said John H. Duvall thirty of the male convict prisoners, such as they have or may have best adapted for his purposes, to be employed by him in the manufacturing of barrels, for the term of five years from the first day of January, eighteen hundred and sixty, and to grant him the privilege of increasing the number, if they be required by him, from time to time, (any increase of prisoners at any time to be kept by John H. Duvall to the end of the term of this agreement,) to the number of seventy-five. The hire of all said prisoners to be at the rate of twenty-five cents per day for the first three months, as they enter his employment, and sixty cents per day thereafter, with the privilege of receiving as many of the prisoners as he may require at any time during the remainder of the year eighteen hundred and fifty-nine.

3rd. That the said Directors grant unto the said John H. Duvall the right to remove at the expiration of this contract all his machinery and building materials, and effects of every kind, he having first discharged to said Directors his debts and obligations under this contract.

These articles of agreement witnesseth, on the second part, that the said John H. Duvall doth agree on his part, and hereby binds himself, to employ the thirty convict prisoners, as provided for above, and to make payment for the same weekly in current funds of the State of Maryland, and to pay for the shop, yard room, &c., herein before specified, at the end of each quarter, in current funds of the State of Maryland, and also that all agents and superintendents of the shops occupied by him, which he may employ at his own expense, shall be subject to the rules and regulations of the prison.

2nd. That the said John H. Duvall agrees to make payment to the Institution monthly for all over work made ·by the prisoners in his employ, and to permit the Directors and Warden to regulate the tasks of said prisoners, said prisoners tasks to correspond, as can be made practicable, with the tasks exacted of the prisoners in the other shops of the establishment.

3rd. That the said John H. Duvall agrees, and hereby binds himself, to a faithful observance of the terms of this contract for the period herein named, under the penalty of one thousand dollars for its violation, and to let his buildings and fixtures remain as security for the fulfilment of his obligations until they are fully discharged.

And lastly, it is understood and agreed upon by and between the Directors of the Maryland Penitentiary and said John H. Duvall, that if either of the parties to this cantract shall desire to terminate the same at the end thereof, it shall be the duty of the party desiring such termination to give notice in writing to the other three months before the expiration of the time for which this contract is now made.

In witness whereof, Wm. J. Bryson, John Hurst, John Hilbert and R. Middleton, Monthly Committee acting for the Board of Directors of Maryland Penitentiary, in behalf of said Board of Directors and said John H. Duvall, have interchangeably set their hand and seals this fourth day of October, eighteen hundred and fifty-nine.

JOHN H. DUVALL, [SEAL.]

Committee. {
WM. J. BRYSON, [SEAL.]
JOHN HURST, [SEAL.]
JOHN HILBERT, [SEAL.]
R. MIDDLETON, [SEAL.]
}

TEST:

JNO. J. C. DOUGHERTY.

Document [M.]

BY THE SENATE,

Auɢᴜsᴛ 6th, 1861.

Read and 25,000 copies ordered to be printed.

By order of Wᴍ. Kɪʟɢᴏᴜʀ, *Sec.*

REPORT AND RESOLUTIONS

OF THE

JOINT COMMITTEE

OF THE

Senate and House of Delegates of Maryland,

UPON THE

REPORTS AND MEMORIALS OF THE POLICE COMMISSIONERS

AND THE

MAYOR AND CITY COUNCIL OF BALTIMORE.

———•———

ADOPTED IN THE HOUSE BY A VOTE OF 42 YEAS TO 7 NAYS,
AND IN THE SENATE BY A VOTE OF 12 YEAS TO 6 NAYS.

———•———

FREDERICK, MD.
B. H. RICHARDSON, PRINTER.
1861.

*To the Honorable the President of the Senate
and the Speaker of the House of Delegates:*

The Joint Committee on Federal Relations, to whom was referred the Report of the Police Board of Baltimore, enclosing a Memorial of Charles Howard, William H. Gatchell and John W. Davis, Esqs., members thereof, to the Congress of the United States, together with a communication from the Mayor of Baltimore, enclosing a Memorial of the Mayor and City Council of Baltimore to Congress, with accompanying documents; respectfully ask leave to submit the following Report:

REPORT.

It is well known to the members of both Houses, that for several years prior to the commencement of the regular session of the Legislature of Maryland in January, 1860, a state of things had existed and been developing itself in the city of Baltimore, which imperatively demanded the interposition of the law-making power. It is needless to dwell upon the causes or magnify the degree of the evils referred to, it being matter of public notoriety that the laws for the personal protection of the citizen, and especially those which guaranteed the free and inviolate exercise of the elective franchise, had almost wholly ceased to be practically operative, and an organized system of lawlessness, violence and terror had usurped their place. The extent to which the city of Baltimore had suffered, not only in her good name, but in her material prosperity, from the causes referred to, is familiar to the public at large, and the subject had for some time occupied the serious attention, as it largely concerned the interests, of the whole people of the State. At the elections held in the Autumn of 1859, the outrages in Baltimore, under the eyes of the municipal authorities, were of so flagrant and insufferable a character, as to raise the direct and unavoidable issue between anarchy and civil government. Proofs of the most overwhelming conclusiveness having been furnished to the General Assembly at its regular session referred to, there was no recourse but to take vigorous steps to re-establish the supremacy of the laws. By the Act of 1860, ch. 7, (incorporated in the 4th article of the Code of Public Local Laws, beginning at section 806,) all police authority previously delegated to the corporation of Baltimore was accordingly withdrawn, and the same was conferred, with greatly enlarged powers, upon a Board, called the Board of Police, composed of five members. Of these, it was provided that four, who were called "Commissioners," should be elected by the Legislature for designated terms of years, at the expiration of which, their successors were to be appointed in the same manner. It was further enacted, that the Mayor of the city, for the time being, should *ex-officio* be a member of the Board. Messrs. Charles Howard, William H.

Gatchell, Charles D. Hinks and John W. Davis, citizens
of Baltimore, gentlemen of great intelligence and fitness
and of the most approved integrity and purity of character, were chosen by the Senate and House of Delegates as
the first Commissioners, and their names appear in the
statute-book accordingly. The official term of Messrs.
Howard and Davis will expire on the 10th of May, 1862;
that of Messrs. Gatchell and Hinks continues until the 10th
of May, 1864.

The extent of the powers conferred upon the Board
by the law creating it, is so well known to both Houses
as to supersede the necessity of recapitulation. It is
sufficient to say, in general terms, that their authority is of the amplest description, embracing the entire
police power of the State, within the limits of Baltimore,
and the right of pursuit and arrest, in certain cases,
throughout the whole of the State. By a subsequent Act,
passed at the same session, (ch. 9,) and incorporated in the
same article of the Local Code, beginning at section 199,
the division and re-division of the city into election precincts: the appointment of judges of election in the city,
and the holding of all elections therein, whether Federal, State or Municipal: were added to the powers and
duties of the Police Board; and it was expressly enacted,
that no election should be valid unless held in conformity
with the provisions of the two statutes referred to, and
unless under and subject to the exclusive control and direction of the Board. The enforcement of the general and
local election laws, in many enumerated particulars, and
the recovery of penalties affixed to their violation, were
comprehended within the scope of the responsible obligations thus imposed on the officers in question. Everything, in fine, in the way of legal enactment, which could
guarantee the freedom and purity of the ballot-box, protect the rights of person and property, and secure the
maintenance of public order in the chief city of the State,
was committed to the Board for execution. All the penal
sanctions which could be reasonably devised, to strengthen
their hands for usefulness and protect them from unlawful interruption and interference, will be found to have
been fully provided, for it was the express and especial
purpose of the Legislature, for sufficient and well known
reasons, to guard against any and every unauthorized intrusion upon the important functions, which the State of
Maryland had deemed it necessary to exercise through officers of her own selection. It is matter of public notoriety,
that the laws in question were assailed with all the bitter-
ness of partisanship, and that the police law, in particular,

was resisted by the then municipal authorities of Baltimore. A legal proceeding was the consequence, in which the validity of the new enactments, under the Constitution of the State and the Union, was put to all the tests which professional ingenuity and ability could devise. The controversy resulted in the complete triumph of the new system, its constitutionality having been placed beyond controversy by the prompt and unanimous decisions of all the Judges, in the Appellate as well as the inferior tribunal.

Sanctioned thus by the Legislative and Judicial departments of our State Government—confessedly within the constitutional limits of State authority, and beyond all pretence of objection or invalidity, upon any ground of antagonism to the Federal Constitution—the police system, inaugurated as has been said, was put into successful operation in the Spring of 1860. That it was faithfully, fairly and honestly administered, with great ability and vigor, and in the spirit of impartiality and freedom from political influences and corruption, which most especially suggested its enactment, your Committee would be wanting to truth and justice were they not emphatically to declare. So undeniably was this the case, that perhaps the warmest and most repeated testimonials to such effect were furnished by the presses most hostile, upon party grounds, to the creation of the Board, and originally most violent in its denunciation. No candid person, let his political opinions or feelings be what they may, will venture to deny, that the organization and administration of the Police Board, under the laws referred to, were at last hailed by the whole community of Baltimore as a blessing, and that a sense of security and good government, never felt there before, had diffused itself among all classes in consequence, and had already given a new impulse to the industry and prosperity of the city. Never had any Legislature better reason than the present, to congratulate itself upon having set in motion a perfectly successful scheme of large and beneficial public policy. Every election which has been held in the city since the police law was passed, has not only illustrated the fidelity and integrity of its administration, but has given it the most conclusive endorsement of popular approval.

Your Committee have deemed this brief review of the creation and functions of the Board of Police and of the manner in which its general duties have been discharged, not only an act of justice to the members of the Board, but necessary to the public and thorough understanding of the grievances which are more particularly the object of the memorials under consideration. The more recent and absorbing facts connected with the case of the memorialists are, in substance, as follows:

On the 27th day of June last, the city of Baltimore and State of Maryland being in the enjoyment of entire tranquility, except in so far as the same was interrupted by the presence and transit of large bodies of troops in the service of the General Government, a proclamation was issued by Major General Banks, of the U. S. Army, commanding the Department of Annapolis, in which he informed the public that " by virtue of authority vested in him, and in obedience to orders as Commanding General of the Military Department " alluded to, he had arrested and detained in custody Col. George P. Kane, the Marshal of Police of the city of Baltimore. Disclaiming all purpose, and announcing that his instructions did not authorize him, " to interfere in any manner with the legitimate government of the people of Baltimore or Maryland," Gen. Banks went on to charge the existence, in his Department, of unlawful combinations of men, organized for resistance to the laws of the United States and of Maryland, providing hidden deposits of arms and ammunition, encouraging contraband traffic with the enemies of the country, and stealthily waiting opportunity to combine their means and forces with those in rebellion against the authority of the Government. Of these combinations he charged that Col. Kane was " believed " to be cognizant, and that he was " both witness and protector to the transactions and parties engaged therein," and consequently could not be regarded by the Government as " otherwise than at the head of an armed force hostile to its authority, and acting in concert with its avowed enemies." The Proclamation then announced that " for this reason " Gen. Banks, " superseding " Col. Kane's " official authority and that of the Commissioners of Police," had arrested and detained Col. Kane, and " in further pursuance of my instructions," he added, " I have appointed, for the time being, Col. Kenly, of the first regiment of the Maryland Volunteers, Provost Marshal in and for the city of Baltimore, to superintend and cause to be executed the Police Laws provided by the Legislature of Maryland, with the aid and assistance of the subordinate officers of the Police Department. And he will be respected accordingly."

On the morning of the same day, Col. Kenly proceeded, by the orders of Gen. Banks, to the office of the Board, and read them this Proclamation, by way of notifying them that their authority was at an end. He then took immediate possession of the Marshal's office and the Police stations, (all belonging to the Corporation,) and assumed the execution of all police power within the city limits. The Board being of course unable to resist the military power of the Government, had no alternative but to submit to force. They however protested, in a dignified and becoming manner, as officers of the State of Maryland, (the Mayor uniting) against the arbitrary subversion of its laws and government by the military authority of the United States, and refused to recognize the right of the officers and men of their police force to receive orders or directions from any authority but their own. Carrying out the obvious spirit, and obeying the letter, of the law which they had sworn to support, and under which, alone, the Board and its officers and men had official existence or authority, they also adopted and published the following resolution:

"*Resolved*, That in the opinion of the Board, the forcible suspension of their functions suspends at the same time the active operation of the Police Law, and puts the officers and men off duty for the present, leaving them subject, however, to the rules and regulations of the service as to their personal conduct and deportment, and to the orders which this Board may see fit hereafter to issue when the present illegal suspension of their functions shall be removed."

Having thus asserted, as was their duty, and in the only mode left to them, the supremacy of the local laws of Maryland within their legitimate locality, the Board refrained from all interference with the proceedings of the Provost Marshal, who at once commenced the appointment of individuals, at his discretion, to assume the places and discharge the functions of policemen. Not content with thus supplanting the subordinates of the Police Board, he proceeded further and removed the officers in the Fire Alarm and Police Telegraph Departments, who receive their appointments by law from the Mayor and City Council, and substituted appointees of his own in their stead. Things remaining in this unnatural position, on the morning of the 1st of July the four Commissioners of Police, Messrs. Howard, Gatchell, Hinks and Davis, were arrested at their residences, two or three hours after midnight, by large bodies of troops under the orders of Gen. Banks, and were removed at once to Fort McHenry, and placed for the time under close confinement. When the morning dawned, the principal places of the city were found occupied by masses of artillery and infantry, and sentinels were posted on the lines from the various camps into the heart of the population. In the course of the forenoon a Proclamation appeared from Gen. Banks. It stated the arrest of the Commissioners to have been made "in pursuance of orders issued from the Headquarters of the Army at Washington, for the preservation of the public peace in this Department." By way of justification, it alleged that "the Headquarters under the charge of the Board, when abandoned by the officers, resembled in some respects a concealed arsenal;" that "after recognition and protest against the suspension of their functions," the Board had continued their sessions daily ; that upon a forced and unwarrantable construction of the Proclamation of 27th June they had declared the Police law suspended and the Police officers and men off duty for the present, "intending to leave the city without any Police protection whatever ;" that they had refused to recognize the officers and men appointed as policemen by Col. Kenly, and finally, held, subject to their orders " now and hereafter, the old Police force, a large body of armed men, for some purpose not known to the Government and inconsistent with its peace and security." It then further stated that the troops in the city had been sent there " to anticipate any intentions or orders " on the part of the Police Board, and concluded with a protestation, as in the previous Proclamation, against " all desire, intention and purpose, on the part of the Government, to interfere in any way whatever with the ordinary municipal affairs of the city of Baltimore."

The Commissioners being thus removed, by force, from their sphere of duty, and held in prison to prevent them from discharging it, the military occupation of the city was continued—the Court House and many public places and offices, which belonged to the corporation, being appropriated to the use of the troops, who thronged the streets and squares also, by night and by day. Meanwhile, being the only member of the Board who had not been deprived of liberty, the Mayor of the city, Mr. Brown, in order, if possible, to relieve his fellow-citizens from the embarrassments and perils of their situation, expressed his readiness to Gen. Banks to undertake the management of the Police, and Col. Kane, with great disinterestedness, was willing to make the sacrifice of his position, so that the Mayor might have no difficulty in consummating the arrangements he proposed. Gen. Banks, however, responded unfavorably to the proposition, after some delay, and on July 10th announced the consummation of his plans in the following proclamation :

"To the People of Baltimore:—

Headquarters, Department of Annapolis,
July 10, 1861.

By virtue of authority vested in me, as Commanding Officer of this Department, *I have appointed, and do hereby appoint George R. Dodge, Esq., of Baltimore, Marshal of Police,* vice Col. John R. Kenly, who, being relieved of this service at his own request, now assumes command of the First Regiment of Maryland Volunteers, on the Upper Potomac, in the State of Maryland. I have made this appointment at the suggestion and upon the advice of very many influential and honorable citizens of Baltimore, representing its different sections, parties and interests. And in order that public opinion shall have proper influence, and the civil authority due weight, in all municipal affairs, it is my desire and expectation that the Marshal shall receive suggestion, advice and direction from them and other loyal citizens, as from all the Departments of the Government of the city, and *in all respects to administer every department of the Police law* in full freedom, for the peace and prosperity of the city, and the honor and perpetuity of the United States.

N. P. BANKS, Major General,
Commanding Department of Annapolis."

The names of the "influential and honorable citizens," who committed the grave offense of aiding in the subversion of the civil government of the State, within the limits of Baltimore, by force of arms, have not been given officially to the public, nor has any official disclosure been made of the names of those, under whose "advice and direction" the functions of Mr. Dodge are exercised. These will of course be subjects for judicial inquiry hereafter. The appointment of Mr. Dodge was accompanied by the withdrawal of the troops from the heart of the city, and, from that time to the present, the laws of the State have been silent in Baltimore, so far as concerns its Police Department, and the lives and property of the people have been at the mercy of the organization, thus set on foot by the military power of the Federal Government. On the 21st of July a Bill was introduced in Congress, appropriating one hundred thousand dollars for the payment of "the Police organization of Baltimore employed by the United States." It was passed by the House of Representatives under the pressure of the previous question, one of the representatives from Baltimore (Mr. May) having in vain attempted to obtain the floor to discuss it, and having been sharply reprimanded for a breach of the rules of the House, in protesting against it, as "a bill to provide for the wages of oppression." In the Senate it was adopted with equal precipitancy, against the solemn remonstrance of both of the Senators from Maryland. The Congress of the United States thus ratified the action of General Banks in the premises—so far as such action was susceptible of ratification—and the existing Police government of Baltimore, and the suppression of the State authority therein, may therefore be regarded as the combined and deliberate act of the Executive and Legislative Departments of the United States Government.

It remains only to add, that one of the Police Commissioners (Mr. Hinks) having been released from custody, on account of failing health, the Memorial, of which a copy has been communicated to the Legislature, was presented to Congress on behalf of Messrs. Howard, Gatchell and Davis; protesting against the wrongs inflicted on them, officially and personally; challenging an investigation of any charges against them; and demanding, as matter of right, that their case should be examined by Congress, or remitted, for hearing and determination, to the tribunals of justice. The memorial of the Mayor and City Council of Baltimore, likewise communicated to us and referred to the Committee, and demanding redress from Congress for the grievances which have already been discussed, was also presented to that body, with the full exposition of facts contained in the Message of the Mayor thereunto appended. It is sufficient to say, that the appropriation of money for the support of the Federal police in Baltimore, was made after the presentation of both the memorials in question, and is the only answer which has been given to the prayer of either. In the meantime, the Grand Jury of the District Court of the United States for the Maryland District, then and till lately in session, finally adjourned, without being able to discover any ground of accusation against the members of the Police Board, and the President of the United States, having been called upon to communicate to the House of Representatives the grounds for their arrest and imprisonment, tacitly confessed that there are none, by declining to furnish the information, on the score that it would be "incompatible with the public interests." On the day before the meeting of the General Assembly, (the 29th of July,)—their memorial still pending before Congress—the gentlemen in question, with sundry other citizens of Maryland, against whom no tangible accusation has been lodged or disclosed, were nevertheless removed, under guard, from Fort McHenry to Fort La Fayette, at the entrance to the harbor of New York, where they are now closely confined, by military order, under many privations and restrictions, at a distance from their families and friends. The order itself which directed their removal described them as "State prisoners"—an appellation hitherto happily unknown in the nomenclature of offenders under the laws and Constitution of this Republic. What may be the further destination or ultimate fate of the victims, can be determined only by those who are able to anticipate and fathom the caprices of irresponsible and arbitrary power.

Upon the facts disclosed by this simple and unexaggerated statement, which has been given without coloring or argument, your Committee propose to comment as briefly as they may. The statement itself would be its own best comment, in any ordinary condition of the public mind. But the tide of partisanship and passion, which is now rolling over the land, seems to have swept away the landmarks of our older and better days, and there is scarce a principle of private right or public freedom, so fundamental or so sacred, as to be sure of recognition, or superior to challenge or denial. A little while ago, and all the sympathies and instincts and convictions of the American people, like all the traditions of their own history and of the mighty and free people from which they sprang, were impulsively upon the side of freedom as against power; of law as against prerogative; of self-government as against government imposed. With a strange and fearful revulsion, they appear, of late, to have rushed back a century, to theories which the Declaration of their Independence and the swords of their fathers were supposed to have buried forever. No man therefore knows the acceptance which may greet, to-day, what yesterday was a consecrated axiom of common right and constitutional liberty. It becomes the representatives of the people of Maryland, then, upon an occasion so important as the present, and in contemplation of grievances so monstrous and so galling as those disclosed by the Memorials before them, to re-assert, distinctly and manfully, the principles which their fathers asserted; to claim, as becomes them, the inheritance which their fathers bequeathed; and to protest and remonstrate, and appeal to their countrymen, against the usurpations, of which their soil has been made the theatre, their State the subject, and their citizens the victims.

It is not a question of Union or Disunion, of North or South, of treason or loyalty. It is the naked and desperate alternative of constitutional government and free institutions on the one hand, and State annihilation and individual enslavement on the other.

2*

The wrongs disclosed by the Memorials under consideration are of two classes : the one affecting individual citizens—the other assailing the dignity and rights of the
State of Maryland herself, as a member of the Federal
Union. The principles of constitutional law, which apply
to the latter class, have never been formally questioned,
although in recent executive documents of the Federal
Government a disposition has been manifested to ignore or
invade them, and practically, as in the instances before us,
they have more than once been set at naught. No states-
man or jurist, who respects his reputation, can be found
definitively to deny that in the sphere of the powers not delegated by the Constitution to the Government of the United
States, the States of the Union have exclusive legislation
and supreme jurisdiction within their territorial limits.
The Federal Government has no more right to interfere
with the State Governments, in their sphere, than the
latter to invade the limits assigned to Federal authority. Among the powers not communicated by the Constitution to the General Government are those of internal government and police in the States. Upon so plain a point,
judicial interpretations are superfluous. Repeated adjudica-
tions of the Supreme Court of the United States have nevertheless recognized the powers in question as belonging to
the States exclusively and fundamentally, and have determined that any invasion of them by the Federal Government
is fatally repugnant to the Constitution. If it were otherwise, State Governments would not exist. They would be
without power and without object. Their control over their
own internal polity is, in fact, their very essence as governments, and the only qualification attached to it is, that
they shall legislate in conformity with the few limitations
of the Federal Constitution applicable to the matter.
That done, their sovereignty in the premises is indisputable—a sovereignty not above the Constitution nor against
it, but guaranteed by it, and within it, and part of it.

As has already been stated, the Police law of Maryland,
after passing the ordeal of the courts, was found to be in
strict accordance with the Federal and the State Constitutions, and the officers appointed under it were therefore
constitutionally appointed, and held their offices as constitutionally as the President held his. Mr. Lincoln consequently had no more right to remove the Police Board or
Marshal, or to cause Gen. Banks to remove them, than they
had to remove Mr. Lincoln or Gen. Banks. Congress has
no more constitutional right to appoint or pay Police officers in their stead, than the General Assembly of Maryland would possess, to appoint and pay officers for the

United States Army or Navy. This is a point about which it is impossible for intelligent men honestly to dispute. If the Commissioners or the Marshall of Police had been guilty or were suspected, upon lawful evidence, of crime, their arrest and trial, by the competent authority, would have vindicated public justice. If their arrest or conviction had left their offices vacant, permanently or for the time, it was for the laws and authorities of Maryland to supply their places. If they were criminal at all, they were criminal and punishable, as individuals and not as officers, for their official character could not qualify or affect their crime or its punishment, for better or for worse. The same principle applies to the Police force under them. If any members of that force were guilty of treason or misprision of treason, it was as citizens and not as policemen, and they were punishable as men and not as officers. The Federal authority had only to deal with them as with all individual wrong-doers, and if that created a necessity for their being displaced as officers, it was for the competent State authority of Maryland so to displace them, and to appoint their successors. If an officer of the army of the United States, or a member of the Cabinet, were to commit murder or other crime in Maryland, in violation of the State laws, and were arrested or convicted thereunder, surely the fact of his arrest or conviction would hardly be regarded, at Washington, as authorizing the Governor of Maryland to fill his place in the army or the Cabinet, and the Legislature of Maryland to keep his successor in its pay. And yet the Constitutional authority, in the one instance, would be identically the same as in the other, and the very statement of the proposition, in either case, reduces it to an absurdity. The action of Gen. Banks, therefore—whether regarded as his own action or as that of the Commander-in-Chief of the army, or of the President, or any other officer of the Federal Government—was, in the language of the resolution adopted by the Police Board, "not warranted by any provision of the Constitution or laws of the United States, or of the State of Maryland, but in derogation of all of them." The Board did no more than their duty, as constituted authorities of the State of Maryland, when they protested accordingly against it, and they but obeyed the obligation of the law which created their office, and of the oath which they had sworn under its provisions, when they refused to transfer their officers and men to an unlawful and unauthorized command, and declined to recognize, as a police force, in any sense legitimate, the individuals designated as policemen by the Provost Marshal, in open violation of the express laws of the State, and in subversion of its government and constitutional supremacy. The subsequent proceedings of Congress have only added aggravation to the outrage, for as Congress has no better claim than the Executive to invade the constitutional rights of the States, and its attempted confirmation of an unconstitutional act cannot render such act in any sense more constitutional, its endorsement of the usurpation of the President commits the whole Federal Government to that usurpation, and places it in the attitude of deliberately revolutionizing the fundamental institutions of the country.

The Committee are of course aware of the appeals which have been made to "military necessity," to justify recent encroachments, by the Government, upon public and private right. Self-preservation, it is insisted, is the right and duty of every government, and the Government of the United States is therefore authorized to do all things which may become necessary to preserve it.

If these ideas were recognized by the Constitution, under any circumstances, (which the Committee deny,) they would not apply to the branch of the present case which is now under consideration. Tye State of Maryland has not assumed to withdraw herself from the Union, and is in no position of hostility against the Government. She is neither a foreign State nor a conquered country. She is represented in the Federal Congress, although her representatives are practically silenced, and the processes and judgments of the Federal Courts have been uninterruptedly and cheerfully obeyed and respected by her people. All the customary functions of the Government are freely exercised, by its officers, within her limits. She contributes to its support, through her custom-houses, and is to be heavily taxed for the expenses of the fratricidal war which it is waging, against her remonstrance. No Proclamation of the President has ever declared her to be arrayed against the laws, and no troops have been called out for their enforcement among us. Not only has martial law never been proclaimed in Maryland, but Gen. Banks, in his Proclamation of June 27, in the very act of suppressing the State authority and laws, took singular pains to declare (as has been stated) that it was not his purpose, nor was it in consonance with his instructions, " to interfere, in any manner, with the legitimate government of the people of Baltimore or Maryland." Confessedly therefore—clearly at all events—if any necessity had demanded and could justify the exercise of extraordinary and extra-constitutional powers, it was a necessity which would have been fully met, by the action of the Government against individuals, but which in no way demanded, and in no way could have justified, a gross violation of the Federal compact, by overthrowing the constitutional laws of Maryland and destroying her federal equality and constitutional independence. To say that "military necessity" can justify such acts, is to say, as explicitly as could be said in words, that it justifies the Federal authorities in breaking up the Government themselves, under the guise of preventing it from being broken up by others. The forms of government may outlast such a catastrophe, but the Federal Government known to and created by the Constitution must end with it. What remains is revolution, in the garb of government, and depending for its legitimacy upon bayonets. The State over whose institutions these are lifted, is no longer a State of the Union, in effect, whatever she may be in name. She has no Constitution, no government, no laws, that she can call her own. She is ruled by external and arbitrary power. Her people are no longer free.

With respect to the individual cases of our fellow-citizens, whose memorial is before us, the principles of constitutional right are equally positive and clear. If the charges of General Banks against the Marshal of Police amount to anything and are well founded, they constitute a case of treason or misprision of treason, cognizable under the laws, and furnishing cause for arrest and trial by the competent tribunals. Against the Commissioners there is nothing alleged, in either proclamation, upon which a warrant could be lawfully issued, or an indictment found, and they but state, in their Memorial to Congress, what every well-informed citizen must recognize as obvious—that no legal tribunal would hesitate to discharge them, if brought before it, upon sworn allegations so simply frivolous and futile. But if the Government thought otherwise —if its high officers were really persuaded, that in the nineteenth century, and under the free institutions of the freest nation upon earth, it was lawful to arrest and imprison men of high character and irreproachable integrity— or any other men—upon the mere suspicion of their entertaining "purposes" which were admitted to be "not known to the Government," while they were alleged, in the same breath, to be "inconsistent with its peace or security"—surely the courts of justice, which were open, unobstructed and active, were the rightful tribunals to pass upon the matter. The Commissioners, as well as the Marshal, were either charged with crime, or they were not. If they were not, it was a heinous crime to arrest and imprison them. If they were, their rights and the demands of public justice required imperatively that they should be dealt with according to law. To refer to the constitutional provisions in which principles so vital are embodied, appears like seeking after proof that we see by God's sunlight, or have our breath from his air. "The right of the people," says the 4th Amendment to the Constitution, "to be secure in their persons, houses, papers and effects against unreasonable searches and seizures *shall not be violated*, and no warrants shall issue but upon probable cause, supported by oath or affirmation, and particularly describing the place to be searched and the persons or things to be seized." "No person," says the 5th Amendment, "shall be held to answer for a capital or otherwise infamous crime, unless on a presentment or indictment of a Grand Jury, except in cases arising in the land or naval forces, or in the militia, when in actual service, in time of war or public danger." "In all criminal prosecutions," says Article VI. of the same, " the accused shall enjoy the right to a speedy and public trial, by an impartial Jury of the State and District wherein the crime shall have been committed, which District shall have been previously ascertained by law, and to be informed of the nature and cause of the accusation—to be confronted with the witnesses against him —to have compulsory process for obtaining witnesses in his favor, and to have the assistance of counsel for his defense."

These provisions are the fundamental law of the land—a law to the government as well as to the people—a covenant of right and liberty, and a limitation upon power. They are an essential and indefeasible portion of the compact which created the Union, and of the conditions upon which alone the people of Maryland and of all the States consented to abide by it. Without them everything else in the Government is worthless, for they represent and guard the great principles of human freedom, which the Union was framed to perpetuate, and compared with which all governmental forms—all names and symbols, all institutions, and traditions, and men—shrink away into dust and nothingness. Of these provisions there is not a single one which has not been trampled upon in the cases before us. Themselves arrested and their papers seized, without warrant or oath of probable cause—held to answer, not only without presentment or indictment, but after a Grand Jury had failed to indict or present—denied a speedy and public trial— indeed, refused the privilege of trial altogether—carried away, by force, from the State and district where any offense alleged against them must have been committed, if at all— no information of the nature and cause of the accusation vouchsafed to them—the President of the United States, upon the contrary, refusing to communicate such information even to Congress, on the ground that to do so would be "incompatible with the public interests"—confronted with no witnesses against them—allowed to call no witnesses in their defense—separated from their counsel, as from their homes and friends—the Maryland Commissioners of Police now imprisoned at Fort La Fayette, are a living testimonial of the overthrow, within their State, of every barrier erected by the Constitution between the freedom of the citizen and the onslaught of arbitrary power. Let it be to their honor and the honor of Maryland, that they have not sullied her name or theirs, by unmanly submission or mean compliance. It will be the eternal shame of the whole nation, if its people, as one man, do not demand and compel their deliverance.

Upon the ground of "military necessity," already discussed in another point of view, there is no doubt that defense will be made for the Government, against the grave responsibilities which these overt acts of individual oppression must entail.

But the Committee, now, as before, rely upon the Constitution of the United States as a bar to all such attempted justification or excuse. There is no foundation whatever for it in our history or our institutions, nor is it any part of our Anglo-Saxon inheritance. No mode of reasoning is more false than that which appeals to what are called "general principles of government," to determine the powers of the particular Government under which we live. It is a Government *sui generis;* to be construed according to its own peculiar principles and none other. It is a Government of enumerated and delegated powers, framed expressly upon the theory that it shall exercise no powers except those which are so delegated and enumerated. Where it finds no prerogatives in the Constitution, it was not meant to be clothed with them. There are no "inherent attributes" about it. This principle, recognized by all the Courts of the land, is insisted upon more strenuously and more repeatedly nowhere, than in the Courts of the Northern and Eastern States. The written Constitution of the Union, as all readers of history know, was expressly devised to get rid of inferences and implications, of all sorts, from general principles and abstract reasoning. No other Government is like ours in this, and the analogies of no other Government apply to it. To insist, therefore, that it has the right to preserve itself by any and all means, whether constitutional or unconstitutional—because other governments, which have no written constitutions and no limitations of power, have adopted the rule to keep power, as long as power can be kept, and through any means by which they can retain it—is to reason from an analogy which does not exist, upon principles which are manifestly false, to a conclusion which is subversive of our institutions. This Government was not intended to be kept together, by any means, through the exercise of any powers, or by the application of any principles, except those of its own constitutional providing. To attempt to preserve it, in name, at the expense of the Constitution, is to destroy it, in theory and fact. Once let " necessity," of any sort, be recognized as above the Constitution, and our system is any thing and every thing which it may be found necessary to make it. As " necessity " has no law, so it has no limit. The same logic by which it justifies the suspension of one constitutional provision, will justify, in like case, the overthrow of all. The same pretext which it invokes to suppress the functions of the Judiciary, may call for the suppression of Congress as well. It may demand a limited monarchy to-day, and by the same process of reasoning may legitimize an absolute monarchy, or a dictatorship, to-morrow. It already finds the liberty of citizens in its way—what is to prevent it from finding their lives equally so, a month hence ? If it justifies imprisoning them, in violation of law and Constitution, it will equally justify their assassination. Concede that it has rightfully suppressed the authority of Maryland in Baltimore, and it may, at any time, as rightfully abolish the whole State Government. It is " the tyrant's plea," and constitutional freedom dies with its predominance.

If " military necessity " had been contemplated by those who framed the Constitution, as a justification for suspending or invading its guarantees, would they not have said so in terms? They provided, by special clause, for the suspension of the *Habeas Corpus*—would they have paused at the enumeration of a single case, in which the laws and the Constitution might be temporarily silenced, if they had intended that the Executive or Congress might stifle all the voices of constitutional liberty, at the sound of the trumpet ? Why specify the limits of " military necessity,' in the one isolated case, if they meant it to cover all cases ? Men who honestly reason to the conclusions of the Administration, upon the point in question, seem to labor under the delusion, that the framers of the Constitution were technical men of law and peace, who had never known war or its terrible exigencies, and did not cover its contingencies with their forecast, when they were laying the foundations of a mighty nation. They seem to forget that the men who sat in the Convention, were the men who had planned the Revolution and had just returned from its triumphs: heroes and sages, who had grappled with war and its necessities, in field and camp and council: free men, who knew, from experience, what oppression was: bold men, who had smitten arbitrary power and abhorred it, and meant to build a bulwark against it, in war as well as peace, for evermore. When such men, in the charter of their Government, fenced round the freedom of the citizen with the guarantees which have been cited, and gave to military power no privilege to override them, it was because they meant the citizen to be free, and were resolved that military force should be kept in perpetual subordination to the law. They knew that in peace there is small danger to civil liberty, and they meant to rescue their priceless heritage from the chances and ambitions of war. They had entered upon the Revolution, with the Declaration of Independence before them, charging these, among the oppressions of the British King:—

"He has kept among us, in times of peace, standing armies, without the consent of our Legislature."

"He has affected to render the military independent of and superior to the civil power."

They believed these to be grievances, and took up arms to redress and not to re-establish them. They had passed through the trials and needs of the struggle themselves, therefore, without once overturning the laws of the land they were liberating. When the Father of his country, their champion and leader, had delivered up to Congress his sheathed and honored sword, they had listened, with pride, and his venerable form had bent in acknowledgment, as the President addressed him these remarkable words:

"Called upon by your country to defend its invaded rights, you accepted the sacred charge, before it had formed alliances, and whilst it was without funds or a government to support you. YOU HAVE CONDUCTED THE GREAT MILITARY CONTEST WITH WISDOM AND FORTITUDE, INVARIABLY REGARDING THE RIGHTS OF THE CIVIL POWER, THROUGH ALL DISASTERS AND CHANGES"

They had felt this to be his highest praise and theirs, and when, in the first years of his administration, and with his sanction and approval, they amended the work of the Convention, by adding to the Constitution the comprehensive safeguards of civil liberty which have been referred to, it is midsummer madness to dream that it was in his mind or theirs to leave, still, to military discretion or caprice, the inestimable privileges thus fortified anew. When they declared that "the right of the people to be secure in their persons, &c., *shall not be violated,*" they had no mental or military reservation in favor of such violation. They meant what they said, and thus and there stands the Constitution, as they made it—and as others have broken it!

Our own immediate ancestors, when they framed the Constitution of Maryland in 1776, embodied in their Declaration of Rights two principles, from which they never departed nor allowed departure, and which they transmitted to us, for equal reverence and observance. They are the 2d and 27th Articles of the Declaration which is prefixed to our existing Constitution, and they were part of the fundamental law of the State when she adopted the Constitution of the Union. Their language is as follows:

" *That the people of this State ought to have the sole and exclusive right of regulating the internal government and police thereof;*" and—" *That in all cases and at all times, the military ought to be under strict subordination to, and control of, the civil power.*"

With this authoritative announcement before us, of rights which the citizens of Maryland have at no time surrendered, we can never consent to recognize, in the pretext of " military necessity," anything but an aggravation of the wrong it is meant to justify. Neither can we fail, without disgrace, to denounce as usurpation and outrage, the overthrow of our domestic authorities and institutions, the assumption of our internal government, and the oppression of our citizens—by the Executive, the Congress, and the army of the United States.

The experience of this General Assembly and of the Memorialists before us, must admonish us, the Committee believe, that any application for redress to the Federal Government, in any of its departments, is idle and hopeless now. There is but one recourse left to us, and that is to appeal to the public opinion and sense of right of the whole country : to call upon free and true men, everywhere, in our own State and in our sister States, to lift their voices for the rescue of the Constitution, before it shall have gone down into the vortex, whose narrowing and rapid circles have already swept its great bulwarks from around the rights of the people of Maryland. It is not, we repeat, a question of Union or Disunion. It is a question of Constitution or no Constitution : a question of Freedom or no Freedom. There can be no trust and no safety, for any people, in arbitrary power. It is progressive, untiring, unresting. It never halts or looks backward. Call it by what holy name you will : sanctify it by what pretexts or purposes of patriotism you may—under any flag, in any cause, anywhere and everywhere, it is the foe of human right, and by the law of its being is inca-

pacitated from leading to good. As surely as man's nature
is corrupt and the lust of power the most corrupting and
insatiable of his appetites, so surely will any Government
or system sink into anarchy or despotism, if committed to
his arbitrary will. There is no life for liberty, but in the
supreme and absolute dominion of law. The lesson is
written, in letters of blood and fire, all over the history of
nations. It is the moral of the annals of republics since
their records began. It is legible upon the crumbling
marbles of the elder world—it echoes in the strifes and revolutions of the new. Wherever men have thought great
thoughts and died brave deaths for human progress, its
everlasting truth has been sealed and proclaimed. It will
be true—it is true—for us and for ours, as it has been for
those who have preceded us, and the consequences of its
violation will be upon us, as upon them, unless the Providence whom we are mocking shall break the inevitable
chain which drags effect after cause. And let the people
of no other section shut their eyes to the danger, because
it seems to be impending over us only, and not over them.
Let them not sympathize with usurpation, because its blows
for the present appear aimed only at sections and individuals, whose opinions differ from their own. They know not
what a day may bring forth, and they cannot measure the
harvest which may spring from a seed-time of impunity in
usurpation and wrong. Already the *Habeas Corpus* is suspended in New York, and the District Judge asks the pleasure
of the commanding General, and yields—as if the great writ
were a favor and not a right, and as if it were a luxury of the
Court, and not the privilege of the prisoner. Before long,
the suspension of the laws and the Constitution may cease
to be for the exclusive chastisement of "rebels," and new tests
of "loyalty" may be prescribed in the very States now held
most "loyal." If public opinion re-acts against the policy
of the Administration, it may be the next "military necessity" to strike down public opinion; and men may then
begin to learn, when it is too late, that there is no more
security for friends than for enemies, under a system where
the power which creates the "necessity" is the exclusive
and irresistible judge of its extent and application. Good
motives, ascribed to such a power, are no better security
than bad ones. Mr. Lincoln himself has said, in his Message, when speaking of another thing—what he, at all
events, may not gainsay—"*The little disguise, that the supposed right is to be exercised only for just cause—themselves
to be sole judge of its justice—is too thin to merit any notice.*"
There are those who may hearken to Mr. Lincoln who will
not hearken to Washington; but Washington, in the fare-

well legacy of his affection, has left us these warning
words also:

"LET THERE BE NO CHANGE, BY USURPATION; FOR THOUGH
THIS, IN ONE INSTANCE, MAY BE THE INSTRUMENT OF GOOD, IT IS
THE CUSTOMARY WEAPON BY WHICH FREE GOVERNMENTS ARE DE-
STROYED. THE PRECEDENT MUST ALWAYS GREATLY OVERBALANCE,
IN PERMANENT EVIL, EVERY PARTIAL OR TRANSIENT BENEFIT WHICH
THE USE CAN AT ANY TIME YIELD."

We shall more surely and reverently honor the memory of Washington, by following his precepts and exam-
ple, than even by respecting, under "general orders," the
groves and walks around his tomb.

It is no part of the purpose of the Committee to discuss
the personal and official conduct of the citizens of whose
wrongs they have spoken, for their merits or demerits have
but little to do with the great principles which have been
violated in their persons. It is but just, however, to say,
that the Message of the Mayor of Baltimore—himself fully
cognizant of their official proceedings, and a witness beyond question or suspicion—confirms, in the amplest manner, the asseverations of their Memorial, which their own
high character for truthfulness and honor would suffice, of
itself, to establish. The Memorial of the City Councils
corroborates the statements of the Mayor, and all the testimony which surrounds the case demonstrates, to the satisfaction of the Committee, not only the unfounded nature
of the suspicions under which the Government has acted,
or assumed to act, but the entire good faith in which the
Board had met, and was prepared to fulfill its obligations,
under the laws of the State and the Union. It is made
conspicuously evident, that in the unfortunate affair of the
19th of April, the Mayor, the Commissioners, the Marshal
of Police and his men, at the imminent risk of their own
lives, endeavored to suppress the riot and protect the troops
assailed. Magnanimous acknowledgment of the fact was
made through the public prints by Capt. Dike, a wounded
officer, as soon as he arrived in Boston. The Governor of
this State, (no willing witness,) on page 4 of his Message
of April 25th, bore testimony to it in the following strong
language: "The Mayor and Police Board gave to the
Massachusetts soldiers all the protection they could afford,
acting with the utmost promptness and bravery. But they
were powerless to restrain the mob." The President
of the United States himself in his interview of April
21st, with the Mayor of Baltimore in Washington,
did not hesitate fully to recognize, in the presence of
his cabinet and of the General commanding the army,
the fidelity and loyalty with which the city authorities

had borne themselves, under the trying circumstances referred to. The statement of Mayor Brown, published in the newspapers of April 22d, bears witness to this fact, which is likewise personally known to one of the members of this Committee, and to another member of the House, themselves present at the interview. Mr. Lincoln could not readily have done otherwise, for he knew that on the night of the 19th of April, both Fort McHenry and the United States receiving ship were protected by the troops under the orders of the Police Board, and that the United States officers in command were notified of the fact and put on their guard also by the good faith of the same authorities. In the face of such facts and acknowledgments, it does not appear necessary to re-capitulate the explanation given by the Mayor, concerning the "concealed arsenal" of between two and three hundred muskets and rifles—belonging to the Corporation and hidden from illegal search in the Marshal's office—with which a body of four hundred policemen were denounced by Gen. Banks as dangerous to "the peace or security" of the Government, in a city whose population was disarmed, whose homes were commanded by the formidable batteries of Fort McHenry, and in whose suburbs an army was sta-tioned of five or six thousand well appointed soldiers.

The Committee respectfully recommend the adoption of the following resolutions—

A. A. LYNCH,
JOHN F. GARDINER,   *Committee*
JAS. F. DASHIELL,   *of the*
D. C. BLACKISTON,   *Senate.*
TEAGLE TOWNSEND,

S. T. WALLIS,
J. H. GORDON,
G. W. GOLDSBOROUGH,   *Committee*
BARNES COMPTON,   *of the House*
JAMES T. BRISCOE,   *of Delegates.*
JAMES U. DENNIS,

WHEREAS, The military authorities of the Government of the United States in Baltimore have assumed to remove from office the Marshal of Police of that city, an officer of the State of Maryland, and to appoint his successor; and have further assumed to dismiss from office the Board of Police of Baltimore, a body clothed with high powers by the State of Maryland for the protection of its citizens; and have actually put an end, by force, to the exercise, by said Board, of its lawful and important functions; and have appointed sundry individuals, in large numbers, to govern the said city, as policemen, in contempt of the constitutional rights of the State of Maryland, and in open and flagrant violation of its laws; and

WHEREAS, The Congress of the United States, instead of rebuking the wrong and usurpation aforesaid, has justified and approved the same, under color of a "military necessity" not known to the institutions of the country and fatal to its liberties, and has appropriated large sums of money for the compensation of the said unlawful police force, so that the members thereof are maintained thereby in daily and oppressive hostility to the laws of Maryland and the rights of its citizens, and constitute in fact a civil government, established by Congress over the chief city of this State; and

WHEREAS, Charles Howard, William H. Gatchell and John W. Davis, Police Commissioners aforesaid, having been arrested by order of the General commanding the army of the United States, and imprisoned in Fort McHenry, under frivolous and arbitrary pretexts, without oath, warrant, presentment of a Grand Jury, or lawful cause disclosed or trial had, have since been removed, by military force, under the same orders, to Fort La Fayette, in New York, where they are now held, as "prisoners of State," at the arbitrary pleasure of the President of the United States and the officers under him, at a distance from their homes and families, in utter defiance of law and constitution, and in criminal violation of the plainest and dearest rights to which American citizens are born; now, therefore, it is

Resolved by the General Assembly of Maryland, That we solemnly protest, in the name of the State and her people, against the proceedings aforesaid, in all their parts; pronouncing the same, so far as they affect individuals, a gross and unconstitutional abuse of power, which nothing can palliate or excuse, and, in their bearing upon the authority and constitutional powers and privileges of the State herself, a revolutionary subversion of the Federal compact.

Resolved, That we appeal, in the most earnest manner, to the whole people of the country, of all parties, sections and opinions, to take warning by the usurpations aforementioned, and come to the rescue of the free institutions of the Republic, so that whatever may be the issue of the melancholy conflict which is now covering the land with sacrifice and sorrow, and threatens to overwhelm it with debt and ruin, there may at least survive to us, when it is over, the republican form of government which our fathers

bequeathed to us, and the inestimable rights which they
framed it to perpetuate.

Resolved, That the President of the Senate and Speaker
of the House be, and they are hereby requested to cause
copies of these Resolutions to be transmitted to our Senators
and Representatives in Congress, and also to the Governors
of the several States, with the request that they be submitted by the latter to their respective Legislatures.

The foregoing Report and Resolutions were adopted in
the House of Delegates by the following vote:

AFFIRMATIVE.

E. G. Kilbourn, Speaker,	G. W. Landing,
P. F. Rasin,	A. Kessler,
Albert Medders,	John A. Johnson,
B. A. Welch,	Wm. E. Salmon,
R. C Mackubin,	G. W. Goldsborough,
Jas. T. Briscoe,	H. M. Warfield,
Benj. Parran,	J. C. Brune,
John T. Ford,	Chas. H. Pitts,
R. M. Denison,	Wm. G. Harrison,
L. G. Quinlan,	J. H. Thomas,
Thos. W. Renshaw,	S. T. Wallis,
J. L. Jones, of Talbot,	Lawrence Sangston,
Alex. Chaplain,	H. M. Morfit,
Jas. U. Dennis, of Som't,	T. Parkin Scott,
Z. W. Linthicum,	Joshua Wilson,
Wm. Holland,	Martin Eakle,
Jas. W. Maxwell,	J. C. Brining,
Wm. R. Miller,	Josiah H. Gordon,
Rich. Wootton,	W. R. Barnard,
E. A. Jones, of P. G.,	Bernard Mills,
W. H. Legg,	John R. Brown—42

NEGATIVE.

W. T. Lawson,	R. B. McCoy,
A. McIntire,	L. P. Fiery,
Jonathan Routzahn,	David Roop—7.
Wm. F. Bayless,	

And in the Senate by the following vote:

AFFIRMATIVE.

John B. Brooke, Pres't,	A. A. Lynch,
D. C. Blackiston,	T. J. McKaig,
Washington Duvall,	Oscar Miles,
James F. Dashiell,	Teagle Townsend,
Thos. Franklin,	J. S. Watkins,
John F. Gardiner,	Franklin Whitaker—12.

NEGATIVE.

S. J. Bradley,	Tilghman Nuttle,
H.H.Goldsborough, of Talb.	J. E. Smith,
Anthony Kimmel,	J. G. Stone—6.

www.ingramcontent.com/pod-product-compliance
Lightning Source LLC
Chambersburg PA
CBHW032317280326

41932CB00009B/839